MW01139923

Archaeologies of Listening

UNIVERSITY PRESS OF FLORIDA

Florida A&M University, Tallahassee
Florida Atlantic University, Boca Raton
Florida Gulf Coast University, Ft. Myers
Florida International University, Miami
Florida State University, Tallahassee
New College of Florida, Sarasota
University of Central Florida, Orlando
University of Florida, Gainesville
University of North Florida, Jacksonville
University of South Florida, Tampa
University of West Florida, Pensacola

Archaeologies of Listening

Edited by Peter R. Schmidt
and Alice B. Kehoe

UNIVERSITY PRESS OF FLORIDA

Gainesville / Tallahassee / Tampa / Boca Raton

Pensacola / Orlando / Miami / Jacksonville / Ft. Myers / Sarasota

Copyright 2019 Peter R. Schmidt and Alice B. Kehoe
All rights reserved
Published in the United States of America. Printed on acid-free paper.

This book may be available in an electronic edition.

24 23 22 21 20 19   6 5 4 3 2 1

Library of Congress Cataloging-in-Publication Data
Names: Schmidt, Peter R. (Peter Ridgway), 1942– editor. | Kehoe, Alice Beck,
    1934– editor.
Title: Archaeologies of listening / edited by Peter R. Schmidt and Alice B.
    Kehoe.
Description: Gainesville : University Press of Florida, 2019. | Includes
    bibliographical references and index.
Identifiers: LCCN 2018027816 | ISBN 9780813056241 (cloth : alk. paper)
Subjects: LCSH: Archaeology—Methodology. | Archaeology—Philosophy. |
    Archaeology—Social aspects. | Oral tradition.
Classification: LCC GN33 .A69 2019 | DDC 930.101—dc23
LC record available at https://lccn.loc.gov/2018027816

The University Press of Florida is the scholarly publishing agency for the State
University System of Florida, comprising Florida A&M University, Florida
Atlantic University, Florida Gulf Coast University, Florida International
University, Florida State University, New College of Florida, University of
Central Florida, University of Florida, University of North Florida, University
of South Florida, and University of West Florida.

University Press of Florida
2046 NE Waldo Road
Suite 2100
Gainesville, FL 32609
http://upress.ufl.edu

Contents

Illustrations

Figures

Maps

1

Archaeologies of Listening

Beginning Thoughts

PETER R. SCHMIDT AND ALICE B. KEHOE

Listening is a skill, an art, a means by which knowledge is gained. In anthropology, it is fundamental to evidence-based practice. From the beginning of anthropological practice, we have drawn on millions of years of selection for listening capacity. Our ability to listen effectively derives from our aural mechanism and our human orientation to face-to-face interaction. It is through our human communications that we go beyond our physical bodies into universes of discourse rich with compounded experiences, memories, and thinking. Listening to our fellow humans living at or near our sites, or to those descended from ancestors who once frequented what we call sites, provides a wealth of knowledge about pasts that we could not otherwise understand or even be aware of. We, as anthropologists who practice an archaeology that is both scientific and humanistic, are committed to examining as wide a spectrum of information as we can access. That is why we listen. Yet, as most of us are keenly aware, we archaeologists are so deeply involved in digging "telephone booth" stratigraphic columns, describing data, and comparing artifacts that we often forget the human side of our mission—listening and learning from others who may hold distinctive and important knowledge about the places and objects that we so highly value in the abstract world we inhabit. Indeed, one thing that Thor Heyerdahl got right was his observation that we cannot hear within university walls.

In this introduction, we explain how "archaeologies of listening" bring to the fore a postcolonial standpoint (see Karega-Munene and Schmidt 2010; Schmidt 2009). Its opposite, the imperialist colonial standpoint (not just Western), elevates the paradigm of knowledgeable imperial persons above allegedly ignorant barbarians living in the colonies. Hierarchies of power are simultaneously hierarchies of knowledge. Our familiar Western worldview developed along with Europe's early modern nation-states and the colonizing outreach that was central to our own history. Conventional history lauds Enlightenment principles, notwithstanding the poignant summation of philosopher Joseph Agassi (1981:386): "positivism, inductivism, pure rationality, scientific proof, and all that, are parts of a myth." The social charter myth for "modern society," allegedly superior because it is built on the practices specified by Agassi, denies these practices in subordinated societies.

As Fabian (1983) has argued, the processes of othering that prevail in anthropology carry ancillary baggage that makes the Other irrational, fails to appreciate scientific proof in all its ontological guises, and fails to admit inductive thinking. If that were not the case, those Others might have a claim to participate democratically in the dominant nations' governance. Postwar economics spurred the breakup of administered colonies, without breaking up racist opinions on their peoples' intelligence. Colonialist archaeological projects also continued. White men, funded by imperial nations, directed crews of manual laborers whose counsel, if listened to at all, was seldom acknowledged. Herzfeld (2010:302) addresses this colonial isolation: "these earlier scholars were perhaps blissfully unaware of taking directions from anyone. Anthropologists' failure to treat their informants as intellectual equals, however, makes little sense today." An archaeology of listening addresses what Herzfeld (2010:302) sees as a need to address "a lingering intellectual colonialism [as well as] demand respect for social actors as theorists of, at the very least, their own conditions of life." Accepting local actors as thinkers has yet to gain traction in archaeological practice.

Our position here is that archaeologists, and archaeology as a discipline, benefit from interchange with local and descendant communities through which their deep experience and historical knowledge broaden our base for inference to the best explanations. We address how calling for listening brings up issues of science versus history, focus versus breadth, and neutrality versus advocacy. Listening is much more than speech entering one's ears. Listening, for an anthropological archaeologist, is also perceiving the landscape, close and beyond, feeling the weather, hearing and seeing ambient sounds and activities, tastes of food and smells, tactile sensations of structures, bedding, tools, containers, clothing. Some of these sense receptions are conscious, while some may be stored subliminally, to rise into consciousness when triggered by more listening or later reflection. In these essays, we hope to illustrate that archaeologists who listen evoke the diverse capacities that make us and the people whose residue we investigate fully human.

History and Science

Ethnographers of science recognize "epistemic cultures . . . the different practices of creating and warranting knowledge in different domains" (Knorr-Cetina 1999:246). This is more than differences between scientific disciplines; within a discipline, one sees national differences and "schools" following leaders' paradigms. We see the Western intellectual tradition as a broad, persistent epistemic culture valuing formal logic and classifications, authority in written documents, ostensible observation, and rejection of immaterial sources of knowledge. Within this Western tradition, battles raged between the ancients and the moderns, statisticians and empiricists, functionalists and symbolists, with the common limits less noticed. Listening to people living in communities maintaining non-Western epistemic cultures illuminates those seldom-remarked conventional limits. That other societies have their own limits is not the point: listening to these others adds to our knowledge. Our project is to crumble arbitrary limits to archaeologists' epistemic culture.

Among the fallacies about science that bedevil archaeology are notions that measurement is essential, that statistics reveal relationships, and that replication is the test of validity—all of which militate against recognizing singular occurrences. Regularities are sought, cross-cutting through sites and times, reducing complexity and eliminating particularities. A moment's reflection leads us to realize that cross-cultural regularities cut out huge amounts of information that potentially has significance, leaving us wondering what of importance was lost. Such elisions may hold great significance for recognizing communities that lived in our sites or for understanding ecological histories that may illuminate climate change and sustainable resource production; differences may be more crucial than regularities. Moreover, hypothesized or discovered regularities often arise, tautologically, from within the Western academic tradition, reinforcing its particular worldview.

Again, one way to crumble such reification is to listen, opening out knowledge to alternative epistemic cultures and their capacity to explain. It is informative that few archaeologists have analyzed their field from an STS (Science, Technology, Society) perspective (exceptions are Kehoe 1998; Patterson 1994).

In *Cultures without Culturalism: The Making of Scientific Knowledge*, Chemla and Keller (2017) describe how researchers usually form communities of practice that share a worldview and premises from which research problems are stated and methods made consonant. In archaeology, such analyses reveal a tight, cordoned-off worldview where the representations and conceptualizations of the Other remain deeply entrenched as a form of distancing, preserving the tenets of the discipline. This epistemic culture of distancing provokes much of what follows in this volume, as we seek ways to open attitudes, nurture a capacity to listen, and work toward a transformed practice.

However, we have some key hurdles to acknowledge on our way to implementing this program. First comes recognition that it is the culture of Cold War America and Britain that projects a conflict between history and science that rejects "culture histories" as worthwhile archaeological goals. Anyone who has been following archaeological history understands that change toward nomological science has come with myriad sacrifices imposed on historical sciences. One of our anthropological ancestors, E. E. Evans-Pritchard (1963:26), captured this conflict when he scathingly remarked:

> The concepts of natural system and natural law, modeled on the constructs of the natural sciences, . . . have been responsible for a false scholasticism which has led to one rigid and ambitious formulation after another. . . . Released from these essentially philosophical dogmas [anthropology] can be really empirical and, in the true sense of the word, scientific.

He further noted that some academics have "the feeling that any discipline that does not aim at formulating laws and hence predicting and planning is not worth the labour of a lifetime" (Evans-Pritchard 1963:27). Such hubris was enhanced during the Cold War by the National Science Foundation (NSF) when it became a principal source of funds for archaeology couched in natural science terms, only occasionally deigning to fund proposals intending to examine history and archaeology of local and descendant peoples.

Shifting government funding from NSF dominance toward more support for the National Endowment for the Humanities made history more feasible for archaeologists and conveyed a message that the reductionist approach mimicking the physical sciences is no longer uncritically accepted. Our insistence that we engage with culture histories, particularly as expressed by local interlocutors, uses the methodology of the historical sciences, an approach now widely accepted.

Focus versus Breadth

We would be remiss if we did not reflect on Franz Boas's focus on historical particularities, foundational to our archaeologies of listening. Importantly, his concern over history did not come from a humanities scholar. Rather, Boas was trained in scientific method and always considered himself a scientist (Müller-Wille 2014:134; Spier 1959). During his year with the Baffin Land Inuit (1883–1884), when he was wholly dependent for his very survival on his hosts' knowledge and skills, Boas saw, felt, heard, tasted, and smelled a rich and lively way of life. Despite his scientific training in Germany in physics and its search to discover general laws, he realized it was too narrow for studying human behavior.

Most importantly, as a scientist Boas appreciated sample size. The number of human communities studied by ethnographers is a tiny sample of all that exist, much less all that have existed. The task of anthropologists, including archaeologists, is to enlarge our sample of *well-studied* societies. Contingencies of place, resources, contacts and relations with other societies, climate episodes, and diseases all affect what we confront as archaeologists practicing ethnography. Boas had a keen understanding that community histories often incorporated discourses about these phenomena. To build scientific evidence sufficient for comparing human behavior in *all* its cultural manifestations, listening to the people we encounter in the field adds their knowledge to our own observations.

Simply stated, we find the postcolonial standpoint more fruitful than generalizations deduced from hypothesis testing. Imperial colonizing nations are relatively late in human history and in many respects well documented. Their denial of indigenous histories—propaganda that reifies domination—can be countered by listening to communities imposed on. We now recognize that marginalized peoples such as the San speakers of Botswana are not living fossils of a unilinear evolutionary stage (Denbow and Wilmsen 1986; Wilmsen 1989). What we learn from listening may unveil the stratagems of colonizing empires and the counterstratagems of accommodation, resistance, and resilience. From a strictly pragmatic perspective, since so much has been lost in archaeological sites, it follows that we need to be open to as much information as possible to build pertinent inferences.

Where We Made a Wrong Turn with Science

Many archaeologists who came of age in the era of processual and postprocessual approaches have failed to engage reflexively on how we were duped into thinking that explicitly scientific archaeology is anthropology (Binford 1962). If we read Binford's seminal article closely, then we cannot help but realize that he omitted anthropology from his discourse. Perhaps this was the result of the hastiness with which it was written:

> Frustrated, sitting in my office in Walker Museum late at night, I decided I would fight. I took out a sheet of paper, placed it in the typewriter, and wrote "Archaeology as Anthropology." Before dawn it was finished. The next day I passed it among some of the students who offered the inevitable suggestions of translating my writing into English and encouraged me to publish it. That afternoon it was typed in final draft and mailed to *American Antiquity*. (Binford 1972:10)

A close reading of his hasty screed reveals that the central concept is adaptation and little else. It is chilling from any retrospective that anthropology was distorted into ecological determinism, ignoring how knowledge is acquired. By refocusing archaeologists upon a reductionist principle pulled from biology, Binford created a milieu in which purposeful deafness to the knowledge of others was valorized—a condition that undermines the very foundational principles of method in anthropology. Lest anyone think that we are overstating this observation, let us examine what Binford had to say about how he valued the knowledge of his Nunamiut interlocutors when he was trying to deal with significant data gaps about bone distributions in dog yards: "For a number of reasons I do not have spring output data or actual bone counts from around houses and remaining in dog yards for the contemporary village. I found it nearly impossible to collect such data under contemporary conditions . . . as the winter snow melts the village becomes a very unpleasant mess of mud, debris, and excrement" (Binford 1978:195).[1]

Binford goes on to say that during his absence he tried to set up collection barrels for bones, but residents inevitably hauled these away to the trash. This narrative reveals significant distance between the archaeologist and residents, who very obviously had not been persuaded to work toward Binford's research goals; one can only wonder how they reacted to his appraisal of their surroundings. By not remaining in the village to observe and to listen to local folks, it was he who trashed the data for that season of the annual round.

It is impossible to learn from local collaborators if one avoids entering into a dialogue to develop deeper understanding of cultural attitudes and knowledge (see Nicholas, this volume). Binford seems to have been unaware of this pro-

Peter R. Schmidt and Alice B. Kehoe

cess, again and again privileging his speculative positions over local knowledge, for example, when trying to develop a protocol for assessing which parts of animals would be transported to home residences:

> In order to obtain an accurate evaluation of part selection [of butchered animals] I asked eight Eskimos to rank order the anatomical parts of the caribou . . . into a sequence from 1 to 18 representing the sequence in which they would carry home parts if they carried only one part at a time. I stipulated that the kill was made in late fall, and that they were only to consider meat; they were to assume that they had plenty of marrow bones and bone grease at home. *The informants were not happy with this situation.* They wanted to know if the weather was freezing, if there was meat in storage at home, if their wives were pregnant, and so on—so I further stipulated that the weather was freezing, no meat was at home, and no wives were pregnant. *I must admit that I do not recall all my qualifying answers to their endless questions. At the time I thought that they were simply playing games, and I assumed that they really knew what I wanted to know.* (Binford 1978:40; emphasis added)

We quote this passage at length because it unveils a stony deafness, an incapacity to listen to local reactions to the arbitrary conditions imposed by Binford, who, oblivious to local values and nuanced hunting practices, reluctantly agreed to modifications to his arbitrary protocol. Most telling, though, is his degradation of local people and their invaluable knowledge—labeling it as game playing. His interaction drips with hubris and betrays a profound disrespect for anthropological methods and for learning in a host community. Such deafness speaks to an arrogance that for too long as been an unfortunate legacy among archaeologists.

> The three large cairns . . . *are most certainly* the insurance stores of extended households. The small caches . . . *might represent* partial stores, resulting from minimal success at this location, supplemented by caches located in other places. They *might also represent* late stores . . . , placed in the cairn during the summer. *Perhaps a situation arose* that made it necessary for a group already encamped for that summer to move to another camp. Meat *would be removed* from the meat racks and the most portable parts packed to the new camp. The rest of the meat *would be cached* in the cairn as insurance. (Binford 1978:242; emphasis added)

These speculations—arising within the imagination of the archaeologist—continue ad infinitum for pages, displaying a disregard for how local interlocutors felt about and knew about cairn features. Most instructive is how Binford squandered an opportunity to listen and to learn; to act as an apprentice to Nunamiut elders was contrary to the archaeologist as expert—anathema to someone who saw himself having the final word.

The deafness syndrome exemplified by Binford did not rise spontaneously out of an obsession with science in archaeology during the post-1960s period. Rather, it is a symptom of a deep colonial heritage in North American archaeology and the archaeology of many other world regions (see Weerasinghe, this volume, for examples from Sri Lanka). Disdainful of both history and local knowledge, Binford set an example for others, who, emboldened by his scorn for humanistic science, began to take positions that diminished indigenous knowledge. By the 1990s, we began to see an open challenge to indigenous constructions of history in the broadside launched by Clement Meighan (1992, 1995) against NAGPRA (the Native American Graves Protection and Repatriation Act) and other repatriation policies as "fall[ing] into the anthropological trap of cultural relativism" (Meighan 1992:704). In other words, local representations of history are dangerous abysses, perils to correct interpretations.

This kind of thinking opened a Pandora's box of colonialist thinking, led by Ronald Mason. Writing in *American Antiquity* (2000), Mason argued that there was no significant value in interpretations gained from listening to local or descendant people. He wrote to provoke and, in our view, to resurrect and amplify the nearly century-old denials of anthropologists such as Robert Lowie (1915:598), who once said with as much absolutism as he could muster: "I cannot attach to oral traditions any historical value whatsoever under any conditions whatsoever. We cannot know them to be true except on the basis of extraneous evidence, and in that case they are superfluous since the linguistic, ethnological, or archeological data suffice to establish the conclusions in question." Lowie's assertion foreshadows the cynicism of Mason, who later expanded his views into a book-length manifesto against oral narratives (Mason 2008).

Other, Mostly Ignored Perspectives

This deep-seated trend in North American archaeology, tinged with provincialism, blithely ignored the work of historians (e.g., Miller 1980; Spear 1981; Vansina 1965, 1985) and archaeologists of Africa (e.g., Maggs 1976; McIntosh and

Peter R. Schmidt and Alice B. Kehoe

McIntosh 1980; Posnansky 1966, 1968, 1969; Schmidt 1978, 2006, 2013; Wright and Kus 1979) who carefully labored to develop new methods of analyses that initially sought to verify oral traditions. They later used oral testimonies with a variety of ethnological, linguistic (Ehret and Posnansky 1982), and archaeological data, delving into the structure of narratives to trace out points of political and social origins. This school of thought accepts that the narratives of elders charged with centuries of learning provide critical evidence for understanding the full spectrum of extant knowledge about the past. It also acknowledges that when working in societies omitted from Western historiography it is often important to gain multiple views of the past through local testimonies. This truly multivocal approach leaves behind the notion that testimonies about the deep past are prehistoric or mythological, both labels created under colonial domination and early anthropology (see Schmidt and Mrozowski 2013).

One of the best illustrations of listening in an archaeological landscape comes from Great Zimbabwe. Long the focus of historians and archaeologists, Great Zimbabwe is an example of how the West denied local history and appropriated the materiality of the site and the contemporary Zimbabwe state for cultural, political, and racial motives (Hall 1984). These foci, closely wrapped in the colonial experience, submerged knowledge about how the site figured into local histories. With the considerable erasure of local meaning that occurred during its colonial and postcolonial histories, the site's inscription as a World Heritage Site reified professional and expert interpretation of its architecture and archaeology. Emphasis on the presentation of monumental remains within the central site was dominant until Joost Fontein's (2006) study of deep-time relationships between Great Zimbabwe and competing social groups. Fontein unveils how archaeological obsession with the materiality of Great Zimbabwe masked deeper and more profound meanings held by neighboring social groups. By patiently listening to the testimonies of Shona elders over a four-year period, Fontein exposed cultural dynamics that have been obscured for more than a hundred years of silencing beliefs, activities, and formal policies.

Apprenticing himself to Shona elders, Fontein—an outsider without Shona ancestry—unveiled the alienation of local communities. For example, the site's fencing prevented people's access to conduct sacred rituals and thus cut off ancestors from their communities. Fontein unmasked management policies, overseen by archaeologists, such as this diminishment of ritual life, so central to keeping ancestors engaged with history-making, that deny access and spiritual expression. Expert heritage managers/archaeologists emerge as deaf to the vital and rich testimonies of groups that hold competing clans' claims to custodianship and ownership, steeped in generations of interaction with potent spiritual places at Great Zimbabwe. Great Zimbabwe is deeply embedded within multivocal systems of spirituality intimately connected to this landscape, a revelation that only emerged when someone took the time to listen, understand, and accept the significance of local knowledge.

Biographies of Listening

Fontein's research into the spiritual landscape of Great Zimbabwe is only one of the ways in which listening is germane to unveiling hitherto unknown empirical evidence for the past. One perspective that emerges in this book is an examination of testimonies in the extant archival record. For example, Catherine Carlson (this volume) digs deep into the archival records of the American Museum of Natural History to unveil why indigenous peoples of the Interior Plateau still regard archaeology with deep suspicion.

By reading closely and listening to the private testimonies of Harlan Smith, Carlson learns that the excavation of Native graves occurred without local permission and that skeletal evidence was secretly transported to New York—a legacy that continues to infect indigenous attitudes toward archaeological practice. Official reports privilege a different kind of listening. Smith solicited local interpretations of material culture objects, an approach that gives the false impression that local information was respected, when, in fact, Smith and his superiors were deaf to the desires and sensibilities of Native peoples.

Alice Kehoe (this volume) takes a similar biographical approach, bringing her focus to bear on Frank Speck, whose unorthodox fieldwork ignored the conventions followed by Harlan Smith. Speck's practice of anthropology was very much within a four-field approach with career-long devotion to the testimonies of linguistically marginalized Native Americans—a perspective that arose from this young man's friendship with Mohegan youths. Speck's "indefatigable and superbly documented collecting made him welcome in museums," a proclivity that meant that his documentation of material culture incorporated the worldview of archaeologists. What made Speck special in Kehoe's view was his ability as a "bedside ethnologist," someone who lived with, ate with, and absorbed the daily rhythms of people among whom he worked, a perspective that he passed on to Claude Schaeffer—one of Frank Speck's students at the University of Pennsylvania. When Schaeffer recommended to Thomas Kehoe that he go around and talk to the elders about tipi rings, he was exercising Frank Speck's view of anthropology—live with those inside the family, talk to those whom others marginalized, to gain knowledge about their world.

Kehoe shares a poignant example of a legacy of listening that can be traced back through Tom Kehoe to his mentor Claude Schaeffer. We learn of Speck's radical perspective—listening attentively to the words and representations of forgotten pockets of marginalized First Nations—and the inspiration that this legacy afforded to a young white archaeologist searching for ways to unravel the meaning of landscape features in Blackfoot territory. Kehoe shares what is possible in archaeological practice when one assumes the posture of an apprentice in another culture. Tom Kehoe, who for years worked in an apprentice-like relationship with the Blackfoot people, learned from elders that the countless rings of stones found on the Great Plains were in fact tipi rings, stones used to hold down the bottom edges of tipis, left behind in ring shape once the community had abandoned the camp site (Kehoe 1960). Conventional archaeological wisdom had denied such a function until Kehoe and others brought it to light.

The power of listening is also vividly illustrated in Alice Kehoe's story about listening to a story of a local white resident, who, after working as an archaeological laborer, revealed that his mother's sweeping with a twig broom left behind a fine dust of the sort he had observed in part of the trading post being excavated (Kehoe 1978, 2000). Indeed, similar fine dust was observed in the quarters of what appears to have been the residence of a Native woman married to a trading post owner, suggesting gender markers for specific deposits. Apprenticeship takes on many guises, accepting that those with deep experience have lessons to teach. Vivid is the contrast between listening to those with local knowledge and what Binford did with stone cairns in Alaska.

Apprenticeship

Long-term apprenticeship is one of the themes that cuts across many chapters in *Archaeologies of Listening*. By accepting the mentorship of respected elders, one passes through several transforming stages that enhance listening ability. Kathryn Weedman Arthur's (this volume) exegesis of her transforming experiences is more than instructive; it conveys emotional lessons as well. Initially, Arthur was considered an immature person, arriving in the highlands of Ethiopia without a child—the strong marker for maturity. People accepted her presence, but it was tempered with recognition that she had not yet experienced full adulthood; additionally, she realized that she had not become an apprentice under such conditions. Not until years later when she brought her daughter with her did she begin to gain acceptance as a person with whom serious conversations could be conducted concerning knowledge held by people respected for their mastery. By accepting her original diminished status and then coming to an awareness over time to building trust, Arthur arrived at a point when intimate knowledge about a ritualized landscape could be shared with her. The maturing of her perspective as an observer trusted by local actors meant that she developed the capacity to learn beyond technical studies of lithic manufacture. She began to see the life stages in the production of lithics as an ontology obscured by Western observers preoccupied with the strictly material world of mechanics of chipping, spatial distributions of debitage, and processes of discard. Her long-term interactions with people in highland Ethiopia occurred within a paradigm of learning "bit by bit," a local way of learning that extends over decades.

The value of apprenticeship emerges in Camina Weasel Moccasin's (this volume) narrative about rock art at Writing-on-Stone Provincial Park/Áísínai'pi National Historic Site in Alberta, Canada. Weasel Moccasin's identity as a Blackfoot working in the park is handled in a compellingly reflexive manner. She does not privilege her knowledge (some of which comes from her father's teaching) of the meanings of the rock art; rather, she listens closely to the spontaneous discourses of Blackfoot Elders who visit the park, learning of the reverence that they express for features of a larger landscape that encompasses the space memorialized in the sacred rock art. Patiently listening, she learns that sacred rock art is dynamic, not immutable. Accepting and understanding these indigenous principles of renewal and spiritual expression, she develops a protocol for contemporary inscriptions of rock art to allow an ages-old process of continuous practice to proceed—a controversial approach to some archaeologists preoccupied with conservation of the original at any cost but not an issue in this management approach. Her listening as an apprentice learner extends to Elders who express their desire to inscribe their historical experiences as part of their right to spiritual practice. Like Fontein at Great Zimbabwe, Weasel Moccasin brings us closer to recognizing that access to spiritual places is an integral part of making history—a recognition that now promises to open new interpretive horizons if we open our ears.

Another perspective comes from Peter Schmidt's (this volume) engagement with community heritage studies among the Haya of northwest Tanzania. He entered the field with the goal to first understand how the Haya represented their past, talking with elders about a wide spectrum of traditional knowledge ranging from epic poetry to mythology and legends about the kings and clans of the region (Schmidt 1978, 2006). After several months, Schmidt came to realize that his conversations often went in the direction that the elders wanted, as they patiently led him beyond his original goals, patiently accepting his naivety and inability to see history through their lens, destabilizing his view of the world, and making him realize that his real professors were those daily working with him. In his tenth month of research, the elders embarked on a suite of tales related to the history of King Rugomora Mahe, the most powerful king in Haya antiquity.

King Rugomora was memorialized by the preservation of his burial estate along with a major shrine to iron working, Kaijja (the place of the forge). Oral traditions were tied strongly to place. Elders suggested that they visit the site with Schmidt to explain its characteristics; they wanted to see for themselves what might lie below the surface. From the beginning they framed the inquiry. They took him to the exact place where they believed smiths had forged iron to build an iron tower for King Rugomora. Schmidt took up this indigenous hypothesis in one of the first expressions of community archaeology in Africa, testing it with excavation on the site (Schmidt 2017). The results are now well known: an early iron age forge dating to the late first millennium BCE—a privileging of local knowledge that has led to significant rethinking of the quality of orally transmitted knowledge in contexts with long-term ritual processes.

Among the interpretative enigmas in northern Australian archaeology are large baked-earth mounds, a topic taken up by Billy Ó Foglú (this volume). Because of the presence of shell, they have long been misinterpreted by archaeologists as shell mounds or considered the result of natural fires because of their burned characteristics—rather than inquiring among Aboriginal peoples about their views of the landscape. Ó Foglú broke with archaeological tradition by listening to local views of these distinctive features. Adopting an apprentice role, Ó Foglú worked over a two-year period with traditional owners to understand the cultural and technological characteristics of earth ovens used for food preparation. By working alongside those who practiced food preparation in earth ovens, Ó Foglú brings significant insights into a domain of heritage practice that has long eluded archaeologists. Understanding practice, he is able to set up technological tests that distinguish these critical features from natural phenomena, a spectacular payoff arising from listening.

Jonathan Walz (this volume) also brings long-term apprenticeship to his practice of archaeology. His experience captures the importance of apprenticeship and, particularly, acute listening. As he worked with a local healer, he came to understand that it was critical to understand where the healer obtained the artifacts that he used in his healing protocols. This required Jonathan to apprentice himself to the healer and accompany him on a long trek to various sites along a caravan route discovered to be of great antiquity. As the healer traversed the landscape, he used sight lines, sounds, and other sensations to fix himself in space—all physical processes that Walz calls listening to the landscape, a potent metaphor for using multiple senses to locate caravan sites that the healer had visited on early collecting expeditions. Walz's apprenticeship afforded an opportunity not only to learn from the healer through constant conversation but also to pick up the clues that were used to locate sites. This distinctive apprenticeship expands the meaning of listening, endowing it with a capacity to understand a multivocality arising from actively "listening" with all the senses.

Patience and Epistemic Humility

We find patience to be a significant attribute in listening to our elders, peers, and collaborators. Sincere patience in our practice arises out an epistemic humility (Matthews 2006)—humility about our knowledge, about pronouncements about our practice of science, and about our capacity to reflect critically about the questions that we routinely ask. A state of epistemic humility carries with it a readiness to listen without privileging, referencing, or drawing on one's background and academic training. It is a capacity to subjugate one's "expertness," baggage that we all carry around as principal investigators of grants, expedition leaders, authors, and a whole host of elevated ways of thinking of ourselves. Larry Zimmerman (2005:306) brings this into our conscious practice through his important essay "First, Be Humble: Working with Indigenous Peoples and Other Descendant Communities": "More insidious troubles occur when archaeologists present their findings as truth and the archaeological accounts as the actual story of what happened in the past. Does archaeological truth undercut sacred history that is a foundation for identity?" He goes on to point out that disdain for indigenous oral traditions is one of these insidious problems: "It seem[s] to be a statement that indigenous versions of the past were not true, that oral tradition was limited, inaccurate and misleading. . . . By taking this position, archaeologists usurped Indigenous voice about the past"

(Zimmerman 2005:307). Under the conditions necessary for truly scientific archaeology, to listen requires, first, an acceptance of humility, which within our archaeological collective is about enhancing values of toleration, civility, and the capacity to nurture others and our own need to learn. This is new territory for many and requires the long-term application of patience writ large—not just while digging test pits and writing reports—but by bringing an open willingness to learn into our daily interactions and discourses with those whose pasts we are studying.

Laurajane Smith (2006) addresses epistemic humility indirectly in her analyses of the authorized heritage discourse. Smith finds that the domination of expert determinations of what constitutes and does not constitute heritage militates against local meanings. She argues that the best pathway to understanding how heritage is represented, conceptualized, and valued is to listen closely and patiently to heritage discourses in communities. This prescription challenges the power relationships that heritage experts have long used. The challenge is gaining recognition as it opens an alternative pathway to powerful local ways of understanding heritage that are historically contingent and locally legitimate. Those who adopt an approach that valorizes local discourse on heritage ipso facto embrace an epistemic humility, as they give up the role of expert, defer to local authorities, and listen with patience to learn alternative knowledge.

Let us turn to some additional examples from our contributors. Audrey Horning (this volume) is engaged in strife-torn settings of Northern Ireland, where narratives are highly contested and often an integral part of conflict. She is very much aware that such a setting "requires an ability not only to listen but also to hear and respect the strength of personal and community narratives." When archaeology is used to bridge conflict, it will sometimes contradict strongly held local narratives, a condition that calls for hearing people out, respecting their views and *not taking sides*, that is, *subjugating one's expert knowledge to gain other knowledge*. Significant patience is required, especially when people become angry at archaeological evidence and archaeologists who contradict sometime age-old narratives. Counternarratives are, in fact, critical to bridge building, for they introduce multivocality, a two-way bridge that accepts narrative traffic both ways. Horning observes that deconstruction of sacred narratives and local reaction to such destabilization may elicit anxiety and anger. Knowing the power of archaeology to create negative, hostile reactions requires epistemic humility—not privileging archaeological evidence above cross-collaboration inclusive of multiple identities and communities. Long-term engagement carries with it building trust and appreciation for differing views, laying the foundation for exercise of patience and exacting ethical principles for the practice of archaeology when serious interpretive rifts develop over archaeological evidence.

Patience runs both ways. Communities may initially be reluctant to share their interpretive positions on landscape history, perhaps timid about juxtaposing it to guiding paradigms of expert archaeologists with whom they are collaborating. Stephen Mrozowski's experience with the Nipmuc people (this volume) illustrates this phenomenon. A representative of the Nipmuc, who for decades were represented as descendants of John Eliot's Praying Towns, challenged Mrozowski's acceptance of the narrative found in the historiography of New England. Eliot is said to have founded Praying Towns as new towns, a representation that fit Eliot's need to make Hassanamisco and other Praying Towns into something new and different from indigenous communities. Faced with this challenge to his professionally endorsed assumptions, Mrozowski realized that his way of recognizing community incorrectly accepted that the space these communities inhabited was new to the Nipmuc families, rather than a space occupied for many generations. When Mrozowski put his expert's hat aside and patiently listened to local knowledge about Nipmuc settlement, he learned that the survival of traditional practices alongside English material culture marked resilient communal practices over deep time. Embracing epistemic humility in this instance opened a significant way to recognize the Praying Indian towns as much older communities, a way of seeing and understanding the past that countered the idea that John Eliot's "founding" of these communities represented a historical rupture.

Patience is manifest in yet another guise in Innocent Pikirayi's (this volume) contribution about landscape history in Zimbabwe. Taught that one engages in conventional survey methods to discover archaeological locales, Pikirayi experienced considerable frustration when he could not locate a site mentioned in Portuguese records as a major trading post on the periphery of what was once Great Zimbabwe (Pikirayi 2016). He ended up in a local bar, talking with farmers who were amused at his odd way of doing research and shared their knowledge about locations they had noticed. Had Pikirayi dismissed such talk as the chatter of backward rural folk, he would have missed some of the most important discoveries of his career. Rather, he adopted a posture of epistemic humility and intently listened to the tales they told about their familiarity with the surrounding landscape. Eventually, he followed them through the bush to a location that matched the elusive site described in Portuguese records. By being respectful and patient, he was able to transition into a new phase of his career that accepted local knowledge. Once he had accepted epistemic humility as a modus operandi, it was much easier for Pikirayi to listen to the landscape. By listening to the toponyms, he entered into a new dimension of landscape archaeology that revealed the political history of the region—an unexpected consequence of his transformation to a state of epistemic humility.

We find in the experiences of Jagath Weerasinghe (this volume) that epistemic humility figures significantly in unlocking new knowledge that changes how heritage is thought about and managed in Sri Lanka. Weerasinghe as director of the Postgraduate Institute of Archaeology in Sri Lanka is a prominent member of the established expert heritage community. As one of many elders who are respected as the founders of modern archaeology in Sri Lanka, Weerasinghe's expert status is known to many people who work at and live around the World Heritage Sites of Sri Lanka. Convinced that heritage management of these sites suffered significantly from the exclusion of local governance, Weerasinghe and Peter Schmidt engaged with local heritage knowledge-keepers to learn about their local heritage practices as well as their ideas about reformation of management practices. As a nationally known heritage expert, Weerasinghe was keenly aware of a need to submerge his status and identity and open himself to alternative knowledge—a cathartic exercise in epistemic humility. Though his adoption of epistemic humility initially surprised some collaborators, he soon won trust and an open willingness to share heritage concerns, some of which have helped to reconceptualize how heritage is viewed in Sri Lanka outside of the community of experts.

When Peter Schmidt (this volume) was invited to return to a Haya village to assist the community with its research initiative into documentation of oral traditions and revitalization of sacred places, he recognized that his role as a heritage "expert" could quickly transform a local initiative into an expert-driven research project. Instead, he took a back seat to research conducted by Haya elders, adopting a posture of epistemic humility. Setting aside decades of running projects and being a professor, Schmidt became a supportive friend and eventually a co-producer of those engaging narratives about the past. Local researchers unveiled long-hidden testimonies by elderly women, heretofore masked by androcentric attitudes toward female-related histories. As he and his cohort learned of an important female ritual official who controlled vast burial estates and political power, they also came to understand that this powerful female ritual leader exercised far more power and influence than a "keeper of the jawbone" in the Kingdoms of Buganda and Bunyoro or a Queen Mother—the quintessential "power behind the throne" featured in anthropological literature. By sitting back and listening, he heard and learned of perspectives on history rarely spoken but significantly transformative—changing ideas about the political and religious roles of female ritual officials at ancient shrines, some of which have been documented archaeologically.

When George Nicholas (this volume) talks about listening, he shares how his consciousness expanded as he saw and heard what is considered to be heritage among First Nations peoples and other groups that participated in the IPinCH (Intellectual Property Issues in Cultural Heritage) project that funded a series of community-directed projects and special initiatives around the globe. Trained as an anthropological archaeologist, Nicholas reveals that a significant tension arose between his Western and indigenous conceptions of "heritage": the Western conception emphasizes the tangible, while indigenous concepts focus on the intangible as well as "relationships and responsibilities aligned with knowledge, objects, and places" as well as other societies, individuals, and nonhuman beings (Nicholas, this volume). This learning process required that he sit, listen, and learn through long meetings that cast him in the role of student learner rather than expert—an experience that should be seen in light of his renown as a heritage expert. His successful role as equal participant was impossible without his first accepting the practice of epistemic humility, the willingness to reconsider previous ideas and learning, to put aside his power as an expert in heritage and archaeology and to open himself to new knowledge.

Archaeologies of listening have diverse origins around the globe, ranging from the study of tipi rings on the Great Plains to African oral traditions linked to iron working. These are important threads to understand in the history of archaeology. We have also brought to the fore the role of "explicitly scientific" archaeology and its failure to listen to alternative explanations. The origins of Binford's deafness are not to be traced to the late twentieth century but rather to the culture of Western colonial dominance seen in the Jesup North Pacific Expedition to the northwest coast and interior plateau at the end of the nineteenth century (Catherine Carlson, this volume). Even Franz Boas, scientific director of the expedition, was deaf to the pleas of the subordinated communities.

On several occasions, Alison Wylie has argued that those on the margins, those stigmatized by the mainstream as unreliable or unorthodox, may have an epistemic advantage:

the range of resources used to address new questions and to assess the presuppositions that frame the history making enterprise must be substantially broadened. All "relevant" resources must be deployed, in particular, oral traditions and oral history should be credited not only as important sources of interpretative insight but also as historical accounts in their own right . . . but also in their potential to provide a basis for the reciprocal interrogation of documentary and archaeological sources. (Wylie 1995:266–267)

We follow Wylie's view, pointing to archaeologies of listening as a way to open taken-for-granted assumptions and interpretations about the past to reevaluated and more inclusive empirical assessments. If we adopt archaeologies of listening as part of our daily practice, then we are embracing ways to decolonize the discipline; simultaneously with opening our minds to richer multidimensional views of pasts, we leave behind the rigid and bounded views of a deaf science.

Note

1. We focus on Binford's disdain for the people who are, in his view, technicians setting up a laboratory to produce data. Readers can contrast the severe limitations that Binford imposed on his Nunamiut project with the rich data observed (and experienced) by ethnographers who lived in Nunamiut hunting camps, not in the government village: Helge Ingstad (1954) and Nicholas Gubser (1965). John M. Campbell (2004) records ethnography told by the man who was Ingstad's host in the Nunamiut camp, later than Binford's project (see Blackman 2004; Ingstad 1998; Kakinya, Paneak, and Ingstad 1987).

References Cited

Agassi, J.
1981   *Science and Society: Studies in the Sociology of Science.* Boston Studies in the Philosophy of Science. Vol. 65. Reidel, Dordrecht.
Binford, L. R.
1962   Archaeology as Anthropology. *American Antiquity* 28(2):217–225.
1972   *An Archaeological Perspective.* Seminar Press, New York.
1978   *Nunamiut Ethnoarchaeology.* Academic Press, New York.
Blackman, M. B.
2004   *Upside Down: Seasons among the Nunamiut.* University of Nebraska Press, Lincoln.
Campbell, J. M. (editor)
2004   *In a Hungry Country: Essays by Simon Paneak.* University of Alaska Press, Fairbanks.

Chemla, K., and E. F. Keller (editors)

2017 *Cultures without Culturalism: The Making of Scientific Knowledge.* Duke University Press, Durham, NC.

Denbow, J., and E. Wilmsen

1986 Advent and Course of Pastoralism in the Kalahari. *Science* 234(4783):1509–1515.

Ehret, C., and M. Posnansky

1982 *The Archaeological and Linguistic Reconstruction of African History.* University of California Press, Berkeley.

Evans-Pritchard, E. E.

1963 *Essays in Social Anthropology.* Free Press, Glencoe, IL.

Fabian, J.

1983 *Time and the Other: How Anthropology Makes Its Object.* Columbia University Press, New York.

Fontein, J.

2006 *The Silence of Great Zimbabwe.* UCL Press, London.

Gubser, N. J.

1965 *The Nunamiut Eskimos, Hunters of Caribou.* Yale University Press, New Haven.

Hall, M.

1984 The Burden of Tribalism: The Social Context of Southern African Iron Age Studies. *American Antiquity* 49(3):455–467.

Herzfeld, M.

2010 Purity and Power: Anthropology from Colonialism to the Global Hierarchy of Value. *Reviews in Anthropology* 39:288–312.

Ingstad, H.

1954 *Nunamiut: Among Alaska's Inland Eskimos.* W. W. Norton, New York.

1998 *Songs of the Nunamiut: Historical Recordings of an Alaskan Eskimo Community.* Tano Aschehoug, Oslo.

Kakinya, E., S. Paneak, and H. Ingstad

1987 *Nunamiut Unipkaanich/Nunamiut Stories: Told in Inupiaq Eskimo.* Fairbanks: Alaska Native Language Center.

Karega-Munene, and P. R. Schmidt

2010 Postcolonial Archaeologies in Africa: Breaking the Silence. *African Archaeological Review* 27:333–337.

Kehoe, A. B.

1978 *François' House, an Early Fur Trade Post on the Saskatchewan.* Saskatchewan Ministry of Culture and Youth, Regina.

1998 Appropriate Terms. *Society for American Archaeology Bulletin* 16(2):14.

2000 François' House, a Significant Pedlars' Post on the Saskatchewan. In *Material Contributions to Ethnohistory: Interpretations of Native North American Life*, edited by M. S. Nassaney and Eric S. Johnson, pp. 173–187. Society for Historical Archaeology and University Press of Florida, Gainesville.

Kehoe, T. F.

1960 Stone Tipi Rings in North-Central Montana and the Adjacent Portions of Alberta, Canada: Their Historical, Ethnological, and Archeological Aspects. Anthropological Papers, No. 62. *Smithsonian Institution Bureau of American Ethnology, Bulletin* 173:417–473. Government Printing Office, Washington, DC.

Knorr-Cetina, K.

1999   *Epistemic Communities*. Harvard Education Press, Cambridge, MA.

Lowie, R.

1915   Oral Traditions and History. *American Anthropologist*. new series 17:597–599.

1917   Oral Traditions and History. *Journal of American Folklore* 30(116):161–167.

Maggs, T.

1976   Iron Age Patterns and Sotho History on the Southern High Veld. *World Archaeology* 7(3):318–332.

Mason, R. J.

2000   Archaeology and Native American Oral Traditions. *American Antiquity* 65(2): 239–266.

2008   *Inconstant Companions: Archaeology and Native American and Oral Traditions*. University of Alabama Press, Tuscaloosa.

Matthews, D.

2006   Epistemic Humility. In *Wisdom, Knowledge, and Management*, edited by J. P. van Gigch, pp. 105–137. C. West Churchman and Related Works Series, Vol. 2. Springer, New York.

McIntosh, S. K., and R. J. McIntosh

1980   *Prehistoric Investigations in the Region of Jenne, Mali*. Cambridge Monographs in African Archaeology 2. BAR, Oxford.

Meighan, C.

1992   Some Scholars' Views on Reburial. *American Antiquity* 57(4):704–710.

1995   Burying American Archaeology. *Archaeology* 47(6):64, 66, 68.

Miller, J.

1980   *The African Past Speaks: Essays on Oral Tradition and History*. Archon, Hamden, CT.

Müller-Wille, L.

2014   *The Franz Boas Enigma*. Baraka Books, Montreal.

Patterson, T. C.

1994   Social Archaeology in Latin America: An Appreciation. *American Antiquity* 59(3):531–537.

Pikirayi, I.

2016   Archaeology, Local Knowledge, and Tradition: The Quest for Relevant Approaches to the Study and Use of the Past in Southern Africa. In *Community Archaeology and Heritage in Africa: Decolonizing Practice*, edited by P. R. Schmidt and I. Pikirayi, pp. 112–135. Routledge, New York.

Posnansky, M.

1966   Kingship, Archaeology, and Historical Myth. *Uganda Journal* 30:1–12.

1968   The Excavation of an Ankole Capital Site at Bweyorere. *Uganda Journal* 32:165–182.

1969   Bigo bya Mugenyi. *Uganda Journal* 33:125–150.

Schmidt, P. R.

1978   *Historical Archaeology: A Structural Approach in an African Culture*. Greenwood Press, Westport, CT.

2006   *Historical Archaeology in Africa: Representation, Social Memory, and Oral Traditions.* AltaMira, Walnut Creek, CA.

2013   Oral History, Oral Traditions and Archaeology: Application of Structural Analysis. In *Oxford Handbook of African Archaeology*, edited by P. Mitchell and P. Lane, pp. 37–47. Oxford University Press, Oxford.

2017   *Community-Based Heritage in Africa: Unveiling Local Research and Development Initiatives.* Routledge, New York.

Schmidt, P. R. (editor)

2009   *Postcolonial Archaeologies in Africa.* SAR Press, Santa Fe, NM.

Schmidt, P. R., and S. Mrozowski (editors)

2013   *The Death of Prehistory.* Oxford University Press, New York.

Silliman, S. (editor)

2008   Collaborative Indigenous Archaeology: Troweling at the Edges, Eyeing the Center. In *Collaborating at the Trowel's Edge: Teaching and Learning in Indigenous Archaeology*, pp. 1–21. University of Arizona Press, Tucson.

Smith, L.

2006   *Uses of Heritage.* Routledge, New York.

Spear, T.

1981   Oral Traditions: Whose History? *History in Africa* 8:165–181.

Spier, L.

1959   Some Central Elements in the Legacy. In *The Anthropology of Franz Boas*, vol. 89, edited by W. Goldschmidt, pp. 146–155. American Anthropological Association, Washington, DC.

Vansina, J.

1965   *Oral Tradition: A Study in Historical Methodology.* Aldine, Chicago.

1985   *Oral Tradition as History.* University of Wisconsin Press, Madison.

Wilmsen, E.

1989   *Land Filled with Flies: A Political Economy of the Kalahari.* University of Chicago Press, Chicago.

Wright, H. T., and S. Kus

1979   An Archaeological Reconnaissance of Ancient Imerina. In *Madagascar in History*, edited by R. K. Kent, pp. 1–31. Foundation for Malagasy Studies, Albany, CA.

Wylie, A.

1995   Epistemic Disunity and Political Integrity. In *Making Alternative Histories: The Practice of Archaeology and History in Non-Western Settings*, edited by P. R. Schmidt and T. C. Patterson, pp. 255–272. SAR Press, Santa Fe.

Zimmerman, L.

2005   First, Be Humble: Working with Indigenous Peoples and Other Descendant Communities. In *Indigenous Archaeologies: Decolonizing Theory and Practice*, edited by C. Smith and H. M. Wobst, pp. 301–314. Routledge, New York.

PART I

Listening with Patience

2

Ethnoarchaeologies of Listening

Learning Technological Ontologies Bit by Bit

KATHRYN WEEDMAN ARTHUR

The Ethiopian leatherworker gathered his fingers together, forming a beak near his mouth, and simultaneously flicked his wrist away from his mouth, opening his hand to the air and aspirating a slight puffing sound—engaging body and sound to emphasize that I should leave this topic alone. I asked him about a story that I had heard from his neighbors concerning stone hidescrapers causing harm when they were discovered in their yards or near their houses. Despite his brush-off, I persisted and thought he said something to the effect of *I did not need to know this and it was not old enough now.* At the time, it did not occur to me that what was not old enough was me. After all, I was 31 years old and married and considered myself an adult. In my mind, I thought he was speaking about the practice.

I was a culture-bound listener (Kuhl 2004), not only in the literal sense of having a difficult time distinguishing between words in the Gamo tonal Omotic language. I was also culturally bound in my way of viewing the world. I could not comprehend that I was not old enough to have access to particular knowledge and thus could not hear it. I would also learn slowly, through long-term participant research among the Gamo, that many Gamo perceive that stones are living entities that literally can move and cause harm. At the time, I was caught in my own experiences of being-in-the world, a human-centered perspective in which object agency is relational (Gosden 2005; Meskell 2004; Robb 2010; Sillar 2009). I was unable to discern the Gamo perceptions of the world and how the clashes in our understandings were intimately entangled with differences as to how we related to resources and technology (Clammer, Poirier, and Schwimmer 2004).

I began my studies among the Gamo 20 years ago as an ethnoarchaeologist, determined to access non-Western worldviews of material culture. My goals, though, were external and mimicked the declarations of Western archaeological academia of the era, which emphasized that ethnoarchaeology was a research strategy that observed practices and behaviors in living communities to test Western archaeological theories and academic approaches (Binford 1978; Gould 1978; Hayden and Cannon 1984; Kleindienst and Watson 1956; Yellen 1977)—a perspective that persists today (Lyons and Casey 2016). My hubris as a young scholar held me back. Only after deeper reflection on my methodology and gentle and persistent guidance from many Gamo Elders did I realize that I refused to be caught and begin transforming into a new phase in life—a stage that would provide me with access to a wealth of knowledge.[1]

I was not a true apprentice to the Gamo, which severely hindered my access to the exact knowledge I desired. I realized that I was simply trying to fit what I observed into Western scholarship and validate Western theories as universal rather than recognizing the legitimacy of alternative ontologies (Alberti and Marshall 2009; Henare, Holbraad, and Wastell 2007; Viveiros de Castro 1998). By simply testing and retesting our theories of the world, we severely limit our ability to provide new knowledge and constrain solutions for future action and understanding (Gonzalez 2012). We not only lose substantial understanding when we dismiss the intellectual contributions of non-Westerners and nonacademics, we also are engaged in intellectual imperialism (Gonzalez 2012; Smith 1999:25–28; Viveiros de Castro 1998). If ethnoarchaeology is going be relevant to the future of our discipline and to the publics we serve, we need to "change like a snake" as the Gamo would say and shed our academic skins.

We must move forward and acknowledge a wide range of intellectual contributions concerning peoples' definitions, perspectives, and relationships to other beings in the world. We need to identify and situate ideas and practices within their proper present-day and historic ontology in a given time and place through onto-praxis (Scott 2007:21). Ethnoarchaeologists should engage onto-praxis by embedding material analyses in reference to local histories and lives—creating the space for revealing the vast tapestry of cultural variation, rather than resorting to universals that tend to homogenize creating tensions and conflicts. The Gamo taught me that learning and immersing oneself in an alternative way of knowing the world/a theory of reality/an ontology (Gosden 2008) occurs bit by bit and requires time, maturity, and the skill to listen. We need to position ourselves in longitudinal relationships that build mutual rapport and respect, apprentice ourselves to earn the privilege and honor to be introduced to alternative ways of knowing the world, and consciously listen and adjust the acoustics with which we hear and understand the deeper and variety of meanings of words as they play out in proverbs, rituals, daily practices, and materials.

Longitudinal Investment and Learning to Listen Bit by Bit

The Gamo transmit their philosophy and ontology to the next generation bit by bit. They believe that a person should acquire knowledge by synthesizing information piece by piece through experience, that wisdom is contained in small bits such as proverbs, and that knowledge is accumulated over the course of one's lifespan little by little, according to one's life course status. Experiential learning, storytelling, and age/status-based knowledge are fairly widespread means of education outside Western society (Barnhardt and Kawagley 2005; Cajete 2000; Kunnie and Goduka 2006; Smith 1999). In at least one account, an ethnoarchaeologist noted (and misconstrued as a joke!) that participants informed him that the knowledge he requested required a lifetime of learning (Binford 1984, 157). We continue to believe that our academic credentials create an exception for us and that weekend and short-term studies are viable means for deriving knowledge outside of our own culture.

In the late 1990s, when I first went to study lithic technology among the Gamo, I was confident in my methodological plan and in my status as a competent adult. I was 30 years old and married. Having left home for college at 16, I had long felt independent. Perhaps like many graduate students, I also was secure in my intellect and knowledge-base derived from years in Western academic training. Few publications in the 1990s explicitly discussed ethnoarchaeological research methods and even fewer exemplified longitudinal research. Notable exceptions included the work of Nicholas David (2008, 2012); Susan Kent (1993, 1998); William Longacre (Longacre and Skibo 1994; Skibo, Graves, and Stark 2007); and Peter Schmidt (1996, 1997).

I realized that I needed ethnographic training and spent the bulk of my Ph.D. course work focused on immersing myself in ethnographic and historical methods and case-studies. I was aware of the importance of language competency, cultural relativity, building rapport, census surveys, questionnaires, mapping, in-depth interviews, collecting life histories and oral traditions, engaging in participant observation, and committing to a long-term study (Arthur and Weedman 2005). Two to three years was the recommended time-frame for dissertation-based cultural studies. I was funded for two years, which seemed like a significant portion of time to dedicate to living abroad and adequate time to build rapport and obtain the knowledge I sought. Learning Gamocalay, the local language, was a challenge, and I hired a schoolteacher to improve my vocabulary and sentence structure. To further complicate matters, I was working in 10 different political districts, which all had their own dialect. Already in my thirties, I greatly exceeded the point at which my brain and ear had converted me to a culture-bound listener (Kuhl 2004).

I still need clarification today on several words that sound almost identical to my ear; the difference is that I know that these variations exist and I know to ask. Learning the nuances and variation in meanings within words, phrases, stories, and proverbs that revealed Gamo perceptions of the world and their material culture required a much longer time and the assistance of many patient teachers, including my assistant for the last 10 years, Yohannes Ethiopia Tocha. These intangible aspects of Gamo culture were initially invisible to me not only because of my lack of language skills but because I had naively believed that the Gamo would accept me as an adult and consider my two years living in the highlands substantial enough to demonstrate my commitment and generate close rapport. *It was not.* Although I left with a wealth of knowledge that I previously did not have, I knew very little about their perceptions of the world or their perceptions of material culture, and my publications concerning Gamo material culture were embedded in academic theories common in archaeology (Arthur 2008; Weedman 2002, 2005, 2006).

I returned to the Gamo highlands in 2006 to begin a community-based archaeological project in the Boreda district that would concentrate on places in the landscape that were identified by the Boreda as significant to their heritage (Arthur et al. 2017). My project goals were entwined with personal, political, and academic changes. I grew up with the privilege of not being concerned with my heritage—except that secrets seemed to weigh heavily on us. I learned with the passing of my mother's parents that they had hidden their Jewish and African American heritage to protect us—a decision that left me with the uncomfortable sense of how quickly and easily one's past can be subsumed.

I also was influenced by movements in the United States and Australia by descendants who were demanding control over their histories (Deloria and Wilkins 1999; Funari 2001; La Roche and Blakey 1997; Smith 1999; Watkins 2000; Weiner 1999). For years, I had been teaching a course on non-Western religion learning about the diversity of ways of being and understanding in the world. I was determined that any future research I conducted would be directed by the Gamo and how and what they wanted preserved concerning their heritage and that it would need to forefront their perception of the world. I worked with interested members of the Boreda-Gamo community, including men, women, youth, Elders, farmers, and craft-specialists, recording their historical knowledge recounted in life histories and oral traditions (Arthur et al. 2017). Elder men led me to their Bayira Deriya (ancestral landscapes) and provided details of their ancestors' settlements, wars, and hunting expeditions. Many Boreda-Gamo identified the household and community spaces of their ancestors based on their historical knowledge and on parallels that they drew in space and material culture with their present settlements and households. This led to more ethnoarchaeological research in which we mapped different households. They taught me and demonstrated to me a variety of technological and ritual practices. Boreda-Gamo Elders also requested that I make maps to accompany their narratives, preserving the locations of their sacred places and settlements associated with their Bayira Deriya. In the course of augmenting some GPS (Global Positioning System) readings at one Bayira Derre (singular) at Barena, I met Detcha Umo (Figure 2.1), a spirit medium who caught my ear

Figure 2.1. Detcha Umo, Boreda spirit medium. Photo by author.

when he crystallized the indigenous Boreda-Gamo method of learning in the phrase "little by little."

At the start of a cool and clear day in 2012, I was exasperated, which makes me impatient and less likely to listen; by the end of the day, I had met the spirit medium Detcha Umo and was listening attentively. At the beginning of the day, I was reviewing GPS data for Barena, a subdistrict of the Boreda district, when one of my colleagues informed me that I had not recorded the locations using the correct reference system (hence my annoyed state). I had to return to Barena and revisit the more than 20 sacred places, which meant one more day reading numbers off a device rather than spending time with Elders and learning about the significance of the locations from them. My one solace was that I would have the opportunity to return to the Zala Gago *debusha* (coming together meeting place), one of the best-preserved sacred places in Boreda. I started my day there.

Unexpectedly, I was distracted almost immediately. It was both a market day and the time of year when men were plowing their fields. But when I arrived two men were sitting on the rock wall that enclosed the sacred meeting place. One of the two men was wrapped in a heavy white blanket with a bright red fringe and his hair was arranged in six long braids, atypical for a Boreda man; he was a Maro or spirit medium. A majority of the Boreda spirit mediums are women, who as children are caught in river water by the Dydanta (water spirits), nearly drowned but saved. They recover in seclusion in their father's home, offer a sacrificial sheep to the spirits at a feast at their father's house, and thereafter serve as mediums between the spirit and human world (Arthur 2013).

We accompanied the spirit medium named Detcha to his home and learned that the Dydanta had caught him as he was getting ready for his circumcision ceremony. He began shaking, so the people bathed him in water. Afterward he spent a long time in his father's home recovering. Ever since this event, the spirits have spoken to him. People bring the stories of their misfortunes to mediums like Detcha, who in turn hear from the spirits how people have offended them and the ways in which they can make amends and relieve their misfortunes. During our conversation, Detcha described his practice: "We have a science of religion—all this I do is science, for all answers we try and try again, little by little, it is a process based on observation and experience" (Detcha Umo, personal communication 2012; Arthur 2018:66). Detcha's transformation through water and the phrase "little by little" conjured Zara Yacob, a man considered to be Ethiopia's founding philosopher.

In the seventeenth century Zara Yacob wrote a treatise titled *Hatata*, which argued that it is best to acquire knowledge bit by bit through human rationality, and in doing so broke tradition with his contemporaries in Ethiopia as well as with "Frang" or European scholars (Sumner 1986:38–39). *Hatata* "refers to a mode of thinking marked by penetrating a phenomenon with the tools of inspection and examination piece by piece" (Kiros 2005:45). Zara is recognized as the founder of the African Enlightenment and a rival to Descartes, as he reasoned that wisdom comes not from God but through the process of experience (Kiros 2001, 2005).[2] Zara's emphasis on experiential knowledge irrigated a future course of learning for many Ethiopians that differs from that of the West (Kiros 2005).

Many Boreda taught me how learning bit by bit, building on my experiences, listening to them, and learning the deeper meanings to their words, proverbs, and phrases was essential to my ethnoarchaeological research methods. Boreda wisdom and philosophy are transmitted in small bits, in their proverbs and sayings. Indeed, several scholars of Ethiopian philosophy argue that the wisdom of Ethiopian thought is revealed through proverbs and oral communication rather than through long treatises (Kiros 2005; Sumner 1986). For my own instruction, Gamo Elders doled out information little by little and left me to ponder and sort out meanings and connections for myself (Figure 2.2). When I met them next,

Figure 2.2. K. W. Arthur interviewing Boreda Elders. Photo with permission by Amanda Wilkerson.

they would question me and make adjustments to my knowledge. When I finally correctly expressed their meaning, they would smile, nod their heads, and say, "Now you know our secrets!" Their discourse was infused with proverbs such as "A wise man listens and speaks little" and "The hen does not give birth immediately." A conversation documented by ethnographer Marc Abélès (2012 [1983]:35) illustrates that this method is widespread in the Gamo highlands: "It is not in the course of one day that *woga* [Gamo ontology] can be learnt. Besides how lengthy is the germination process after the seed is sown! Does the hen give birth immediately? Day after day the egg is brooded, and similarly your knowledge will grow little by little."

For many, Gamo knowledge is transmitted slowly through experience, through a process, and throughout one's life time. The importance of the connection of listening, time, and wisdom is expressed in Ethiopian thought as early as the sixteenth century in the *Book of Philosophers*:

> The wise man is he who knows the time, the time to speak, and the time to keep quiet, the time to listen, and the time to reply. (Kiros 2005:4)
> The wise man is like a farmer who knows the time of the maturation of his crops. (Sumner 1974:223)
> A wise man gives up his world and examines the future. (Sumner 1974:226)

Sumner (1974:221–224) argued that sixteenth-century Ethiopian thought diverged from contemporaneous Western thinking in that "time is the creation in process": it has stages and is ordered, though it lacks a predestination controlled by God. Learning and acquiring knowledge requires rationality, piecing together knowledge bit by bit, listening, and knowing when to move forward.

In a biography by Teodros Kiros (2005), Zara Yacob credits his life experience to the development of his wisdom, a description that parallels the Boreda philosophy and acknowledgment of life stages. Zara attributes his wisdom to his life, recalling his birth, his education, his fall into a ravine, more education, and his seclusion in a cave, where he secured refugee from persecution (Kiros 2005). Similarly, many Boreda say that people learn proper behavior and practice, including technological practices, little by little, in accordance with changes in their life course marked by rites of passage that mark new phases of social responsibility (Arthur 2018; for similar rites of passage descriptions, see Freeman 1997, 2001; Hamer 1996; Kassam 1999; Turner 1969; Van Gennep 1960). The Boreda crystallize their philosophy in the proverb "Keep changing like a snake," which conveys to youth that life is a process that changes bit by bit in stages, with the shedding of former lives to move into the future. If individuals fail to transform in life, they are *t'unna* (infertile and wasteful), which has the potential to create chaos and disrupt the world.

Men and women who properly transform into their different life course stages from a human infant to child, circumcised youth, married adult, wise adult/ ritual-political leader (including a Maro; plural Maroti), and ancestor living with seniority and prestige (*bayira*). Each rites of passage ceremony symbolizes the human life cycle and consists of a particular act at each stage of the rite: birth—cleansing with water (*yella*), circumcision—cutting (*katsara*), maturation—seclusion (*dume*), marriage—feasting (*bullacha*), and transition to new being—cleansing with water and anointing with butter (*sofe*). As in the case of the seventeenth-century Ethiopian philosopher Zara Yacob, who acquired new knowledge after falling in a ravine (Sumner 1986), river water is an essential transformative medium in all Boreda ritual practices. Boreda spirit mediums are caught in river water, instigating their transformation into Maroti (Arthur 2013); at birth Boreda newborns are washed with river water; and at puberty young men wash together in the district boundary river prior to their presentation in the community as young adults. In addition, Boreda acquire knowledge during ritual seclusion in forests and households, like Zara Yacob, who secluded himself in a cave. A Boreda person's maturation from a child to a circumcised adult for men and to a mother for women is considered the most important life transformation and is accompanied by a long ritualized period of household seclusion.

Many Boreda recounted in their life histories that they began to learn their trade in life and its connection to their indigenous ontology (Etta Woga: Fig Tree Culture) during seclusion (*dume*) rites of passage for puberty (for men) and marriage (for women). For example, a Boreda leatherworker stated: "When I was a youth, I was circumcised. I began to stand by my father, side by side. During *dume*, I learned and practiced to scrape. I learned to produce my own hidescrapers" (Osha Hanicha, personal communication July 2012; Arthur 2018:78).

When I first began working in the Gamo highlands I was married but without a child. I brushed off persistent comments by women that I should leave and return to my husband's house to produce a child (Arthur 2020). I was unaware that many Boreda perceived me either to be a child or to be infertile (*t'unna*), incapable of change and thus not ripe to receive adult knowledge and responsibilities. The absence of a child signaled that I had not participated in long-term household seclusion after marriage when the first child is often conceived. After a woman births her first child, she acquires a new status and title (*mischer*) in society. During her social reproduction, her seclusion in the married household, she acquires essential technological knowledge from her mother-in-law and sisters-in-law. She learns her future technological responsibilities in society: farming, brewing beer, spinning, basketry and gourd work, and possibly making pottery and its connection to their indigenous ontology, Etta Woga.

Ten years after I began to work in the Boreda highlands, I returned and spent the subsequent eight summers working with Boreda. I brought my child with me. For many Boreda, my return demonstrated my long-term investment in their community and the birth of a child signaled my status change into a responsible adult. Not until a ceremony at the most sacred of all Boreda landscapes in which my daughter was initiated into the Boreda community did Elders express that as her mother I was now *mischer* and also a Boreda adult (Arthur 2020). After this point, ritual specialists made themselves available for me to interview.

As a mother, I understood the responsibility of helping forge an identity for the next generation and quickly realized that two years was a short-term investment in any social relationship. I had a sense of understanding the importance of the past, change, and the future. I was now ready to accept and internalize adult knowledge and mature enough to represent these ideas to others. Boreda men and women, in turn, began to disclose to me their philosophies, foregrounding a deeper understanding of their relationships and perceptions of technology. Today most Boreda practice Orthodox Christianity, but many, particularly Elders, continue to hold to the proscriptions outlined in their indigenous religion, Etta Woga. I came to know how the phrase "bit by bit" was significant to the Boreda of the southern Ethiopian Gamo highlands in terms of their way of knowing the world—their ontology: Etta Woga, particularly their way of acquiring and practicing lithic technology.

Reproductive Ontology: The Birth and Death of Stone Tools

> In old days they celebrated by sacrificing for the Spirits and they assumed the earth has its own spirit . . . they believed in the power of the earth, stone, and tree. Every village had Tsalahay trees and water. (Shara Luga, personal communication, 2007)

In the Boreda-Gamo perception of reality expressed in Etta Woga, humans and nonhumans (including trees, water, mountains, caves, and stone) are alive (Arthur 2018). The essence/life force/spirit (Tsalahay) of being embodied soil, stone, water, rainbows, sun, moon, and wind that came into being through the reproductive forces of the earth without human interference. Evidence of their existence was their ability to change exhibited in the life cycle (*deetha*) and their creation through the reproductive process. Like humans, stone tools shed their skin and proceeded through life-cycle rituals that were parallel in space and action to those of humans to ensure their proper development.

Boreda knappers perceive stone tools to be male. Chert and obsidian began life as parts of the parent raw material, a fetus (*gatchino*), and proceeded to become an infant (*uka*) individual piece of raw material, a boy (*na7a*) tool blank, an unused tool (*pansa*) youth, a married (*wodala*) hafted tool, and an Elder (*chima*) tool ready for discard. *Deetha* organized leatherworking and lithic technology into five stages facilitating proper practice and ensuring the longevity of the stone being. A stone being is birthed and washed in water (*yella*) at the quarry; he is knapped or circumcised (*katsara*) at the quarry and at home; he is secluded (*dume*) in storage at the home; he is married with the haft in the household (*bullacha*); and is reincorporated into the earth (*sofe*) in garden discard. When nonhumans enter Boreda social life, Etta Woga stipulated that humans have a responsibility to respect and properly interact with nonhuman beings, which impacted the practices associated with the birth and death of stone tools.

Give Birth to Stones

The phrase "Give birth to stones" is generally considered a grave insult among *mala*, who define themselves as farmers, working land that they have acquired through agnatic descent. The phrase speaks loudly of the contempt that many Boreda farmers harbor for the status of leatherworkers and their perceived infertility in society as a result of birthing stone. Etta Woga established rules that insist birth is a female activity and that reproduction involves male and female interaction. Knapping and leatherworking are male-controlled technologies among the Boreda. Excluding women from "reproduction," particularly birth, is a transgression of the natural order. Male leatherworkers during their puberty rites of passage formally participate in their first offensive act by birthing knapping stone from the earth—infringing on female reproductive authority as midwives.

In the past, young men were circumcised with stone knives prior to birthing stone. As the knives first transformed a young man, he then gained access to practices and knowledge for transforming stone. Yet his act of birthing stone was a transgression. His neighbors, the *mala* farmers, prohibited him from completing the final ritual stage of puberty rites of passage, which is public incorporation at the marketplace (*sofe*). Consequently, stone tool–using leatherworkers do not fully transform and shed their skins, reinforcing publicly their impure and infertile status. Within Boreda communities, leatherworkers historically were referred to as *tsoma*, who inherited their trade and were forced to live segregated lives from *mala* in marriage, diet, resources, and community, and household space. Their perceived impure status prohibited leatherworkers and other craft specialist *tsoma* from entering the sacred forests and caves with springs at the ancestral landscapes (Bayira Deriya) and from participation in historic ritual festivals, such as the summer solstice renewal bonfire or light festival (Tompe).

Leatherworkers, though, birth their own light (*tompe*) in the form of chalcedonies at their sacred grounds—quarries (Figure 2.3). Quarries are located in river gorges. Like Bayira Deriya, which are located on mountaintops and caves hollowed and eroded by the rain, quarries are direct evidence of the vitality of the earth. In river gorges of the lowlands, the earth as womb is penetrated by

Figure 2.3. Boreda knappers working at a quarry. Photo by author.

the rain, creating chert nodules. Quarries are a part of a knapper's patrimony: access to quarries is restricted based on a man's patrilineage just as *mala* restrict access to Bayira Deriya based on their claims of direct descent from the founding settlers (Arthur et al. 2017). Knappers travel to quarries in small groups, usually consisting of an experienced Elder and his sons or grandsons. Inexperienced and younger men never travel to quarries alone due to the potential for danger.

Elder leatherworkers often place bowls of porridge in tree hallows or at the edge of the river at the quarry, as offerings to the spirits (Tsalahay) to protect the quarrying group from the earth's harmful forces. Flooding waters have swept men to their deaths, landslides buried them in early graves, and illness often inflicts a man after he has quarried. As a living entity under the Boreda way of knowing, Etta Woga, a stone has the potential to cause harm and also earns the right to be properly cared for from the moment it is born to ensure its proper development. With the guidance of experienced knappers, men work to remove nodular cherts from the earth, dismissing surface materials. They select only nodular cherts, which exude a shine or light (*tompe*) as evidence of their life force (Tsalahay) to be birthed. These small nodules are considered to be fetuses (*gatchinotta*). Knappers in each community prefer particular colors of chert, which they believe are more developed than others. Stones not only communicate through light and color but also issue sound.

At the quarry after birth, the infant stone is circumcised (*katsara*) or knapped and is perceived to emanate a sound. A nearly blind leatherworker stated that he selected proper knapping stone by the sound that the stone makes when he knaps/circumcises it. He whispered that when he struck the stone it spoke Odetsa, the secret ritualized language of the leatherworkers. Leatherworkers use the word *tekata* to refer to knapping, which literally means "to protect," and the debitage that is removed is referred to as the "infertile waste" (*chacha*). The implication is that the act of knapping, like circumcision at puberty and removing the umbilical cord at birth, is an act of protection. Knapping protects the future of the infant stone and allows it to develop by removing the impure infertile aspects. Knapping is considered the most difficult aspect of leatherworking and requires years of listening, observing, learning, and practicing with expert and master knappers. Just as they would not leave a human youth to mature on his own or alone in the presence of other youths, expert knappers do not leave knapping to the whim of youths. Stone is protected, and youths practice for at least 10 years in the presence of experts, who directly intercede on the behalf of the stone and may even take over production. The Boreda perception that stone is a living entity encourages long-term apprenticeships and control of lithic reproduction by experts. Western archaeologists and narratives often assume that lithic technology can be self-taught or learned through experimental attempts to mimic a tool's form (Bordes 1947, 1961; Flenniken 1984; Tixier 1974; Tostevin 2012). This approach amplifies the perspective that stone, clay, and other earthly materials are nonliving, resulting in a lack of concern for nonproductive events. In the absence of direct instruction from experts in experimental studies, novices produce a large amount of debitage and often do not produce actual tools or produce nonfunctional tools. Their knapping results in production errors (for a collected list of errors, see Bamforth and Finlay 2008). Expert Elder Boreda leatherworkers closely monitor and assist youth for at least 10 years before apprentices are encouraged to knap, engage, and bury stone scrapers on their own. Boreda experts take over production of tools from novices, resulting in fewer production errors, a consistent production of viable stone being (tools), and community standardization in tool form that is contrary to experimental studies (Arthur 2018; Weedman 2002). The Boreda perception of stone tools as living beings ensures that skilled knappers have a responsibility to protect the birth and the development of stone tools. As stone tools mature and reach an age when they are no longer productive, skilled knappers carefully bury them in household gardens.

The Spirit Mediums Are Never Fools, the Leatherworker's Neighbors Are Strong

What is seemingly hidden from the unacultured ear in this proverb is the power of discarded/deceased hidescrapers. Leatherworkers' neighbors are the *mala*-farmers, who are strong because they have the protection of the spirit medium. Historically and to some extent today, leatherworkers and their stone hidescrapers are considered the source of many misfortunes and problems in a community. To contain the perceived pollution of leatherworkers, they reside separately from farmers at the edge of communities on grades that are too steep for agriculture. Their segregation may be considered a symbolic state of persistent seclusion (*dume*) and their inability to transform and shed their skin. Stone tools as beings associated with leatherworkers spend their lives in a leatherworker's household compound and are also considered by many *mala* to be the source of infertility and pollution.

When a stone hidescraper is no longer functional or dies, he is buried with other hidescrapers near the base of a tree in the leatherworkers' garden. It is common practice even today to plant a tree at the burial site of a deceased family member. In the past, leatherworkers, other craft-specialists, and even the children of *mala* who did not complete their puberty rites of passage ceremonies were buried in household gardens rather than in the cemeteries at Bayira Deriya. Final discard or incorporation (*sofe*) of all lithic materials, the deceased scraper (*hayikes*), and the debitage or infertile waste (*chacha*) takes place in the household garden (Figure 2.4). The *hayikes* return to the earth and rejuvenate the life-cycle process, supplying the essence for new stone beings, like the essence of the leatherworker who transforms into an ancestral being.

The leatherworkers intentionally and carefully bury stone beings in their household gardens to respect the stones and prevent them from wondering and settling elsewhere, where they may inflict harm. As noted at the beginning of this chapter, chert and obsidian sometimes are perceived to bury themselves in the houses or household gardens of the *mala*, who believe that the stones, particularly obsidian, contain a bad spirit (Bita) that will bring them misfortune through infertility of fields, domestic stock, and people. "The black one [obsidian] was only used on hoofed animals with wounds, not people. The black one, like a dead cat

Figure 2.4. Boreda stone hidescrapers rest together in the garden. Photo by author.

or rat or wood on someone's land, can cause bad things to happen; it can have a bad spirit" (Badheso Tera, personal communication June 2008; Arthur 2018:70).

A *mala* who finds the offending item in his house or compound consulted the community spirit medium, who prescribed the diagnosis as Bita practices. The spirit medium suggested how the Bita could be removed, usually by offering a goat and placing enset leaves full of roasted barley around the person's property. Enset and barley are perceived to be among the oldest of crops and have a seniority featured prominently in many Boreda rituals in association with fertility and well-being. Leatherworkers said that whenever they acquired some small bit of wealth, they would be accused of encouraging the stone to move out of their household to bring misfortune. The community's punishment for Bita practices was either to ask the offender to provide a small feast for the community or to impose further sanctions restricting interaction between the leatherworker and other community members. The perceived impure status of male knapping-leatherworkers and the recognized vitality of the stone tools ensures that both are spatially segregated from the larger community. Learning slowly, bit by bit over decades, through proverbs and observations, eventually led to my exposure to Boreda ontology or perceptions of their relationships with nonhuman beings and clarified the Boreda lithic technological practices and status of the male leatherworker.

Conclusion

Longitudinal research among the Boreda has awakened me to the importance of letting oneself become a cultural apprentice who develops sensitivity to the existence of a wide variety of historical and present-day ontologies that inform technologies. By listening and submitting to the Boreda practice of learning bit by bit through proverbs and experience and by maturing in my own time, I eventually was given access and the responsibility of learning their ontology, Etta Woga. Etta Woga is significantly different from the ontology of most archaeologists. In the past and some Boreda today perceive that stone tools have a biography and the power to change in the presence or absence of humans as well as the power to impact humans. The living status of stone tools sets a moral order for interaction. Male conscription of "reproduction" results in low status of the male toolmaker, contrary to Western tropes. Etta Woga also ensures that apprenticeships are long term, emphasizing community investment in the care and well-being of nonhuman beings.

The Boreda ontology Etta Woga shapes the life of both the knapper and the stone tool. According to the tenets of Etta Woga, all matter is in existence, sharing an empowering essence, which most closely resembles other African ontologies (Diop 1974; Karenga 2004, 178, 186; Obenga 2004). All beings demonstrate their existence through their ability to change, which is instigated by a reproductive process that may or may not involve humans. Knapping stone is born and comes into existence without human interference through other earthly life forces in a kind of vitalism. The stone has a power to cut and circumcise a youth, to enter households and fields causing infertility, and to influence other earthly agents resulting in harm. Once a stone enters human social life in a seemingly relational alliance, the stone experiences a life course that includes circumcision (knapping), rest in the house (storage), marriage (hafting), activity in the house (use), and burial (discard) in a knapper's garden. I am hesitant to categorize Etta Woga as either animistic (Tylor 1871), vitalist (Bergson 1998 [1907]), or relational (Astor-Aguilera 2010). Like many African ontologies, it incorporates aspects of all of these. Subsuming it under one would eliminate the space for recognizing non-Western ontologies as legitimate alternative realities. The Boreda ontology through which many perceive stone as alive cannot be subsumed under animism, vitalism, or relational theories. It is a unique ontology.

Gaining the knowledge and the permission to relate alternative ways of knowing the world requires longitudinal studies and a willingness to shed academic training and theories, deferring to listening and experience. I am not unaware of the voices of students and current practitioners of ethnoarchaeology. I understand that most scholars who practice ethnoarchaeology do so in departments or programs in archaeology and that ethnography and the four-field approach emphasized in some U.S.-based anthropology departments may not be widespread. I am cognizant of the simultaneous emphasis on STEM (Science, Technology, Engineering, and Math) programming and funding that shrinks money and resources for long-term humanistic research. Archaeologists are increasingly aware that descendants have a human right to control their heritage; they equally have the right for their present-day materials to be kept in the context of the ontologies in which they came into existence—to be accredited for their theories of reality. Longitudinal research and accepting that communities may have other status criteria for transmitting knowledge to researchers in spite of their academic ones is essential for engaging in ethical ethnoarchaeological practice.

Notes

1. I use the word "caught" intentionally as a reference to Gamo perceptions. Individuals are caught by others and encouraged to transition to new phases in their lives.

2. In Ethiopia, people are respectfully addressed by using their first name rather than their surname or father's name.

References Cited

Abélès, M.

2012 [1983] *Placing Politics*. Translated by D. Lussier. Barwell Press, Oxford.

Alberti, B., and Y. Marshall

2009 Animating Archaeology: Local Theories and Conceptually Open-Ended Methodologies. *Cambridge Archaeological Journal* 19(3):344–356.

Arthur, J. W., and K. Weedman

2005 Chapter 7: Ethnoarchaeology. In *Handbook for Archaeological Methods*, vol. 1, edited by H. Maschner and C. Chippindale, pp. 216–269. AltaMira Press, Walnut Creek, CA.

Arthur, K. W.

2008 Stone-Tool Hide Production: The Gamo of Southwestern Ethiopia and Cross-Cultural Comparisons. *Anthropozoologica* 43(1):67–98.

2013 Material Entanglements: Gender, Ritual, and Politics among the Boreda of Southern Ethiopia. *African Study Monographs* 47 (Supplemental):53–80.

2018 *The Lives of Stone Tools: Crafting the Status, Skill, and Identity of Flintknappers*. University of Arizona Press, Tucson.

2020 Preserving and Reconstituting Feminine Prestige and Dignity through Heritage in the Gamo Highlands. In *Engendering Heritage: Contemporary Feminist Approaches to Archaeological Heritage Practice*, edited by T. C. Cain and T. P. Raczek. Archaeological Papers of the American Anthropological Association, Volume 31. Washington D.C.

Arthur, K. W., Y. E. Tocha, M. C. Curtis, B. Lakew, and J. W. Arthur

2017 Seniority through Ancestral Landscapes: Community Archaeology in the Highlands of Southern Ethiopia. *Journal of Community Archaeology and Heritage* 4(1):101–114.

Astor-Aguilera, M. A.

2010 *The Maya World of Communicating Objects: Quadripartite Crosses, Trees, and Stones*. University of New Mexico Press, Albuquerque.

Bamforth, D., and N. Finlay

2008 Introduction: Archaeological Approaches to Lithic Production Skill and Craft Learning. *Journal of Archaeological Method and Theory* 15(1):1–27.

Barnhardt, R. and A. O. Kawagley

2005 Indigenous Knowledge Systems and Alaska Native Ways of Knowing. *Anthropology and Education Quarterly* 36(1):8–23.

Bergson, H.

1998 [1907] *Creative Evolution*. Translated by A. Mitchell. Dover, Mineola, NY.

Binford, L. R.

1978   *Nunamiut Ethnoarchaeology.* Academic Press, New York.

1984   An Alyawara Day: Flour, Spinifix Gum and Shifting Perspectives. *Journal of Anthropological Research* 40(1):157–182.

Bordes, F.

1947   Étude comparative des différentes techniques de taille du silex et des roches dures. *L'Anthropologie* 51:1–29.

1961   *Typologie du Paléolithique Ancien et Moyen.* Imprimeries Delmas, Bordeaux, France.

Cajete, G.

2000   *Native Science: Natural Laws of Interdependence.* Clear Lights Publisher, Santa Fe, NM.

Clammer, J., S. Poirier, and E. Schwimmer

2004   Introduction: The Relevance of Ontologies in Anthropology: Reflections on a New Anthropological Field. In *Figured World: Ontological Obstacles in Intercultural Relations,* edited by J. Clammer, S. Poirier, and E. Schwimmer, pp. 3–24. University of Toronto Press, Toronto, Canada.

David, N.

2008   *Performance and Agency: The DGB Sites of Northern Cameroon* (Vol. 1830). British Archaeological Reports Ltd., Oxford.

2012   *Metals in Mandara Mountains Society and Culture.* Africa World Press, Trenton, NJ.

Deloria, V., Jr., and D. E. Wilkins

1999   *Tribes, Treaties, and Constitutional Tribulations.* University of Texas Press, Austin.

Diop, C. A.

1974   *African Origin of Civilization: Myth or Reality.* Chicago Review Press, Chicago.

Flenniken, J. J.

1984   The Past, Present, and Future of Flintknapping: An Anthropological Perspective. *Annual Review of Anthropology* 13 (1984):187–203.

Freeman, D.

1997   Images of Fertility: The Indigenous Concept of Power in Doko Masho, Southwest Ethiopia. In *Ethiopia in Broader Perspectives: Papers of the XIIth International Conference of Ethiopian Studies, Volume II,* edited by K. Fukui, E. Kurimoto, and M. Shigeta, pp. 342–357. Ethiopian Studies Association, Kyoto, Japan.

2001   *Initiating Change in Highland Ethiopia: Causes and Consequences of Cultural Transformation.* Cambridge University Press, Cambridge.

Funari, P. P.

2001   Public Archaeology from a Latin American Perspective. *Public Archaeology* 1(4):239–243.

Gonzalez, W. J.

2012   Methodological Universalism in Science and Its Limits, Imperialism versus Complexity. In *Thinking about Provincialism in Thinking,* edited by K. Bryzechczyn and K. Paprzychka, pp. 155–176. Rodopi, Amsterdam.

Gosden, C.

2005   What Do Objects Want? *Journal of Archaeological Method and Theory* 12(3):193–211.

2008   Social Ontologies. *Philosophical Transactions of the Royal Society: Biological Sciences* 363(1499):2003–2010.

Gould, R. A.

1978   Beyond Analogy in Ethnoarchaeology. In *Explanations in Ethnoarchaeology*, edited by R. Gould, pp. 249–293. University of New Mexico Press, Albuquerque.

Hamer, J. H.

1996   Inculcation of Ideology among the Sidama of Ethiopia. *Journal of the International African Institute* 66 (4):526–551.

Hayden, B., and A. Cannon

1984   *The Structure of Material Systems: Ethnoarchaeology in the Maya Highlands*. Society for American Archaeology Papers No. 3. Society for American Archaeology, Washington, DC.

Henare, A., M. Holbraad, and S. Wastell

2007   *Thinking through Things*. Routledge, London.

Karenga, M.

2004   *Maat, the Moral Ideal in Ancient Egypt: A Study in Classical African Ethics*. Taylor and Francis, Hoboken, NJ.

Kassam, A.

1999   Ritual and Classification: A Study of the Booran Oromo Terminal Sacred Grade Rites of Passage. *Bulletin of the School of Oriental and African Studies* 62(3):484–503.

Kent, S.

1993   *Domestic Architecture and the Use of Space: An Interdisciplinary Cross-cultural Study*. Cambridge University Press, Cambridge.

1998   Gender and Prehistory in Africa. In *Gender in African Prehistory*, edited by S. Kent, pp. 9–24. Sage, New Delhi.

Kiros, T.

2001   Zara Yacob: A Seventeenth-Century Ethiopian Founder of Modernity in Africa. In *Explorations in African Political Thought*, edited by T. Kiros, pp. 69–80. Routledge, New York.

2005   *Zara Yacob: Rationality of the Human Heart*. Red Sea Press, Lawrenceville, NJ.

Kleindienst, M. R., and P. J. Watson

1956   Action Archaeology: The Archaeological Inventory of a Living Community. *Anthropology Tomorrow* 5(1):75–78.

Kuhl, P. K.

2004   Early Language Acquisition: Cracking the Speech Code. *Nature Reviews Neuroscience* 5(2004):831–843.

Kunnie, J. E., and N. I. Goduka (editors)

2006   *Indigenous Peoples' Wisdom and Power: Affirming Our Knowledge through Narratives*. Ashgate, Burlington, VT.

La Roche, C. J., and M. L. Blakey

1997   Seizing Intellectual Power: The Dialogue at the New York African Burial Ground. *Historical Archaeology* 31(3):84–106.

Longacre, W. A., and J. Skibo

1994   *Kalinga Ethnoarchaeology*. Smithsonian Institution, Washington, DC.

Lyons, D., and J. Casey

2016 It's a Material World: The Critical and On-going Value of Ethnoarchaeology in Understanding Variation, Change, and Materiality. *World Archaeology* 48(5): 609–627.

Meskell, L.

2004 *Object Worlds in Ancient Egypt: Material Biographies Past and Present*. Bloomsbury Academic Press, London.

Obenga, T.

2004 Egypt: Ancient History of African Philosophy. In *A Companion to African Philosophy*, edited by Kwasi Wiredu, pp. 31–49. Wiley-Blackwell, Malden, MA.

Robb, J.

2010 Beyond Agency. *World Archaeology* 42(4):493–520.

Schmidt, P. R. (editor)

1996 *The Culture and Technology of African Iron Production*. University Press of Florida, Gainesville.

1997 *Iron Technology in East Africa: Symbolism, Science, and Archaeology*. Indiana University Press, Bloomington.

Scott, M. W.

2007 *The Severed Snake: Matrilineages, Making Place, and Melanesian Christianity in Southeast Solomon Islands*. Carolina Academic Press, Durham, NC.

Sillar, B.

2009 The Social Agency of Things? Animism and Materiality in the Andes. *Cambridge Archaeological Journal* 19(3):369–379.

Skibo, J. M., M. W. Graves, and M. T. Stark (editors)

2007 *Archaeological Anthropology: Perspectives on Method and Theory*. University of Arizona Press, Tucson.

Smith, L. T.

1999 *Decolonizing Methodologies: Research and Indigenous Peoples*. Zed Books, London.

Sumner, C.

1974 *Ethiopian Philosophy. Volume 1: The Book of the Wise Philosophers*. Central Printing Press, Addis Ababa, Ethiopia.

1986 *The Sources of African Philosophy: The Ethiopian Philosophy of Man*. Franz Steiner Verlag, Wiesbaden/Stuttgart, Germany.

Tixier, J.

1974 *Glossary for the Description of Stone Tools with Special Reference to the Epipalaeolithic of the Maghreb*. Special Publication 1, Newsletter of Lithic Technology, Pullman, WA.

Tostevin, G. B.

2012 *Seeing Lithics: A Middle-Range Theory for Testing for Cultural Transmission in the Pleistocene*. Oxbow Books, Oxford.

Turner, V.

1969 *The Ritual Process: Structure and Anti-structure*. Aldine Publishing, Chicago.

Tylor, E. B.

1871 *Primitive Culture*. J. Murray, London.

Van Gennep, A.

1960 *The Rites of Passage.* University of Chicago Press, Chicago.

Viveiros de Castro, E.

1998 Cosmological Deixis and Amerindian Perspectivism. *Journal of the Royal Anthropological Institute* 4(3):469–488.

Watkins, J.

2000 *Indigenous Archaeology: American Indian Values and Scientific Practice.* AltaMira, Walnut Creek, CA.

Weedman, K. J.

2002 On the Spur of the Moment: Effects of Age and Experience on Hafted Stone Scraper Morphology. *American Antiquity* 67(4):731–744.

2005 Gender and Stone Tools: An Ethnographic Study of the Konso and Gamo Hideworkers of Southern Ethiopia. In *Gender and Hide Production*, edited by L. Frink and K. J. Weedman, pp. 175–196. AltaMira, Walnut Creek, CA.

2006 An Ethnoarchaeological Study of Hafting and Stone Tool Diversity among the Gamo of Ethiopia. *Journal of Archaeological Method and Theory* 13(3):188–237.

Weiner, J. F.

1999 Culture in a Sealed Envelope: The Concealment of Australian Aboriginal Heritage and Tradition in the Hindmarsh Island Bridge Affair. *Journal of the Royal Anthropological Institute* 5(2):193–210.

Yellen, J.

1977 *Archaeological Approaches to the Present: Models for Reconstructing the Past.* Academic Press, New York.

3

Continuing Writings on Stone

CAMINA WEASEL MOCCASIN

Scholars acknowledge that all cultures contain both tangible and intangible heritage. So far, discussions of appropriation and repatriation have principally focused on tangible objects, those items held in museum and private collections. Here I address the issue of appropriating and repatriating that which cannot be seen, the intangible cultural heritage. Specifically, I discuss repatriation of the spiritual connection associated with the making of rock art. My personal experience with the proactive relationship between the Blackfoot community and Writing-on-Stone Provincial Park/Áísínai'pi National Historic Site is my case study.

My first encounter with Áísínai'pi took place when I was 16 years old. My father took my brother and me to see a pictograph called the Thunderbird, located in a cave among the sandstone cliffs of Writing-on-Stone Provincial Park. As we drove through the main entrance of the park, I was immediately awestruck by the landscape that Iihtsipáítapiiyo'pa (creator) created. The prairie broke into a beautiful, lush riparian environment surrounded by sandstone cliffs and oddly shaped hoodoos (rock spires with an eroded narrow column and a cap resembling a mushroom), backdropped by the Sweetgrass Hills dominating the southern horizon (Figure 3.1). We proceeded into the campground area and found a trailer labeled "Interpreters."

A woman in a park uniform walked out of the trailer, and my father began speaking to her in Blackfoot, essentially telling her that he was looking for an interpreter. She wore a large grin and replied, "*Oki*, I am Bonnie Moffett." My father seemed pleased that she knew the basic greeting in Blackfoot. He explained that he heard about the Thunderbird pictograph and brought his children to see it. She said that it was located in an area of the park known as the Restricted

Figure 3.1. View of the Milk River valley from the Writing-on-Stone park entrance. Photo by author.

Area. I immediately thought that there would be no way they would allow us to see it, at least not that day. Bonnie went on to give my father directions on the best access point for us to enter the Restricted Area with some privacy and kindly asked if we would return after our trip to let her know that we had made it back safely. I remember feeling impressed by the level of respect and trust that the park staff had shown us that day.

My father, brother, and I followed Bonnie's directions and after some searching came upon Ksiistsikómiipi'kssii. The impressive image is made of red ochre and measures 1 m across. Immediately my father pulled out his cigarettes and began rolling out the tobacco in his hand to leave as an offering; we were instructed to do the same. My brother and I sat and rested as my father explained the symbols and interpreted the rock art image for us. That day made me realize the importance of rock art to Siksikaitsitapii (Blackfoot people) and our way of life. After spending some time exploring and searching for rock art, we returned to the Interpreter trailer, where my father had a short visit with Bonnie. I had no idea at the time that I would one day work as an interpreter at Writing-on-Stone/Áísínai'pi.

In June 2015 I began an Indigenous Internship Program provided through the Indigenous Relations Ministry of the Alberta Government. Due to my cultural and academic background, I was pleased to be placed at Writing-on-Stone/ Áísínai'pi. This provincial park is located in southeastern Alberta, Canada, along the Milk River. Áísínai'pi is central within traditional Blackfoot territory, which, my Elders tell me, runs from Ponoka'sisaahta, the North Saskatchewan River in Edmonton, Alberta, to Otahkoiitahtaa, the Yellowstone River in southern Montana and northern Wyoming. West to east, the territory runs from Miistakistsi, the Rocky Mountains, to Omahksspatsiko, the Great Sandhills in southwestern Saskatchewan. Blackfoot Elders assert that the people have occupied this land since time immemorial. Áísínai'pi is not only a geographical center for Siksikaitsitapii but also a significant ceremonial center.

The area is well known for its dramatic landscape, which is part of the Canadian Badlands, and has one of the harshest climates in southern Alberta. Approximately 85 million years ago, the Bears Paw/Western Interior Sea sat over most of what is today the interior of North America. In this ocean environment began the depositional processes of the sand grains that would become the sandstone cliffs of the Milk River basin. These cliffs, which now contain thousands of individual rock art images, are more than 35 m high in some areas (Campbell 1991).

My work at Writing-on-Stone/Áísínai'pi has made me a witness to the fact that the rock art is heavily affected by natural transformations. Campbell (1991) describes the Milk River formation as a very weak, closely jointed and fractured, Cretaceous sandstone composed mainly of quartz grains weakly cemented in a clay matrix. When walking along the interpretive trails, visitors can easily see the effects of the wind plucking sand grains from the cliff face, especially at higher elevations.

Moisture is also an issue. At a certain point along the Main Rock Art Cliff, I would point out a unique feature in the rock that looks like the profile of a bison face. While giving a tour one day in September 2016, I noticed that the high rate of rain received in one week had caused part of the bison nose to fall off. Not only does the water runoff wash away loose particles of rock, but the increased moisture allows for the growth of lichen, which, in turn, speeds up the breakdown of the sandstone.

Brink (2007:66) points out that running water also carries with it a variety of chemicals and minerals derived from local soils, from the bedrock itself, or from the water source. The chemicals and minerals brought with the water are deposited on the rock art surface and can leave deposits, which, over time, obscure the artwork. He also mentions the effects of the freeze-thaw cycle. Seasonal temperatures at Writing-on-Stone are known to be extreme. During my employment in the summer of 2015, I recorded a temperature reading, done at panel 14 of DgOv-2, of an astounding 67° Celsius (152.6° Fahrenheit), whereas a winter temperature below -30° Celsius (-22° Fahrenheit) is common. These temperature extremes likely induce thermal expansion and contraction of the sand grains and the cementing clay particles, which ultimately results in mass wasting (Brink 2007:64).

Áísínai'pi is an associative cultural landscape that can be understood in the Siksikaitsitapiiksi deep history of the land. The horizon south of the park is dominated by the presence of the Sweetgrass Hills, in the United States just south of the 49th parallel. These landforms are considered part of the larger landscape of Áísínai'pi and are said by Blackfoot to be the place that spirits often travel to. The hills began their formation nearly 45–50 million years ago, when magma from earth's core began to rise and collect under the surface. Eventually, this magma cooled and solidified, becoming porphyry. The Blackfoot know these features as Kaatoyis, which means Blood Clot. This is the name of a hero in Blackfoot oral traditions.

Like most First Nations cultures in North America, the Blackfoot have an impulsive, foolish character, named Napi. It will be no surprise to hear that Napi was notorious for mischief and wreaking havoc in our world. Eventually, Napi left the people, leaving the world in disarray. At this time, Creator sent Kaatoyis to the people. This person was born from the blood clot (miscarried fetus) of a bison, hence the name. He was a strong young man described by some today as a superhero. Kaatoyis walked the earth, ridding the land of evil spirits and making this world a safe place for Siksikaitsitapii to live.

Nearly 2.6 million years ago, the earth's temperature began to decline and the ice age began. The Cordillera and Laurentide ice sheets covered all of what is today Canada, with the glacial maximum reaching the present-day northern United States. With a height of 2,128 m, the tops of the Sweetgrass Hills stood above the glacier, creating an island in the sea of ice. Global temperatures began to rise approximately 13,000 years ago, causing the glaciers to retreat. Meltwater emitted from the glacier in huge amounts carved out the coulee systems and river channels that characterize southern Alberta today. Most importantly, the meltwater created the Milk River basin, cutting through layers of sandstone and exposing the cliff faces where rock art is found today and forming the hoodoo formations for which the park is well known.

The hoodoos were created when water entered the top layer of ironstone and eroded the softer sandstone below at a relatively more rapid pace. The result is many oddly shaped formations, some of which seem to take on human forms. The Blackfoot refer to these formations as Maatapiiksi, which means "the people" or "the beings." One oral tradition speaks of a bad spirit coming to the people and teaching them bad habits. What really worried the Elders was that young mothers were not taking proper care of their children. The young mothers and fathers were leaving their children alone most of the time, and they became unruly when they grew up. Creator told the people they needed to revert to the traditional ways and take proper care of their children or they would be punished. Those who followed the good ways chased out those who did not. Some went to the area where the Badlands are today and were never heard from again. It is said that those disobedient parents were transformed into hoodoos as their punishment.

Another type of spiritual land formation that occurs at Áísínai'pi is a clay bentonite mound. These are referred to as spirit lodges by the Blackfoot people. Blackfoot Elders have explained that spirits dwell within these mounds during the day. Once the sun has gone down below the horizon, the spirits come out from these lodges and walk along the river valley. In some cases, the spirits are the ones who have left rock art for Siksikaitsitapii to find and interpret at a later time. In one written account by Roland H. Wilcomb, an Elder from the Blackfeet in Montana, describes the multicolored conical butte as the "painted lodge of the Earth Spirits responsible for the 'writings'" (Klassen, Keyser, and Loendorf 2000:194).

The Blackfeet in Montana signed the Lame Bull Treaty on October 17, 1855. The Blackfoot Tribes in Canada signed Treaty 7 on September 22, 1877. Within 10 years of each signing, the tribes were placed on separate reserves. During this early reserve period, First Nations people were not allowed to leave the boundaries of the reserve unless they had written permission by the Indian agent (Barron 1988). As a result, by the 1890s, Siksikaitsitapii use of the site known as Writing-on-Stone was greatly diminished, although by no means entirely discontinued (Klassen, Keyser, and Loendorf 2000, 196).

During the early twentieth century, the Euro-Canadian population increased in the west. The land now known as Writing-on-Stone/Áísínai'pi became privately owned by the O'Hara family. Recognizing the significance of the rock art, they decided to sell the land to the government of Alberta, giving Writing-on-Stone the status of a provincial park in 1957. Currently there are 94 registered rock art sites within the park, many of which contain multiple panels as well as multiple faces, equating to over two thousand single images.

In addition to this quantity, Writing-on-Stone/Áísínai'pi also exhibits one of the best cultural records of the Blackfoot over millennia. The oldest known rock art within the park boundaries is referred to as En Toto Pecked, which was accomplished by using percussion tools to strike the cliff face and remove small chunks of sandstone. The image depicts multiple male and female human figures and is the earliest remnant of a tradition that has existed for thousands of years (Brink and Blood 2008).

Shield-bearing warriors are a common motif at Áísínai'pi, occurring in both pictograph and petroglyph form (Figure 3.2). These human figures are often depicted in conjunction with the bow spear, a weapon attributed to the prehistoric period (Keyser 1977:39). Other rock art images depict the arrival of Europeans with the presence of horses, guns, and wagons. Through the images left behind, we can see the culmination of an account of a whole people. Writing-on-Stone/ Áísínai'pi was, and still is, considered a place for guidance from the *ohkotokitapiiksi* (rock beings). If warriors were brave enough to seek the outcome of a battle or another life event, they would make the voyage to Áísínai'pi and interpret the images that have been left behind by these beings.

Another form of guidance was exercised through a vision quest. This required an individual to sit in isolation in a sacred spot for four days and nights with no food or water. Blackfoot Elders have shared that after completing a

Figure 3.2. Pictograph telling the story of a battle. Photo by author.

vision quest the person would travel to the cliff face and leave a record of the experience in the stone. There are multiple vision quest sites within the park boundaries that are known to staff and registered with the Government of Alberta Ministry of Culture and Tourism. The locations are kept confidential, with restricted access.

During the first two decades of the park (1957–1977), visitors had unfettered access to the main rock art area (DgOv-2). People could freely walk up to the sandstone cliffs and inspect the rock art images. Unfortunately, some of these people decided to leave their own mark behind, sometimes on top of existing rock art. Recognizing that the cultural material was threatened, the provincial government rezoned an area and closed it to the public, declaring it an archaeological preserve, and has since restricted access.

Fortunately, people have always recognized that the impressive art should be viewed and appreciated and the associated stories should be shared. With the designation as a provincial park, this can now take place through public programming. To assist with the development of an interpretive program at Writing-on-Stone Provincial Park, an inventory of the rock art was conducted in the summer of 1976 (Keyser 1977:15).

Today paid interpretive tours to the cliff face take place three times a day during the peak summer months (May–August). The park provides employment opportunities for Blackfoot descendants, who are often the ones providing these tours. All interpretive staff members are encouraged to use Blackfoot traditional knowledge and the culmination of Western scientific knowledge to help the visitors gain a deeper understanding of the ancient images they view. As an acknowledgment of respect for the long history between the Blackfoot people and Áísínai'pi, the park does not charge visitors of First Nations ancestry to view the work of their ancestors.

Writing-on-Stone/Áísínai'pi: A Case Study in Listening

My position at the park has allowed me not only to learn the relationship between the Blackfoot and the landscape but also to learn about the relationship between the Blackfoot and parks management staff. Since 2001 the park has worked with and consulted the Mookaakin Cultural Heritage Society, a group of Elders from the Blood (Kainai) Reserve. This not-for-profit society was created as a response to repatriating ceremonial items. According to the Province of Alberta's First Nations Sacred Ceremonial Objects Repatriation Act, a First

Nation may apply for repatriation of a sacred ceremonial object. The specific wording of this policy states that items being repatriated cannot be given to an individual but can be passed into the care of an organization. Elders from the Kainai community created the Mookaakin Cultural Heritage Society and became the entity that allowed the homecoming of many sacred and important items (Conaty 2015). Today the Mookaakin society continues to meet with Writing-on-Stone staff and offer guidance and support in regard to the management of the park.

During my time as a staff member of the park, I have been privileged to meet with and learn from these Elders. One visit in particular stands out in my memory. We took a group of Elders to a new section of the park recently purchased. They stood at the crest of a coulee looking down on a group of three or four hoodoos that stood at the bend of the meandering river (Figure 3.3). Speaking in Blackfoot, they discussed how the position of the hoodoos meant that those Maatapiiksi had the responsibility of watching over that bend in the river. Listening to their words and watching their gestures, I could see the deep spiritual connection that they felt to the land. In addition to repatriating tangible items, Mookaakin contributes to, practices, and fights for the repatriation

Figure 3.3. Mookaakin members visiting a new area of the park. Photo by author.

of the intangible as well. This is most evident when Mookaakin and the park staff discuss the management/preservation of the rock art images.

"Rock Art Conservation Research at Writing-on-Stone Provincial Park, Alberta" (Brink 2007) summarizes experimental research done to help preserve the rock art. Two methods of conservation have been employed over 15 years. The first was a passive method where rock art was protected but with no direct contact with the ancient images (Brink 2007:66–75). This included drip lines that diverted running water, spot welding, which reinforced sandstone veneers separating from the underlying bedrock, and roof capping/rain diversion. The other method was active, making irreversible changes to the rock surface, such as applying the chemical Conservare OH, which replaces "lost" cementing agents, producing a chemically inert, strong grain-to-grain contact. On average, the chemical penetrates 2.5 cm into the rock (Brink 2007:75–82). This method has been tested on samples of local sandstone but has not been applied to natural surfaces in situ.

These conservation experiments were deemed necessary because the park was inevitably losing rock art, sometimes slowly, other times quickly and dramatically. However, Birks et al. (1988:8) state that conservation of the cultural landscape is not solely nature conservation, as it requires preservation of traditional land use practices. Writing-on-Stone is an associative cultural landscape, which recognizes a continuing relationship between people and the land, expressed through spiritual and other associated means. Klassen (1995) describes the act of creating rock art as not only a means of storytelling and recounting important events but also a means of communicating with the spirit world. Brink and Blood (2008) draw attention to a Blood Tribe Elder's concern that the hardening of the rock surface with Conservare might prevent the spirits from continuing to create rock art for Siksikaitsitapiiksi. This concern highlights the relationship between the Blackfoot people and the spirit world that is still alive today and continues to be practiced at Áísínai'pi.

When I entered the Indigenous Internship Program, I was introduced to the United Nations Declaration on the Rights of Indigenous Peoples. I felt that many of the articles had already been practiced by Writing-on-Stone/Áísínai'pi for decades. As part of the Heritage Appreciation section of the 1997 Management Plan, the park included providing "opportunities for the Blackfoot people to visit the rock art sites in a manner that is in accordance with their own ways and to provide means to permit ongoing ceremonial and spiritual use of the site" (Prairie Region Natural Resources Service Department of Environmental

Protection 1997:16). Evidence of continued ceremonial and spiritual use is seen in the various offerings found throughout the landscape. Every year, the park receives requests from Blackfoot members to access restricted areas of the park, such as table rock and/or Thunderbird cave. There are also requests to conduct certain ceremonies within the park, such as a bundle-opening ceremony held by Blood Tribe Elder Pete Standing Alone in 2006, and requests to conduct sweat-lodge ceremonies, as on September 11, 2015.

My cultural background allows me to understand fully, and to appreciate, the level of spiritual connection that Siksikaitsitapii feel with the landscape and the rock art that is left behind. I respect, and agree with, the Mookaakin Elders' opinion that we should not interfere with the natural processes of such a spiritual place. In addition, my archaeological background allows me to understand the threat of everyday erosional processes and their effect on the irreplaceable rock art. As a Blackfoot archaeologist, I can come to only one conclusion: in order for rock art to continue guiding Siksikaitsitapii, and for archaeologists to continue studying it, we must begin to encourage the continued creation of rock art. This understanding is ultimately what led me to begin crafting the Ceremonial Access Protocols document, which is intended to be implemented into Writing-on-Stone/Áísínai'pi management practices.

When requests to hold a ceremony within the park are made, they are often passed on to the seasonal frontline staff. To create consistency among the ever-changing seasonal staff of Áísínai'pi, the Ceremonial Access Protocols will be implemented in visitor services staff training. The document lays out step-by-step actions for park staff to assist applicants and encourages collaboration among all park teams. Protocols have been established for managing requests for sweat lodge ceremonies, bundle-opening ceremonies, collecting (plants and/or minerals), vision quests, making rock formations/effigies, and making new rock art.

The making of contemporary rock art is still highly contested (Bowdler 1988; Mowaljarlai et al 1988; O'Connor, Barham, and Woolagoodja 2008; Sundstrom 1999). Writing-on-Stone Park is unique in that it is the only institution proactively looking at how this practice can be accommodated and continued. The idea seems to be supported by the local archaeological community, although not without apprehension regarding the integrity of the traditional rock art. The act of making new rock art at an archaeological site can understandably be a concern, especially for those who consider these sites to be the cultural heritage not just of one cultural group but of all humankind (Bowdler 1988). Although the park would like to accommodate contemporary requests to make rock art, ultimately it is the park's responsibility to ensure that the integrity of existing rock art will not be compromised in any circumstances. The Ceremonial Access Protocols explicitly instruct staff to ensure that this is explained to and understood by the artist who is making the request.

A staff member will introduce the individual to the visitor experience programmer, who will become the primary contact. If the visitor experience programmer is not on site, a permanent staff member will become the primary contact. The first action of the primary contact is to notify the permanent conservation officer, who will assist with the process, as soon as possible. Individuals making the request will be asked if they would be willing to let the park record general information about their visit, including name, birth date, tribal affiliation, and clan affiliation if known.

To respect the relationship with the Blackfoot people, it has been suggested that any future making of rock art should be discussed with and supported by a Blackfoot Elder from the community. It would be ideal for the Elder to accompany the individual to the site; if this cannot be arranged, the individual will be asked for the Elder's contact information. It will be explained that, as part of the park's protocol, staff must personally contact the Elder in order to move forward with the request, which can take place over the phone if necessary.

If the staff members receive confirmation of the Elder's approval, the individual will be informed that the park needs to know in which area he or she intends to leave the image. If the individual has not already chosen a specific place, then the staff will point out the options in designated areas on a map. Regardless of whether the individual has chosen a specific place or not, it is the staff member's responsibility to ensure that the area chosen is void of traditional rock art. If it is not, the staff will explain that the integrity of the traditional rock art is of utmost importance and assure the individual that the staff will help to find an alternative space.

Once a place has been chosen (and designated on a map), the individual will be given a GPS system, to pinpoint the location of the rock art, as well as a satellite phone for safety. He or she will be instructed to return to the visitor center after the task and asked for an approximate return time. This is standard safety protocol for anyone who is planning to spend time in more remote areas of the park; if someone does not return when expected, a conservation officer or park ranger will be sent to look for the person to ensure that he or she is safe.

After the individual has returned to the visitor center, staff will continue recording information on the coordinates of the new rock art site, a sketch of the image that was created, and, if the individual is willing, the story or the meaning behind the image. The individual is informed that all information is kept confidential and that it is being collected to assist park staff with improving management practices. The literal meaning of rock art images is an aspect missing from most traditional rock art; by explaining their image, the artist is helping researchers understand the cognitive reasoning of the art left behind. Education is the best way to get individuals to understand that human art is part of a dynamic experience, and if we are going to oppose the creation of new rock art, we are condemning Native art to the status of cultural relic (O'Connor, Barham, and Woolagoodja 2008).

It should be fully understood that these protocols in no way give a person the right to make rock art, which is an inherent right held by the Blackfoot people. The sole purpose of the protocol document is to assist staff with accommodating this inherent right. If we value the tradition of studying and appreciating rock art, there is no future except to encourage its continuation (Brink and Blood 2008).

Repatriating the Intangible

The Blackfoot consider every aspect of Writing-on-Stone/Áísínai'pi to be imbued with spirit. This spiritual influence is seen in the animals, in the plants, and especially in the sandstone. One way the people consulted with these spirits is through the rock art, tangible evidence of the people's long connection with the land. Although the earliest datable rock art (En Toto Pecked figures) is approximately 2,000 years old, the earliest in situ archaeological evidence at Áísínai'pi dates to approximately 4,500–3,500 years BPE (Brink 1979:19). My experience in listening to Blackfoot Elders had led me to realize that our ancestors have been leaving rock art on these cliffs for much longer, but many of these images have left this world due to the fragile nature of the sandstone. In essence, what we see and are able to study today is a small snapshot of what has been placed at Áísínai'pi over a long period. Siksikaitsitapii use of the site continued until the signing of the treaties in both Canada and the United States, when visitation was largely restricted but by no means entirely discontinued.

The enforcement of the Indian Pass system, a political instrument of confinement, caused many Blackfoot to assert Indianness in opposition to forced assimilation (Barron 1988:31). Individuals and families continued to travel to

Áísínai'pi to visit and consult with the spirit world. One such visit was recorded by Roland H. Wilcomb, an engineer who was overseeing the construction of roads across the Blackfeet Reservation in Montana. Wilcomb was friends with a man from the reservation named Bird Rattle, who told him where to find writings on the stone. Wilcomb was so intrigued by these stories that he planned a journey to Writing-on-Stone with three Blackfeet, Jack Wagner, Bird Rattle, and Split Ears, as well as two acquaintances from Great Falls, John Stevenson and O. I. Deshon (Klassen, Keyser, and Loendorf 2000:193).

The group arrived at Writing-on-Stone on September 13, 1924, and set up camp near the cliffs. The next morning, to mark the significance of the event, Bird Rattle and Split Ears donned full ceremonial regalia while inspecting and photographing the rock art (Klassen, Keyser, and Loendorf 2000). At one point during the day, Bird Rattle took a hard piece of quartz and selected a rock face to carve a record of his trip to Áísínai'pi, thus continuing the record of his people into the twentieth century. Klassen, Keyser, and Loendorf (2000, 195) explain that Bird Rattle demonstrated the relationship between narrative expression and the spirit powers of a sacred place. Bird Rattle's petroglyph is a regular stop on the rock art tours today.

Both Canada and the United States are guilty of creating and enforcing oppressive policies toward the Native peoples of North America. Many of these policies suppressed traditional and sacred practices, making them illegal, and forced assimilation on the people (Barron 1988; Nicholas and Wylie 2012). As a result, much of the traditional knowledge about the landscape was lost when the people became physically separated from their traditional environment (Sundstrom 1999, 74).

Writing-on-Stone/Áísínai'pi is a unique site because of the park's close relationship with the Blackfoot community. Although the park has sectioned off the area that holds the largest concentration of rock art and declared it a restricted access area, First Nations descendants are given access to view and consult the rock art. Traditional ceremonial activities have taken place within the park, many of these occurring with staff support and/or involvement. Members of the park staff believe it is a matter of time before Blackfoot descendants travel to Áísínai'pi with the intention of leaving rock art in a traditional manner. Rock art is a symbol of the continuity of Native cultures and has a role to play in cultural revitalization (Sundstrom 1999:74).

The park exhibits signs notifying visitors of a fine of $50,000 or one year in jail for anyone caught defacing the cultural material. This policy is intended to protect existing rock art; many Native Americans generally agree that rock art sites should be protected from vandalism and desecration, but that is not the same as preservation (Sundstrom 1999:74). According to law, the continued traditional practice of recording one's deeds and/or visions is illegal and subject to legal action. I would argue that this is a form of cultural appropriation; although this policy protects cultural material, it has also become another policy that oppresses First Nations peoples' traditional rights, particularly the right to make rock art.

The topic of descendants making additions and/or changes to rock art sites is not only discussed in North America. Since the late 1980s, the act of repainting rock art sites has been a highly contested topic in Australia (Bowdler 1988; Mowaljarlai et al. 1988; O'Connor, Barham, and Woolagoodja 2008). This is largely due to the Western paradigm constraining nonindigenous people's understanding of the intangible. Western priorities lie in preserving the images with an aura of antiquity. Aboriginal priorities lie in the spiritual power of the ancestral paintings, which, to remain powerful and meaningful to present and future generations, need to be spiritually recharged and freshened by repainting (Mowaljarlai et al. 1988, 693).

For the people of western Australia, repainting sacred sites is how the spirit within is renewed and rejuvenated. This innate, living, evolving spirit of the rock art is similar to the Blackfoot worldview of Áísínai'pi. Blackfoot Elders believe that the rock art images of Áísínai'pi are animate and can move their position. The images appear and carry a specific meaning and/or message for the individual who is looking at them. I have experienced this myself while working in the park. When standing in front of a rock art panel that I have visited countless times, all of a sudden I see images that I had not noticed before, some of which have not even been officially recorded.

The last few years I have enjoyed visiting with Elders from my community, sharing stories of my experiences at Áísínai'pi, and learning the history that they know. In one conversation with an Elder who is a Vietnam veteran I informed him of my place of work. He was immediately interested and told me: "You know what I always wanted to do? I want to travel to Áísínai'pi and leave some rock art that shows me in battle in Vietnam." I began to tell him about the protocols I had developed and said that perhaps in a few years he could easily do that. He looked at me with a twinkle in his eye and said, "I just thought of sneaking in there and doing it anyway." I immediately recognized that this Elder did not consider it necessary to ask for permission, as he saw the making of rock art as an inherent right.

It is well known and documented that some of the most prominent people to leave markings at Áísínai'pi were warriors. The warrior spirit and the willingness to lay down their lives for their people and their land resonates with many indigenous peoples today. Blackfoot people have served in and fought in, both the Canadian and American militaries. Some of these veterans are still around today and hold prominent positions in their communities. Along with all veterans, once a year these Blackfoot warriors, both men and women, are honored by their countries and given thanks for the sacrifices that they have made. These warriors should also be honored in a traditional sense and be able to leave their mark in the cliffs of Áísínai'pi for many future generations to see and consult. The concept of making new rock art should not be a frightening one. At Writing-on-Stone/Áísínai'pi adequate monitoring of the site would allow researchers easily to distinguish between ancient and more contemporary rock art images.

Managing the Living Use of Áísínai'pi

During my internship at Writing-on-Stone, I was responsible for managing the Rock Art Monitoring Program, which had been implemented since 2010. This comprehensive program requires parks staff and volunteers regularly to monitor registered rock art sites within the boundary of Writing-on-Stone/Áísínai'pi. The main objective is to record and preserve the integrity of these ancient images. Using coordinates, baseline photographs, baseline tracings, and site inventory forms, park staff members are able to locate a specific site and determine the severity of natural and cultural transformations that have occurred since the last visit. Using site location and accessibility as factors, all sites have been placed on an annual, two-year, or five-year rotation for monitoring. The program not only helps in making management decisions in terms of protecting existing rock art but has also contributed to the discovery of new rock art sites/ images. Monitoring teams use various computer software, such as Photoshop and DStretch (decorrelation stretch), to assist with monitoring less visible attributes of the rock art. The creation of new programs such as DStretch not only helps find these "new" images at previously recorded panels but also assists in finding images where rock art was not previously known and hence was not being protected (Brink 2016:12).

The Writing-on-Stone/Áísínai'pi Rock Art Monitoring Program is managed and led by permanent park staff members, who are assisted by archaeology students from the University of Lethbridge and volunteers (Figure 3.4). Students

Figure 3.4. Volunteers of the Rock Art Monitoring Program surveying the effects of a mass waste event. Photo by author.

have the opportunity to participate in the program as an independent study course earning credits toward their degree. Rock Art Monitoring volunteers are mainly locals with a deep appreciation for archaeology. More recently, park staff members are looking for opportunities to include Blackfoot descendants in the monitoring process, to make the cultural material more accessible to members of all ages and strengthen the feeling of heritage responsibility. The biggest strength of archaeology, and arguably the least utilized, is the profession's capacity to involve and inspire people at the community level. The best chance for the long-term preservation of rock art in its original setting lies in public education of potential visitors (Macleod 2000). Involving the public in programs like the Writing-on-Stone/Áísínai'pi Rock Art Monitoring Program is the best way to educate and foster a sense of responsibility. According to traditional Blackfoot customs, education is a collective responsibility (Little Bear 2000:81).

Conclusion

The Blackfoot people have a long and powerful connection to the landscape of Áísínai'pi. This is evidenced in the archaeological history, the thousands of rock art images, and the continued ceremonial use of the site today. Writing-on-

Stone Provincial Park has been a leading example for creating and maintaining respectful and engaging relationships with descendant communities, enriching all parties involved. Blackfoot members are given employment opportunities to ensure that the appropriate cultural information is being shared in an appropriate way, creating a positive, enriching experience for thousands of local and international visitors every year. It also creates a trusting relationship between the Blackfoot community and the staff of Writing-on-Stone/Áísínai'pi, leading to the park's proactive measures in creating ceremonial access protocols. A section of these protocols lays out a step-by-step process to assist park staff with accommodating the making of new rock art images. Although this continues to be a highly contested topic, Writing-on-Stone/Áísínai'pi has proven that engaging descendant communities in cultural education leads to deeper understandings and helps foster positive relationships.

Governments and entities all over the world need to look to this example to reevaluate their policies on rock art protection and learn to accommodate the inherent right of descendant communities to continue making rock art. The ceremonial connection that the Blackfoot people practice at Writing-on-Stone/Áísínai'pi is one example of how many First Nations groups are repatriating their intangible spiritual heritage. It is an example of the benefits to both indigenous and settler descendants accruing from postcolonial recognition of the nation-state's mosaic of cultural realities.

References Cited

Barron, F. L.
1988   The Indian Pass System in the Canadian West, 1882–1935. *Prairie Forum* 13(1):25–42.
Birks, H. H., H.J.B. Birks, P. E. Kaland, and D. Moe
1988   *The Cultural Landscape: Past, Present, and Future.* Cambridge University Press, Cambridge.
Bowdler, S.
1988   Repainting Australian Rock Art. *Antiquity* 62(236):517–523.
Brink, J. W.
1979   Archaeological Investigations at Writing-on-Stone. In *Archaeology in Southern Alberta,* pp. 1–74. Occasional Paper No. 12/13. Archaeological Survey of Alberta, Edmonton.
2007   Rock Art Conservation Research at Writing-on-Stone Provincial Park, Alberta. *Revistade Arqueologia Americana,* 25:55–99.
2016   DStretch and New Discoveries in Alberta Rock Art. *La Pintura* 42(4):9–13.
Brink, J. W., and N. Blood
2008   Perspectives on Rock Art Conservation at Writing-on-Stone Provincial Park,

Alberta. In *Preserving Aboriginal Heritage: Technical and Traditional Approaches,* edited by C. Dignard, K. Helwig, J. Mason, K. Nanowin, and T. Stone, pp. 341–349. Canadian Conservation Institute, Ottawa.

Campbell, I. A.

1991   Classification of Rock Weathering at Writing-on-Stone Provincial Park, Alberta, Canada: A Study in Applied Geomorphology. *Earth Surface Processes and Landforms* 16:701–711.

Conaty, G. T.

2015   Niitsitapiisinni: Our Way of Life. In *We Are Coming Home: Repatriation of Blackfoot Cultural Confidence,* edited by G. T. Conaty, pp. 71–117. Alberta University Press, Edmonton.

Keyser, J. D.

1977   Writing-on-Stone: Rock Art on the Northwestern Plains. *Canadian Journal of Archaeology* 1:15–80.

Klassen, M. A.

1995   Icons of Power, Narratives of Glory: Ethnic Continuity and Cultural Change in the Contact Period Rock Art of Writing-on-Stone. Unpublished master's thesis, Faculty of Arts and Science, Trent University, Peterborough, Canada.

Klassen, M. A., J. D. Keyser, and L. L. Loendorf

2000   Bird Rattle's Petroglyphs at Writing-on-Stone: Continuity in the Biographic Rock Art Tradition. *Plains Anthropology* 45(172):189–201.

Little Bear, L.

2000   Jagged Worldviews Colliding. In *Reclaiming Indigenous Voice and Vision,* edited by M. Battiste, pp. 77–85. University of British Columbia Press, Vancouver.

Macleod, I.

2000   Rock Art Conservation and Management: The Past, Present and Future Options. *Reviews in Conservation* 1:32–42.

Mowaljarlai, D., P. Vinnicombe, G. K. Ward, and C. Chippindale

1988   Repainting of Images on Rock in Australia and the Maintenance of Aboriginal Culture. *Antiquity* 62(237):690–696.

Nicholas, G. P., and A. Wylie

2012   Do Not Do unto Others: Cultural Misrecognition and the Harms of Appropriation in an Open Source World. In *Appropriating the Past: Philosophical Perspectives on Archaeological Practice,* edited by R. Coningham and G. Scarre, pp. 195–221. Cambridge University Press, Cambridge.

O'Connor, S., A. Barham, and D. Woolagoodja

2008   Painting and Repainting in the West Kimberley. *Australian Aboriginal Studies* 1:22–38.

Prairie Region Natural Resources Service Department of Environmental Protection

1997   Writing-on-Stone Provincial Park Management Plan.

Sundstrom, L.

1999   Rock Art and Native Americans: A View from South Dakota. *Plains Anthropologist* 44(170):71–80.

4

Listening and Learning

The Benefits of Collaboration

STEPHEN A. MROZOWSKI

The essence of collaboration in any field is listening. Over the past decade, I have overseen the Hassanamesit Woods Project, a collaborative effort involving the Fiske Center for Archaeological Research at the University of Massachusetts, Boston, the Nipmuc Nation, and the Town of Grafton, Massachusetts, where Keith Hill—the main focus of our archaeological investigations—is located (Map 4.1). From the beginning, the collaboration grew organically through the relationships that developed during the project. Working with a variety of stakeholders, from the residents of Grafton who voted to support the project with their tax dollars, to the members of the Hassanamesit Woods Management Committee who oversaw the project for the town, to the tribal council of the Nipmuc Nation, our investigations involved communication and negotiation. When I originally met with the tribal council, some questioned the need for an archaeology that they saw, correctly, as disruptive. Others were willing to support the project as long as the process was handled respectfully. Rae Gould, who served as the tribal historic preservation officer, and was then a graduate student in the Ph.D. program in anthropology at the University of Connecticut, was the liaison for the project and played a critical role in helping chart the course of research.

In this chapter I want to outline some of the concrete benefits that resulted from listening to the Nipmuc perspective through Rae, the tribal council, and other Nipmuc tribal members, including Ray Vickers and Cheryll Toney Holley, who have served as chief while the project has been ongoing. It was Cheryll—then a member of the tribal council—who raised questions concerning the disturbance that archaeology would cause. I acknowledged that she was right to have such a concern because the archaeological process was indeed disturbing.

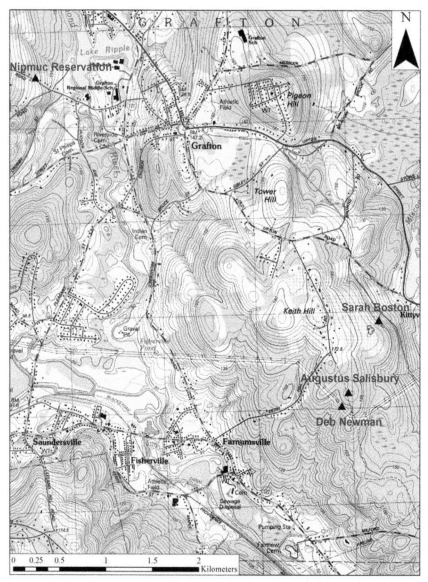

Map 4.1. USGS Quadrangle Map of Grafton, showing Keith Hill and Nipmuc Reservation.

Over time, Cheryll came to support the work at Hassanamesit Woods. There were several reasons for this, which I discuss below, but overall I think it was because we listened to each other. That helped us develop a level of trust because our overall goals were the same.

The protocol for the project involved the Nipmuc, particularly Rae Gould, who provided feedback on research plans and publications, collaborated with scholarly and public presentations, helped interpret materials, and suggested questions that the project sought to pursue. Having begun as a heritage-based project to determine if any Native American or Euro-American sites were located on a 202-acre parcel that the Town of Grafton decided to purchase for conservation and recreational uses, the project has expanded into a comprehensive inquiry of Nipmuc history, with a particular focus on the community of Hassanamisco. One of the earliest and largest "Praying Indian" communities

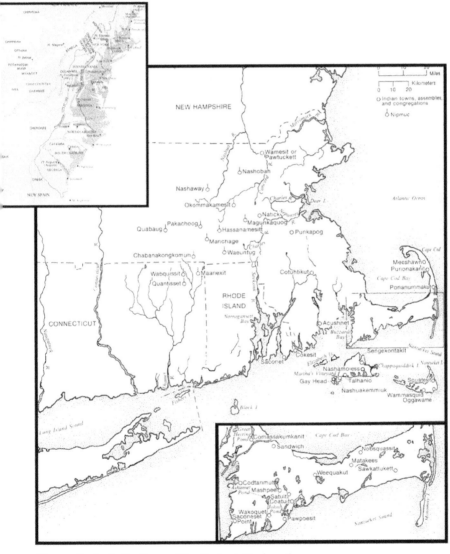

Map 4.2. Praying Indian Towns of New England. Map by author.

in the Massachusetts Bay Colony, Hassanamesit was first acknowledged by the colony's general court in the 1660s (Map 4.2).

Most of the archaeology carried out in Grafton has focused on the later members of the community who survived King Philip's War of 1675–1676 and returned to a postwar landscape (Gould 2010, 2013a, 2013b; Law 2008; Law Pezzarossi 2014a, 2014b, 2015a, 2015b; Mrozowski 2012, 2013, 2014; Mrozowski, Gould, and Law Pezzarossi 2015; Mrozowski and Law Pezzarossi 2015; Pezzarossi 2008, 2014). The narratives that have emerged from that work and the intellectual exchanges that have been and continue to be an essential part of the project provide a detailed picture of Nipmuc life over the past 1,000 years, with a particular focus on the last 300. Listening has been a particularly critical piece of the process. Here I want to highlight just a few of the more meaningful examples. The scale of these contributions varies, but in each instance, it involved a sharing of information and perspectives that I believe has resulted in a much stronger, more robust form of inquiry than some (such as McGhee 2008, 2010) suggest is possible (but see Colwell-Chanthaphonh et al. 2010; Mrozowski et al. 2009; Nicholas 2010; Silliman 2010; Wylie 2015).

The Pragmatic Quality of Collaboration

Having come to collaborative research rather late in my career, I have been aided by the lens of pragmatism—a philosophical tradition that traces its roots to the United States of the late nineteenth and early twentieth centuries. In fairly stark contrast to European philosophical traditions that deal extensively with the mind as a plane of reality or the detachment inherent in most positivist epistemologies, pragmatism values engaged research that seeks to improve the human condition. A distinctly American philosophical tradition, pragmatism developed during the later stages of the nineteenth century out of the work of Charles Peirce, William James, and John Dewey (see Baert 2005; Preucel and Bauer 2001).

Peirce is the scholar most identified with pragmatism's initial development, including his own highly complex conceptualization that contributed to the growth of semiotics today (see Preucel 2006; Preucel and Bauer 2001). It is, however, the work of William James (1898, 1907) and John Dewey (1916, 1925) that has continued to inspire advocates, most notably Richard Rorty (1979, 1982, 1998, 1999) but more recently Philip Baert (2005) to argue for a return to the activism that was a hallmark of early pragmatism. For Dewey, inquiry and truth were not separate realities. Indeed, the differences between belief and reality were hotly contested topics during the early years of the twentieth century (Dykuizen 1973; Taylor 1973). Within this context, Dewey argued for the kind of self-referential knowledge that scholars influenced by postmodernism today take for granted. He felt that the intellectual process of inquiry helped in shaping human perceptions of realities that, while existing outside human experience, nevertheless gained meaning or importance through human experience (Dewey 1906a, 1906b, 1907). In this regard, Dewey's argument concerning reality and human experience presaged the same point that Henri Bergson (1999 [1922]) would offer in defense of his own criticism of Albert Einstein's concepts of time.

Einstein published his theory of relativity in 1916. Bergson did not agree with his ideas concerning time and summarized his opinions in his book *Duration and Simultaneity* (Bergson 1999 [1922]), in which he attempted to address the implications of Einstein's theories. Bergson had tried to address time in his doctoral dissertation entitled *Time and Free Will* (Bergson 2001 [1889]), in which he distinguished between real time and measurable time. The difference revolved around the idea that there was actually no way to define the present, because time always involved a time before and a time afterward but never really an actual present that could be temporally isolated (Scott 2006:186). In *Duration and Simultaneity* Bergson (1999 [1922]) formulated the idea of "durée" that would influence Braudel (1980), suggesting that time could not truly be separated from consciousness and human experience. According to Scott (2006:185–188), Einstein and Bergson met at a meeting of the Philosophical Society in Paris in 1922. Bergson was quite popular at the time; despite some reservations, he was persuaded to "extemporaneously outline" his views on Einstein's ideas concerning time. As Scott (2006:185) notes, Bergson assumed that Einstein "was giving us not only a new physics but also certain new ways of thinking," yet as a philosopher he felt the need to pursue the question of whether a notion of time existed outside such experience.

Scott (2006:188) concludes his recounting of the encounter between the two men by stating: "After listening patiently to Bergson, Einstein articulates the essential conflict between them in terms of a question: 'So, the question before us is this: Is the philosopher's time the same as the physicist's?' The answer that Einstein gives is a resounding 'No.'" Despite Einstein's apparent acceptance of the legitimacy of these different views of time—that of the philosopher who grounded time in human experience and that of the physicist who believed in a time that existed "independent of individual consciousness"—he nevertheless insisted "on the primacy of the physicist's time" (Scott 2006:188).

In the same way that Bergson saw the meaning of time linked to human experience, Dewey saw truth as something realized primarily through daily life. For him, inquiry was more important than truth because he did not believe in truth as something that preexisted human inquiry. Dewey envisioned a social science that stressed the ceaseless process of inquiry, seeing himself "as an instrument of continuous learning" (Taylor 1973:xx). The purpose and ultimate goal of such learning, however, was not some transcendent truth that only the philosopher or physicist could comprehend, but rather an understanding of human existence that had some practical benefit or application to a problem of everyday life.

It was the concern for everyday experience and the open quality of intellectual inquiry of Dewey's pragmatism that would later inspire Richard Rorty (1979, 1982, 1998, 1999) to revitalize the approach. Rorty's pragmatism raises two points concerning the goals and process of inquiry. First, he argues against the postmodernist proclivity to critique rather than engage. He is particularly disdainful of postmodernist critiques of modernity that are celebrated for their erudition rather than their practical benefit. Second, he echoes the earlier calls of both James and Dewey to maintain a never-ending process of inquiry that must remain open to all forms of knowing as long as the epistemologies that underpin these forms of knowledge are not closed systems (see Baert 2005; Preucel and Mrozowski 2010).

Pragmatism provides a sound philosophical grounding for collaborative research because of its insistence on maintaining an open intellectual process. Part of that process involves an open dialogue with descendant populations on a whole host of levels. It also aids in fostering communication that helps in decolonizing the academic as intellectual authority. The broader movement of decolonizing Western intellectual practice is proving to be one of the more important developments for the social sciences (see Harding 2016) but is particularly relevant for academically trained archaeologists working with indigenous and/or descendant communities (see Atalay 2006; Lightfoot et al. 2013; Nicholas 2010; Panich 2013; Silliman 2009). This process of decolonization can take many forms, but chief among them is the growth of collaborative research projects. From the terminology employed to the questions we pursue, the benefits of collaborative research are beginning to prove their worth in creating an archaeology that is intellectually sound and politically sensitive. There is a salutary dimension to this process that is essential to doing other people's history. Trigger (1980) posed this question almost 40 years ago, and the growth of collaborative indigenous archaeology is the logical outgrowth of concerns he raised about the questions archaeologists asked of other people's history.

The Hassanamesit Woods Project

Each of the processes noted above has contributed to the growth of the Hassanamesit Woods Project. One of the more gratifying parts of this collaboration has been working with Rae Gould—a Nipmuc scholar who has worked as a review officer for the advisory council in Washington, DC, and now serves as university tribal liaison and senior lecturer at the University of Massachusetts, Amherst. Rae proved to be the ideal interlocutor for the project, combining her own experience growing up Nipmuc with her perceptions of the academic world while completing her Ph.D. in anthropology. One of the most fundamental benefits of the collaboration has involved drawing comparisons between our own work and Rae's on several properties that were linked to the seventeenth-century Nipmuc community of Hassanamisco. As a descendant of that community, Rae is uniquely situated to examine the deep connections between today's Nipmuc community and its long history in the area (Gould 2010, 2013a, 2013b). Of particular interest has been her fieldwork and ethnographic work associated with the 2.5-acre Hassanamisco Nipmuc Reservation less than a mile from the focus of our fieldwork on what is today Keith Hill in Grafton (Map 4.1).

Hassanamesit was one of the "Christianized Communities" that were established with the help of English missionary John Eliot. Fourteen such "Praying Indian" towns were said to have been "established" by Eliot during the period before King Philip's War (see Map 4.2; Cogley 1998; Kawashima 1969; O'Brien 1997, 26–30).

When we were writing an article together, Rae asked me why I had written that English missionary John Eliot had established the Praying Indian Communities of Massachusetts and Connecticut during the seventeenth century. To me, this was common knowledge and had been an accepted assumption on the part of both historians and archaeologists who had researched these communities. I use the term "common knowledge" purposefully to characterize a form of knowledge that has indeed been in common use by academics who have studied and written about the history of these Praying Indian communities (see Cogley 1998; Kawashima 1969; Pierce 1879:20). Given that most secondary discussions of these communities had consistently included a statement to this effect, I assumed that it was correct and have to admit that I had never put much thought into the process of precisely how these communities were indeed established.

When I asked Rae what she thought about the subject, she said that she saw these "towns" as being located within long-standing Native communities. Rae also raised the deeper question of just what constituted community beyond the space they inhabited. That space, until recently, had eluded archaeologists' attempts to locate the Praying Indian communities (see Mrozowski 2009). Concerted efforts during the 1980s proved fruitless, forcing some to ask why these well-documented communities had such low archaeological visibility (see, e.g., Brenner 1984, 1986; Carlson 1986; Cogley 1998; Thorbahn 1988). Cemeteries associated with the Praying Indian communities of Natick, Ponkapoag (Canton, Massachusetts), and Okommakamesit (Marlboro, Massachusetts) had been discovered as a direct result of construction activities in Natick and Okommakamesit during the 1960s, but these discoveries were poorly documented (see Kelley 1999). A cemetery thought to be associated with the community of Ponkapoag was uncovered by preliminary construction for a development that was never completed (Kelley 1999; Mrozowski 2009).

Systematic attempts to locate other communities were unsuccessful, leading the archaeologists involved to question the accuracy of the descriptions of the early communities written by Eliot (1655, 1670, 1834) and Daniel Gookin (1972 [1674]), who served as the supervisor for the Indian towns of the Massachusetts Bay Colony (Brenner 1980, 1984, 1986; Carlson 1986). Brenner (1984:169) argued that even a community such as Natick, the largest and oldest of the towns, may have been more of a seasonal village that might contain a central meeting house described as being present by Gookin (1972 [1674]; also see Cogley 1998, 31 who uses the term "fair house"). Cogley disagrees with Brenner's interpretation in arguing that the towns were continuously occupied residential communities (Cogley 1998:31–33, 1999). O'Brien's (1997:2010) extensive research on Natick and other Praying Indian communities also tends to counter the notion that these were only seasonal occupations. She does note that documentary evidence indicates divisions within Native communities between those willing to adopt English cultural practices and those who resisted such changes (O'Brien 1997:93; see also Mrozowski, Gould, and Law Pezzarossi 2015). The fluid nature of Native practices described by O'Brien raises questions about the veracity of Daniel Gookin's 1674 descriptions of communities composed of streets, houses built in the English style, and meeting houses. Despite the concerted efforts of archaeologists to find the remains of these communities (e.g., Brenner 1984, 1986; Carlson 1986), it was not until the late 1990s that evidence of the settlement of Magunkaquog was unearthed during a cultural resource management survey in Ashland, Massachusetts (Herbster and Garman 1996). Subsequent investigations in 1997 and 1998 revealed the remains of what is believed to be the community's meeting house and its adjoining yard (Mrozowski 2009; Mrozowski et al. 2009).

Since the discovery of the Magunkaquog meeting house, additional investigations of several Nipmuc households associated with the eighteenth-century community of Hassanamesit—consisting of families associated with the seventeenth-century Praying Indian settlement of the same name—have been conducted (Gould 2010, 2013a, 2013b; Mrozowski and Law Pezzarossi 2015). Combined with the results from Magunkaquog, the Hassanamisco research has provided a wealth of detail about daily life as well as strong evidence of cultural dynamism and continuity. It has also provided evidence of the deeper history of Hassanamisco that has implications for Gould's point concerning the gathering of these communities. In his original request for land for the Natives interested in Christianity, Eliot noted that the education they needed as part of their conversion was best taught them "where they dwell," noting later in the same passage: "A place must be found . . . some what remote from the English where they must have the word constantly taught, and government constantly exercised, means of subsistence provided, incouragements for the industrious [and a] means of instructing them in Letters, Trades, and Labours" (O'Brien 1997:28). There is nothing in this passage that is discordant with Rae Gould's point concerning the Praying Indian towns being parts of well-established communities. In fact, the archaeology of these communities provides a fairly rich picture that supports this interpretation (Mrozowski 2009; Mrozowski et al. 2009; Mrozowski and Law Pezzarossi 2015).

Reimagining the seventeenth-century Praying Indian towns as much older communities presented a picture that countered the notion of historical rupture that had influenced my own perceptions of that past. It led me to realize the falsehood embedded in the concept of prehistory as constituting a period severed from the more recent past and the need to abandon the notion. Fortunately, I found answers to what could have been a quandary in the philosophy of pragmatism. If the notion of prehistory was to become a barrier to collaboration because my Nipmuc partners found it offensive or, more importantly, basically inaccurate, then I needed to find my own new way of carrying out my research (see Mrozowski 2013; Schmidt and Mrozowski 2013). Once the artificial boundary between history and prehistory was removed, it was conceptually much easier to see the experience of the Nipmuc through the lens of deep history. This made it easier to see the dialectical qualities of change and continuity in Nipmuc cultural practices. Even more profoundly, it forced me to reexamine the epistemological underpinnings of concepts of time and space employed in scientific inquiry, making it possible to dismantle the boundaries between past, present, and future (see Mrozowski 2014). Viewed as a continuum—a duration of time experienced by the Nipmuc—their own pragmatic needs concerning their future and the purpose of our broader archaeological inquiry became complementary.

The primary focus of the Hassanamesit Woods Project has been the area of Keith Hill in Grafton (Map 4.1). The project began with an intensive survey of a 202-acre parcel that the town had purchased. Surveys carried out in 2003 and 2005 found early evidence of Native American quarrying in the area as well as a single concentration of material culture associated with the remains of the Sarah Burnee/Sarah Boston (hereafter SB/SB) farmstead (see Gary 2005). This mid-eighteenth-century farmstead was the home to four generations of Nipmuc women who can trace their lineage directly from the Sachem Petavit, who was the political leader of the Hassanamisco community during the seventeenth century. Petavit was known as Robin by the English, and it is his heir, Sarah Robins, along with her husband, Peter Muckamugg, who first appears as one of the owners of a 106-acre parcel granted to them as part of the 1727 sale and redistribution of Hassanamisco lands, designed to provide up to 40 lots for English families. As a result of King Philip's War, all Native lands in the Massachusetts Bay Colony became subject to the control of colonial authorities. While they did not take full ownership of these lands at this time, the 1727 redistribution represented a forced sale of Hassanamisco lands to provide land for the English families (see Map 4.3).

The 1727 map that documents the Hassanamesit sale contains the uniformly abstracted English lots as well as seven Native lots that were set aside for the most prominent members of the former Praying Indian community. These included Sarah Robins and Peter Muckamugg as well as Moses Printer, whose original 1727 parcel contained what is today the last remaining piece of Hassananisco land, the Nipmuc Reservation. This parcel has been the subject of intensive research by Rae Gould, which has helped in developing

Figure 4.1. Excavated foundation of the Sarah Burnee/Sarah Boston house. Photo by author.

larger narratives of Hassanamisco history based on our research on Keith Hill (Gould 2013a, 2013b; Mrozowski, Gould, and Law Pezzarossi 2015). There is also one additional 120-acre lot on the 1727 map that is labeled "For Indians Overplus." I believe "overplus" makes use of a Middle English term for excess land or grains accorded to tenants. Recent excavations in this lot have found evidence of another possible Nipmuc household—that of Deborah Newman,

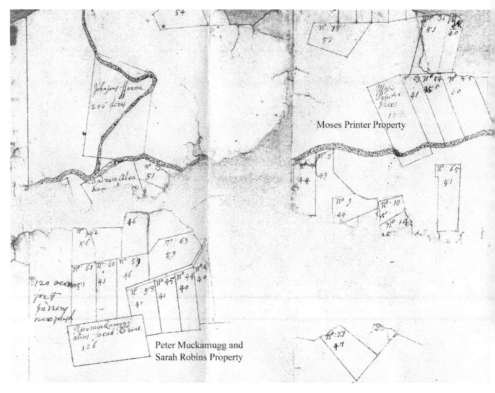

Map 4.3. A 1727 Hassanamisco Lands Distribution Map, showing Lots of Peter Muckamugg and Sarah Robins, Moses Printer, and "Indian Overplus" lots. Map by author.

who was a contemporary of Sarah Boston—and what might be the foundation of a circa 1730 meetinghouse/school for both English and Native children. The school was to be constructed, maintained, and provided with a teacher at the expense of the 40 English families who were purchasing the former Hassanamisco lands in 1727.

The documentary record of the events surrounding the purchase of the Hassanamisco lands is a prophetic example of the kinds of tactics that the English employed over the course of the seventeenth and eighteenth centuries to take control of Native property (Mrozowski 2019; see also Massachusetts Archives Collections [hereafter MAC], vol. 30, 1603–1705:117–118, 746–748). Through a combination of legal manipulation that was often constructed on the assumption of eventual Native extinction, these documents represent a good example of the kind of governmentality that Foucault envisioned. The instrumentality to the process was a challenge to the Nipmuc, but they did avail themselves of the courts to argue for fairer treatment. Contrary to the inevitability implicit in much of the archive, the archaeology from Hassanamesit Woods presents an interesting history of survivance.

The location of the SB/SB farmstead within the original Sarah Robins lot on the Eastern Slope of Keith Hill is identical to that of the Magunkaquog Meeting House. This is not a coincidence in my estimation. What they share is a building technique that takes advantage of the downslope to buttress the western walls of the structures. It is possible that this is a continuation of a long-standing Native building tradition that often made use of large outcrops along hillsides to create temporary shelters or more permanent structures. Our search for the Deborah Newman farmstead, for example, has found the remains of such a structure that we believe to be an animal pen, quite possibly a lambing pen. However, nine-teenth-century descriptions of similar structures suggest that they could have been Native dwellings. Law Pezzarossi (2014a) has raised a series of extremely interesting questions about these descriptions and the very real possibility that such structures are indeed Native, but that their descriptions in nineteenth-century local histories are part of an Anglo-American narrative that views them as impermanent. According to Law Pezzarossi (2014a) the English viewed this impermanence in stark contrast to the "fixity and place" that O'Brien (2010:84) argues provided justification for the acquisition and improvement of Native lands by English colonists.

The landscapes of New England during the early to mid-eighteenth century remained contested space. The challenge of deciphering the difference between the descriptions compiled by Eliot and Gookin and the archaeology on the ground leads me to conclude that the eighteenth- and nineteenth-century land-scape of Grafton remained very much an indigenous landscape, in the same way that parts of it remain so today. The Nipmuc never disappeared; they remained a self-identified group that has retained indigenous cultural practices. While these are different from those that were part of daily practice in the deep or recent past, Anglo-American cultural practices have themselves changed over the past 300 years. Beyond the more academic questions that this raises about notions such as hybridity and its value in describing the cultural processes that are linked to colonialism, issues of identity and authenticity are critically linked to the struggles of Native groups such as the Hassanamisco Nipmuc to gain fed-eral recognition (Den Ouden 2005; Gould 2010, 2013b; Mrozowski 2012, 2014; Mrozowski et al. 2009).

The original Nipmuc petition was granted in the later phases of the Bill Clinton administration, only to see the positive designation reversed by the Bureau of Indian Affairs (BIA) under the George W. Bush administration on the grounds that the Nipmuc had failed to provide written documentation of political continuity over the past 300 years (Adams 2004; Gould 2013b). Given that one of the baseline goals of our research in Grafton was to chronicle the occupation of Hassanamisco families, it seemed quite logical to ask whether there was archaeological evidence or oral testimony that might counter the government's denial of the Nipmuc petition. After all, archaeology provides an empirically powerful set of techniques with which it can document both the chronology of occupation and the cultural practices of the Hassanamisco community since at least the seventeenth century, if not earlier. In what remains of this chapter, I provide an overview of the multiple lines of evidence that confirm the kind of political continuity that the BIA denied could be documented.

The Archaeology of Hassanamesit

The major focus of our work in Grafton has been the SB/SB farmstead that was located in the original 1727 plot of Sarah Robins and Peter Muckamugg. This original 106-acre parcel was home to four generations of Nipmuc households, all headed by women named Sarah. Over time, the lot was slowly reduced in size by a combination of sales to raise capital and a land dispute between Sarah Boston and her brother Joseph Aaron that resulted in part of the land going to him (Law Pezzarossi 2015a, 24–28). Over a period of roughly 100 years, the 106-acre parcel was reduced to approximately 20 acres (Map 4.4). These last 20 acres have received the bulk of our attention over the past decade.

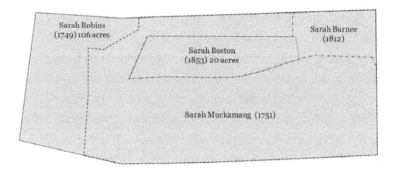

Map 4.4. Hassanamesit Woods Site Plan, showing Sarah Burnee/Sarah Boston farmstead home lot, pasture, and "Swago." Map by author.

This took place in a phased manner, starting with survey to identify archaeological deposits within the 203 acres that the Town of Grafton purchased (Gary 2005). This resulted in the identification of several sites, including a quarry site used in the deep past and the remains of the SB/SB farmstead that was occupied between 1750 and 1840. In addition to the home lot that contained a dry-laid stone foundation and the possible remains of a barn, investigations were also carried out in a large pasture area to the south of the home lot and an area known as "Swago" that was referenced in several primary sources (Map 4.5); Mrozowski and Law Pezzarossi 2015). According to local folklore, this area of rocky, wooded streams was where Sarah Boston would collect herbs (Law Pezzarossi 2014a). In addition to our work at the SB/SB farmstead, we also conducted geophysical survey, archaeological testing, and large-scale excavations in the area of Salisbury Street on Keith Hill that would have been part of the 120-acre overplus lot mentioned earlier. I provide a brief discussion of our recent work in this area below after presenting the results of analysis of the material from the SB/SB farmstead.

Using a combination of field testing and geophysical survey, it was possible to identify the remains of a deep, dry-laid foundation that had been filled with a small bulldozer after the 1938 hurricane. Much of the spatial, stratigraphic macro-botanical and micro-stratigraphic analysis carried out at the SB/SB farmstead was geared toward determining how much damage the hurricane had done to the foundation and surrounding yard (see Mrozowski and Law Pezzarossi 2015). Fortunately, it was possible to determine that much of the damage to the yard deposits was restricted to the southern side of the foundation and yard. Intact yard deposits included a primary trash deposit that appears to have been located beneath part of the structure (perhaps a lean-to or porch) as well as a cooking hearth and food-preparation area and a sizable midden to the east and downslope from the foundation (Mrozowski and Law Pezzarossi 2015). Much of the fill of the foundation was excavated by hand—a truly daunting task—yet it uncovered evidence of an interior hearth area and possible corner chimney in what we believe to be the rear or west portion of the building. The foundation was also constructed with a drainage system that appears to have channeled hill runoff through the cellar floor and through a stone-lined drain that terminated west and downslope from the foundation (Figure 4.1).

Using a combination of soil chemistry, geophysical testing, and additional excavation, it was possible to gain a rough idea of the configuration of the home lot, but some of this remains speculative. The house itself rests on a terrace that

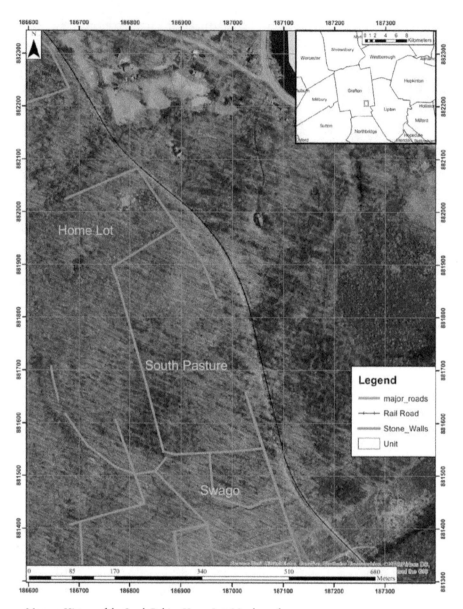

Map 4.5. History of the Sarah Robins Home Lot. Map by author.

was probably augmented by landscaping. The midden noted above contained material culture spanning the period 1750–1840 and was clearly deposited downslope of the house. No concrete evidence of a barn that is noted in some primary documents was uncovered, but geophysical testing did identity an area of scattered stones that coincides with slightly elevated phosphate levels to the south of the foundation. A similar configuration along the wall that separates the home lot from the south pasture suggests that animals were traveling over the wall in this area. This is not a high level of detail about the home lot, but it does lend itself to some level of spatial activities.

By far the most interesting result of our excavations is the more than 100,000 artifacts recovered from within the foundation and the surrounding yard. There was also a rich faunal assemblage and more limited macrobotanical assemblage that added to the picture of life at this Nipmuc household. The bulk of the material recovered was tightly dated to the period 1790–1840—when both Sarah Burnee and Sarah Boston were active in the community—but a steady percentage of material culture from the mid-eighteenth century is probably linked to the Sarah Muckamugg household.

Anything approaching a comprehensive discussion of the assemblage is beyond the scope of this chapter (but see Allard 2010, 2015; Law 2008; Mrozowski and Law Pezzarossi 2015; Pezzarossi 2008, 2014; Pezzarossi, Kennedy, and Law 2012), so instead I focus here on the results that pertain to the question of political continuity. The sheer size and the diversity of the assemblage reflect what is best described as a well-appointed household with the fine earthenware to provide servings for a large number of people. In his analysis of a large sample of the ceramics from the site, Pezzarossi (2014) compared the SB/SB material with assemblages from eight Anglo-American sites from the surrounding area. In terms of ware types and patterns of decoration, he notes that the SB/SB assemblage is perhaps most notable because of its "insignificance or commonness" (Pezzarossi 2014:165). He makes two additional points that warrant mentioning. The first is that the SB/SB assemblage compares most favorably with Anglo households that practiced a mixture of farming and artisan work (Pezzarossi 2014). This is consistent with a large iron assemblage that contained numerous examples of tools that Law Pezzarossi (2014a, 2014b) has linked to basketmaking as well as woodworking more generally. Some of these tools appear to have been repurposed—a scythe made into a possible draw knife for cutting splints, for example, as well as several examples of bent knives also used in basketmaking. Other tools, such as small drill bits, may have been used for repairing chairs (see Law Pezzarossi 2014a, 2014b; Mrozowski, Law Pezzarossi, et al. 2015:176), suggesting another possible economic activity carried out by the members of the SB/SB household. One of the most common trees used in basketmaking and chair repair was ash. Although Trigg (2015:135–136) recovered charred ash along with other woods commonly using in cooking such as oak, hickory, and chestnut, at best it might represent residue of basketmaking that was thrown into the fire for kindling (Mrozowski, Law Pezzarossi, et al. 2015; Trig 2015; Heather Trigg, personal communication 2017).

The ceramics and glassware from the SB/SB site are most notable for the large number of food-serving and drinking vessels. The remains of between 15 and 20 tumblers were recovered, including one that displayed evidence of microflaking so it could be used as a cutting tool (Bagley 2013; Bagley et al. 2015; Law 2008). Another notable class of glass artifact was decanters: remains of several were recovered from the site (Mrozowski, Law Pezzarossi, et al. 2015:160). The assemblage of glass and ceramics is consistent with urban households in terms of vessel diversity and overall size (Mrozowski 2006; Mrozowski, Law Pezzarossi, et al. 2015). An impressive array of refined earthenware, especially coffee and tea wares, also reflect a "middle-class" sensibility for entertaining that was comparable with English and American households in rural Massachusetts (see Pezzarossi 2014) as well as those in the region's urban centers (Mrozowski 2006). There is a notable departure from other assemblages in the region in the large number of metal eating utensils recovered from the SB/SB farmstead; 31 knives and 12 forks were recovered, along with a collection of iron cooking pots. These included remains of no less than 12 cooking vessels, including kettles, a skillet, and the lid for a Dutch oven. Most of the iron vessels were recovered from deposits associated with what we believe to have been an interior hearth that collapsed into the cellar after the building fell into disrepair (Mrozowski, Law Pezzarossi, et al. 2015:170–171).

Faunal analysis indicates that food preparation took place both in the house and in the yard area. The one clearly defined exterior hearth contained both calcined bone and maize remains (Allard 2010; Trigg 2015). In her analysis of the faunal material from the site, Allard (2010, 2015) found that the bone from the yard represented both food preparation and food consumption, while the bone recovered from the foundation was residue of food preparation alone. Most of the faunal remains were from domesticated animals, especially cattle, caprines, and pigs, which Allard thinks were husbanded on site. Evidence that all three species were being butchered on the site supports this interpretation, as do the age ranges of the domesticated animals. Cattle and sheep of all ages were being slaughtered on site, indicating that they were part of a varied household economy: cows provided dairy products as well as meat, while caprines, including sheep, were raised both for wool, or milked in the case of goals, and to be eaten. Some of the cattle remains were from individuals of prime age, indicating that they could have been consumed or traded. Only pigs appear to have been raised purely for consumption (Allard 2010, 2015).

Although the bulk of the faunal material represents domesticated animals, a rather rich collection of wild animal remains indicates that hunting and trapping were an important part of the household economy. In addition to deer, Allard identified wild fowl remains, including duck, pigeons, turkeys, and possibly pheasants. The remains of nine individual turtles were recovered from the site, suggesting that these highly prized animals were probably available in the ponds and streams in and around Keith Hill. In contrast to this fairly localized activity, the presence of saltwater fish on the site is evidence of trade with the coast (Allard 2010, 2015). Both Allard (2010, 2015) and Pezzarossi (2008, 2014) argue that local traders exchanged their catches with local shopkeepers who were themselves linked to commercial ties to Boston and beyond.

Taken as a whole, the rich assemblage from the SB/SB site presents a picture of a well-appointed household that practiced a varied economic strategy of farming, hunting, trapping, woodworking, and basket production that was linked to local and regional economies. The large ceramic assemblage and the unusually large number of eating utensils suggest that large dinners, sometimes consumed outside, were commonplace. The varied nature of the assemblage indicates entertaining with food and drink. Smoking is also evident from the pipe remains recovered from the site. In her analysis of pipes Rymer (2015) offered two observations suggesting that smoking behavior among the Nipmuc was in some ways different from that of their English neighbors while in other ways quite comparable. Her first observation concerns dating. While most of the pipes date to 1790–1830—the peak period of ceramic consumption—she suggests that some earlier pipes were being purposely curated (Rymer 2015:169). Her second observation is that smoking seems to have been done within the house and yard at the SB/SB farmstead much more than during work in the area surrounding the site (Rymer 2015:165). This observation is supported by statistical spatial analysis indicating that smoking and drinking vessels correlated favorably in the area of the house.

English culture also showed a strong preference for the consumption of tobacco, food, and drink, especially in taverns. Taverns were places of entertainment and frivolity, but they were also places where politics were discussed and, in Massachusetts, where rebellions were planned (see Bragdon 1981; Bridenbaugh 1938; Conroy 1995; Thompson 1998). Smoking played a more serious role in Native culture, often as part of political discussions as in the case of the

English, but of a more religious nature—something that was not part of the culture of tobacco use in Europe (Rymer 2015). Combined with the other classes of material culture and their distribution on the site, I believe the data strongly suggest that gatherings at the SB/SB farmstead served an important political purpose. During the eighteenth and nineteenth centuries, the Hassanamisco community would have been particularly close knit. The documentary record is replete with case after case of expressions of communal identity that support Nipmuc scholar Thomas Doughton's (1997) argument for a resilient and vibrant Nipmuc community throughout central Massachusetts (see also Gould 2010, 2013a, 2013b). One of the more important conclusions reached by the combined work of the Hassanamesit Woods Project participants (Allard 2010, 2015; Law 2008; Law Pezzarossi 2014a, 2014b; Mrozowski 2012, 2014; Mrozowski, Gould, and Law Pezzarossi 2015; Mrozowski and Law Pezzarossi 2015; Pezzarossi 2014) is that the SB/SB farmstead served as a community gathering place for a self-identified political group. When combined with the work of Gould (2010, 2013a, 2013b), it provides strong evidence of political continuity between both the SB/SB farmstead and the Moses Printer property—the current Nipmuc Reservation. This evidence stands in stark contrast to the conclusions reached by the BIA in denying the Nipmuc petition in 2004.

Conclusion

The collaboration that has been a major feature of the Hassanamesit Woods Project has demonstrated the value of pragmatic archaeology. The techniques and methods brought to the fieldwork and analysis of the SB/SB farmstead are rigorous and sophisticated. And I would argue that the quality of the research is not compromised by the collaboration but strengthened. This is especially true of the questions that have driven the overall research program that are consistent with long-standing strengths of basic archaeological research, such as the duration of the occupation. Further, what kinds of activities were carried out at the farmstead? What was the nature of the interaction between the Nipmuc and their English neighbors and how did it change over time? How did the life of the Nipmuc change as English colonialism unfolded? These are the kinds of base questions that any archaeologist would ask.

As the nature of our collaboration deepened, these questions were both interrogated and refined as a result of two facets of our work with the Nipmuc. First, we were introduced to the oral history of the Hassnamisco Nipmuc that has been kept alive by tribal members, in particular Rae Gould. This provided both a Native perspective and a Native voice. More deeply, however, it brought a different history to our larger inquiry than we could access through our standard approach. Second, it raised questions about the larger intellectual inquiry, especially its ultimate purpose. In this instance, the collective goal of the project participants was most broadly to make the history resulting from the collaboration address questions of cultural and political importance to the Nipmuc—it is their history. The history generated from the work at Hassanamesit Woods and Gould's work on the Moses Printer property (2010; 2013a, 2013b; Mrozowski, Gould, and Law Pezzarossi 2015) provides a rich picture that will form the corpus of a book being prepared for the University Press of Florida, which is designed to be primarily descriptive and accessible to a broader audience.

The questions and results outlined in this chapter capture only a small part of the picture that emerges from the research, but they do stress a convergence of archaeology and pragmatic philosophy that reinforces the benefits of collaborative research. At its core, the openness of the inquiry and the significance it places on all forms of knowledge make for a dynamically creative intellectual environment in which innovation can be fostered. That effort continues on a variety of levels. The focus of the project has now shifted to other Nipmuc and English households around Keith Hill. Most of these are located within the boundaries of the 1727 overplus lot (see Map 4.6). Some evidence, in the form of a slate writing board with the days of the week on either side and several slate pencils, could be linked to a circa 1730 meeting house and school that the general court stipulated would be built and maintained by the 40 English families who were allowed to purchase Hassanamisco land (MAC, vol. 31, 1701–1750:117–118, 746–748). Additional archaeological evidence appears to be linked to other members of the Nipmuc community living on Keith Hill, including the household of Deborah Newman—a contemporary of Sarah Boston—and her husband, Isaac Newman. Despite several seasons of geophysical and archaeological testing and excavations, definitive evidence of the house site of Deborah Newman has not been found. There is a scattering of material culture that dates to the late eighteenth/early nineteenth century—precisely when documentary evidence suggests that the Newmans were living on Keith Hill. But several attempts to find what was described by nineteenth-century historians as Deb Newman's cellar hole (Pierce 1879) have failed to find such a structure.

The most recent discovery made in the area is an oval-shaped (2 × 3 m) stone surface that includes fire-cracked rock and circa 1730–1750 ceramics, which is

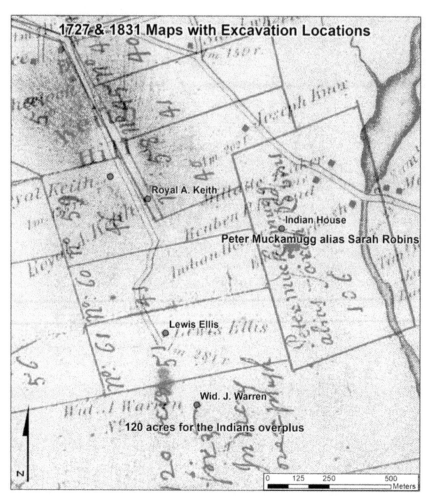

Map 4.6. Overlay of 1727 Hassanamisco Lands Distribution Map and 1831 Map of Grafton, showing excavations at the Deborah Newman and Augustus Salisbury properties. Map by author.

much earlier than any of the English farmsteads established close to 50–70 years later within the bounds of 120-acre overplus lot. I believe that this deposit is linked to Deborah Newman and her mother, Elizabeth Samson, and may represent family members who resided in the same area. It is possible that the extra land was used for other Nipmuc families; by the early nineteenth century, however, the vast majority of the land on Keith Hill was owned by English and then American farmers and artisans.

In the mid-nineteenth century the Commonwealth of Massachusetts enlisted John Milton Earle to assess the disposition of the Indians in the state. His report, published in 1861, focused on many groups, but his largest chapter focused on the Nipmuc. The picture that he paints of a small group of Native descendants whose treatment did not reflect well on the commonwealth, despite its sympathetic tone, nevertheless reinforced the notion of a dying people. The Hassanamisco Nipmuc continue to deal with the legacy of this troubled history in their struggle for federal recognition. If the archaeology of Hassanamesit Woods and at their own reservation helps them in making their case, I believe that this is a worthy purpose. Archaeology is a sophisticated form of inquiry that can examine historical questions that remain contested territory. Some of its more traditional strengths, such as temporal clarity and breadth, allow archaeologists to document the past in an empirically sound manner that can be used to answer sensitive historical questions. This is not the only advantage of collaboration, but it does provide a concrete example of the benefit and mutual respect that it embodies. That fact alone bodes well for the future of both communities.

References Cited

Adams, J.
2004   Nipmuc Say BIA Got the Facts Wrong Indian Country: http://www.indiancountrytoday.com/archive/28175229.html; accessed October 6, 2008.
Allard, A
2010   Foodways, Commensality and Nipmuc Identity: An Analysis of Faunal Remains from Sarah Boston's Farmstead, Grafton, MA, 1790–1840. Unpublished master's thesis, Department of Anthropology, University of Massachusetts, Boston.
2015   Foodways, Animal Husbandry and Nipmuc Identity: Faunal Analysis from Sarah Boston's Farmstead, Grafton, MA, 1790–1840. *International Journal of Historical Archaeology* 19(1):208–231.
Atalay, S.
2006   Indigenous Archaeology as Decolonizing Practice. *American Indian Quarterly* 30(3–4):280–310.
Baert, P.
2005   *Philosophy of the Social Sciences: Towards Pragmatism.* Polity Press, Cambridge.
Bagley, J.
2013   Cultural Continuity in a Nipmuc Landscape. Unpublished master's thesis, Department of Anthropology, University of Massachusetts, Boston.
Bagley, J. M., S. A. Mrozowski, H. Law Pezzarossi, and J. Steinberg
2015   Continuity of Lithic Practice at the Eighteenth- through Nineteenth-Century Nipmuc Homestead of Sarah Boston, Grafton, Massachusetts. *Northeast Historical Archaeology* 43(1):121–142.

Bergson, H.

1999 [1922] *Duration and Simultaneity, with Reference to Einstein's Theory*. Clinamen Press Ltd, Manchester, UK.

2001 [1889] *Time and Free Will: An Essay on the Immediate Data of Consciousness*. New York: Dover.

Bragdon, K. J.

1981 Occupational Differences Reflected in Material Culture. *Northeast Historical Archaeology* 10(1):27–39.

Braudel, F.

1980 *On History*. University of Chicago Press, Chicago.

Brenner, E.

1980 To Pray or to Prey: That Is the Question, Strategies for Cultural Autonomy of Massachusetts Praying Town Indians. *Ethnohistory* 27(2):135–152.

1984 Strategies for Autonomy: An Analysis of Ethnic Mobilization in Seventeenth Century Southern New England. Ph.D. dissertation, Department of Anthropology, University of Massachusetts, Amherst.

1986 Archaeological Investigations at a Massachusetts Praying Indian Town. *Bulletin of the Massachusetts Archaeological Society* 47(2):69–78.

Bridenbaugh, C.

1938 *Cities in the Wilderness: The First Century of Urban Life, 1625–1742*. Oxford University Press, New York.

Carlson, C.

1986 Archival and Archaeological Research Report on the Configuration of the Seven Original 17th Century Praying Indian Towns of the Massachusetts Bay Colony. University of Massachusetts Archaeological Services, Amherst.

Cogley, R. W.

1998 Was Natick a Residential Praying Town in the Period before King Philip's War? *Bulletin of the Massachusetts Archaeological Society* 59(1):31–35.

1999 *John Eliot's Mission to the Indians before King Phillips War*. Harvard University Press, Cambridge, MA.

Colwell-Chanthaphonh, C., T. J. Ferguson, D. Lippert, R. H. McGuire, G. P. Nicholas, J. E. Watkins, and L. Zimmerman

2010 The Premise and Promise of Indigenous Archaeology *American Antiquity* 75(2): 228–238.

Conroy, D. W.

1995 *In Public Houses: Drinks and the Revolution of Authority in Colonial Massachusetts*. University of North Carolina Press, Chapel Hill.

Den Ouden, A. E.

2005 *Beyond Conquest: Native Peoples and the Struggle for History in New England*. University of Nebraska Press, Lincoln.

Dewey, J.

1906a The Experimental Field of Knowledge. *Mind* 15(59):293–307.

1906b Beliefs and Realities. *Philosophical Review* 15(2):113–129.

1907 Reality and the Criterion for the Truth of Ideas. *Mind* 16(63):317–342.

1916   *Democracy and Education: An Introduction to the Philosophy of Education.* Text-Book Series in Education, edited by P. Monroe. Macmillan, New York.

1925   *Experience and Nature.* Open Court, Chicago.

Doughton, T. L.

1997   Unseen Neighbors: Native Americans of Central Massachusetts, People Who Had "Vanished." In *After King Philip's War: Presence and Persistence in Indian New England*, edited by C. Collaway, pp. 207–230. University Press of New England, Hanover, NH.

Dykuizen, G.

1973   *The Life and Mind of John Dewey.* Southern Illinois University Press, Carbondale.

Earle, J. M.

1861   *Report to the Governor and Council, Concerning the Indians of the Commonwealth, under the Act of April 6, 1859* (No. 96). White, Printer to the State, Boston.

Eliot, J.

1655   *A Late and Further Manifestation of the Progress of the Gospel amongst the Indians in New England.* Corporation for the Propagating of the Gospel in New England, London.

1670   *A Brief Narrative of the Progress of the Gospel Amongst the Indians in New England.* J. Allen, London.

1834   *The Day-breaking, If Not the Sun-rising of the Gospel with the Indians in New England.* Reprinted in *Massachusetts Historical Society Collections*, 3rd series, 4:1–23.

Gary, J.

2005   Phase 1 Archaeological Intensive Survey of Hassanamesit Woods, Grafton, Massachusetts. Cultural Resources Management Study No. 14. Center for Cultural and Environmental History, University of Massachusetts, Boston.

Gookin, D.

1972 [1674] *Historical Collections of the Indians in New England: Of Their Several Nations, Numbers, Customs, Manners, Religion and Government, before the English Planted There.* Collections of the Massachusetts Historical Society for the Year 1792, Vol. 1. Arno Press, New York.

Gould, D. R.

2010   Contested Places: The History and Meaning of Hassanamisco. Unpublished Ph.D. dissertation, Department of Anthropology, University of Connecticut, Storrs, CT.

2013a   Cultural Practice and Authenticity: The Search for Real Indians in New England in the "Historical" Period. In *The Death of Prehistory*, edited by P. Schmidt and S. A. Mrozowski, pp. 241–266. Oxford University Press, Oxford.

2013b   The Nipmuc Nation, Federal Acknowledgment, and a Case of Mistaken Identity. In *Recognition, Sovereignty Struggles, and Indigenous Rights in the United States: A Sourcebook*, edited by J. O'Brien and A. E. Den Ouden, pp. 213–231. University of North Carolina Press, Chapel Hill.

Harding, S.

2016   Latin American Decolonial Social Studies of Scientific Knowledge: Alliances and Tensions. *Science, Technology & Human Values* 41(6):1063–1087.

Herbster, H., and J. C. Garman

1996   Results of an Intensive (Locational) Archaeological Survey and a Burial Verifica-
        tion Study, Apple Ridge III Project, Ashland, Massachusetts. Public Archaeology
        Laboratory, Inc. Report No. 690. Submitted to Richmond Development, Ash-
        land, MA.

James, W.

1898   Philosophical Conceptions and Practical Results. *University Chronicle* 1(4):287–
        310.

1907   *Pragmatism: A New Name for an Old Way of Thinking.* Longmans Green, New
        York.

Kawashima, Y.

1969   Legal Origins of the Indian Reservation in Colonial Massachusetts. *American
        Journal of Legal History* 13(1):42–56.

Kelley, J. W.

1999   Burial Practices of the Praying Indians of Natick, Panokapoag, and Marlboro.
        Unpublished master's thesis, Department of Anthropology, University of Mas-
        sachusetts, Boston.

Law, H.

2008   Daily Negotiations and the Creation of an Alternative Discourse: The Legacy
        of a Colonial Nipmuc Farmstead. Unpublished master's thesis, Department of
        Anthropology, University of Massachusetts, Boston.

Law, H., G. Pezzarossi, and S. Mrozowski

2008   *Archaeological Intensive Excavations: Hassanamesit Woods Property, the Sarah
        Boston Farmstead, Grafton, Massachusetts.* Andrew Fiske Memorial Center for
        Archaeological Research, Cultural Resource Management Study 24. University
        of Massachusetts, Boston.

Law Pezzarossi, H.

2014a   *Traces of Residence: Indigenous Mobility and Materiality in 19th C. New Eng-
        land.* Unpublished Ph.D. dissertation, Department of Anthropology, University
        of California, Berkeley.

2014b   Assembling Indigeneity: Rethinking Innovation, Tradition and Indigenous Ma-
        teriality in a 19th-Century Native Toolkit. *Journal of Social Archaeology* 14(3):
        340–360.

2015a   Hassanamesit History. In *The Archaeology of Hassanamesit Woods: The Sarah
        Burnee/Sarah Boston Farmstead,* edited by S. A. Mrozowski and H. Law Pez-
        zarossi, pp. 11–34. Andrew Fiske Memorial Center for Archaeological Research
        Cultural Resource Management Study No. 69. University of Massachusetts,
        Boston.

2015b   Native Basketry and the Dynamics of Social Landscape in Southern New Eng-
        land. In *Things in Motion: Object Histories, Biographies and Itineraries,* edited by
        R. Joyce and S. Gillespie, pp. 179–199. School of Advanced Research Press, Santa
        Fe, NM.

Lightfoot, K. G., L. M. Panich, T. D. Schneider, S. L. Gonzalez, M. A. Russell, D.
Modzelewski, T. Molino, and E. H. Blair

2013   The Study of Indigenous Political Economies and Colonialism in Native California: Implications for Contemporary Tribal Groups and Federal Recognition. *American Antiquity* 78(1):89–103.

Massachusetts Archives Collection (MAC)

1603–1705 *Indians.* Vol. 30. Massachusetts State Archives, Boston.

1701–1750 *Indians.* Vol. 31. Massachusetts States Archives, Boston.

McGhee, R.

2008 Aborginalism and the Problems of Indigenous Archaeology. *American Antiquity* 73(4):579–597.

2010 Of Strawmen, Herrings, and Frustrated Expectations. *American Antiquity* 75(2): 239–243.

Mrozowski, S. A.

2006 *The Archaeology of Class in Urban America.* Cambridge University Press, London.

2009 Christian Indian Communities in New England after King Philip's War. In *Archaeology in America: An Encyclopedia*, edited by F. P. McManomon, pp. 143–147. Greenwood, Westport, CT.

2012 Pragmatism and the Relevancy of Archaeology for Contemporary Society. In *Archaeology in Society: Its Relevance in the Modern World,* edited by M. Rockman and J. Flatman, pp. 239–256. Springer, New York.

2013 The Tyranny of Prehistory and the Search for a Deeper History. In *The Death of Prehistory*, edited by P. R. Schmidt and S. A. Mrozowski, pp. 220–240. Oxford University Press, Oxford.

2014 Imagining an Archaeology of the Future: Capitalism and Colonialism Past and Present. *International Journal of Historical Archaeology* 18(2):340–360.

2019 Violence and Dispossession at the Intersection of Colonialism and Capitalist Accumulation. *Historical Archaeology.*

Mrozowski, S. A., R. Gould, and H. Law Pezzarossi

2015 Rethinking Colonialism: Indigenous Innovation and Colonial Inevitability. In *Colonial Narratives*, edited by K. Howlett-Hayes and C. Cipolla, pp. 121–142. University Press of Florida, Gainesville.

Mrozowski, S. A., H. Herbster, D. Brown, and K. L. Priddy

2009 Magunkaquog Materiality, Federal Recognition, and the Search for a Deeper History. *International Journal of Historical Archaeology* 13(4):430–463.

Mrozowski, S. A., and H. Law Pezzarossi (editors)

2015 *The Archaeology of Hassanamesit Woods: The Sarah Burnee/Sarah Boston Farmstead.* Andrew Fiske Memorial Center for Archaeological Research Cultural Resource Management Study No. 69. University of Massachusetts, Boston.

Mrozowski, S. A., H. Law Pezzarossi, J. Bagley, G. Pezzarossi, J. Rymer, and J. Warner

2015 Material Culture, in *The Archaeology of Hassanamesit Woods: The Sarah Burnee/ Sarah Boston Farmstead*, edited by S. A. Mrozowski and H. Law Pezzoarossi, pp. 145–184. Andrew Fiske Memorial Center for Archaeological Research Cultural Resource Management Study No. 69. University of Massachusetts, Boston.

Nicholas, G. (editor)

2010 *Being and Becoming Indigenous Archaeologists.* Left Coast Press, Walnut Creek, CA.

O'Brien, Jean M.

1997 *Dispossession by Degrees: Indian Land and Identity in Natick, Massachusetts, 1650–1790*. University of Nebraska Press, Lincoln.

2010 *Firsting and Lasting: Writing Indians Out of Existence in New England*. University of Minnesota Press, Minneapolis.

Panich, L. M.

2013 Archaeologies of Persistence: Reconsidering the Legacies of Colonialism in Native North America. *American Antiquity* 78:105–122.

Pezzarossi, G.

2008 Consumption as Social Camouflage: "Mimicry" and Nipmuc Survival Strategies in the Colonial World. Unpublished master's thesis, Department of Anthropology, University of Massachusetts, Boston.

2014 Camouflaging Consumption and Colonial Mimicry: The Materiality of a Colonial Nipmuc Household. *International Journal of Historical Archaeology* 18(1):146–174.

Pezzarossi, G., R. Kennedy, and H. Law

2012 "Hoe Cake and Pickerel": Cooking Traditions and Community at a Nineteenth-Century Nipmuc Farmstead. In *The Menial Art of Cooking: Archaeological Studies of Cooking and Food Preparation*, edited by S. R. Graff and E. Rodríguez-Alegría, pp. 201–230. University of Colorado Press, Boulder.

Pierce, F. C.

1879 *The History of Grafton, Worcester County, Massachusetts, from Its Early Settlement by the Indians in 1647 to the Present Time, 1879, Including the Genealogies of Seventy-Nine of the Older Families*. Press of Chas. Hamilton, Worcester, MA.

Preucel, R. W.

2006 *Archaeological Semiotics*. Blackwell, Malden, MA.

Preucel, R. W., and A. A. Bauer

2001 Archaeological Pragmatics. *Norwegian Archaeological Review* 34:85–96.

Preucel, R. W., and S. A. Mrozowski (editors)

2010 *Contemporary Archaeology in Theory: The New Pragmatism*. Wiley-Blackwell, Malden, MA.

Rorty, R.

1979 *Philosophy and the Mirror of Nature*. Princeton University Press, Princeton, NJ.

1982 *Consequences of Pragmatism*. University of Minnesota Press, Minneapolis.

1998 *Achieving Our Country: Leftist Thought in Twentieth-Century America*. Harvard University Press, Cambridge, MA.

1999 *Philosophy and Social Hope*. Penguin Books, London.

Rymer, J.

2015 Pipe Dating and Implications. In *The Archaeology of Hassanamesit Woods: The Sarah Burnee/Sarah Boston Farmstead*, edited by S. A. Mrozowski and S. Law Pezzarossi, pp. 163–169. Andrew Fiske Memorial Center for Archaeological Research Cultural Resource Management Study No. 69. University of Massachusetts, Boston.

Schmidt, P. R., and S. A. Mrozowski

2013 The Death of Prehistory: Reforming the Past, Looking to the Future. In *The*

Death of Prehistory, edited by P. R. Schmidt and S. A. Mrozowski, pp. 1–28. Oxford University Press, Oxford.

Scott, D.

2006   The "Concept of Time" and the "Being of the Clock": Bergson, Einstein, Heidegger, and the Interrogation of the Temporality of Modernism. *Continental Philosophy Review* 39:183–213.

Silliman, S. W.

2009   Change and Continuity, Practice and Memory: Native American Persistence in Colonial New England. *American Antiquity* 74(2):211–230.

2010   The Value and Diversity of Indigenous Archaeology: A Response to McGhee. *American Antiquity* 75(2):217–220.

Taylor, H.

1973   Introduction. In *The Life and Mind of John Dewey*, edited by G. Dykhuizen, pp. xi–xxv. Southern Illinois University Press, Carbondale.

Thompson, P.

1998   *Rum Punch Revolution: Tavern Going and Public Life in Eighteenth-Century Philadelphia*. University of Pennsylvania Press, Philadelphia.

Thorbahn, P.

1988   Where Are the Late Woodland Villages in Southern New England? *Bulletin of the Massachusetts Archaeological Society* 49(2):46–57.

Trigg, H.

2015   Analysis of the Botanical Materials from the Sarah Burnee/Sarah Boston Farmstead. In *The Archaeology of Hassanamesit Woods: The Sarah Burnee/Sarah Boston Farmstead*, edited by S. A. Mrozowski and H. Law Pezzarossi, pp. 129–143. Andrew Fiske Memorial Center for Archaeological Research Cultural Resource Management Study No. 69. University of Massachusetts, Boston.

Trigger, B.

1980   Archaeology and the Image of the American Indian. *American Antiquity* 45(4):662–667.

Wylie, A.

2015   Plurality of Pluralisms: Collaborative Practice in Archaeology in Archaeology. In *Objectivity Science: New Perspectives from Science and Technology Studies*, edited by F. Padovani, A. Richardson, and J. Y. Tsou, pp. 189–210. Dondrecht, Netherlands, Springer.

5

Listening to Experts

The Directions Indigenous Experience Has Taken
the Study of Earth Mounds in Northern Australia

BILLY Ó FOGHLÚ

In north Australian archaeological discourse, the term "earth mound" refers to
a specific archaeological site type. Earth mounds are typically shallow, anthropogenic mounds of soil, sand, and fine sediment that can be found alongside
creeks, along the margins of swamplands, and on alluvial plains that experience
seasonal flooding. These sites can be oval to circular in plan, range from 10 m
to 40 m in diameter, and on average reach 0.8 m at their highest point (see
Brockwell 2006). There are essentially two fundamental problems at the heart
of north Australian earth mound analysis.

The first problem is that it is difficult to obtain interpretable data from these
sites. Large sites can initially appear to be very similar in form to natural features like collapsed termite mounds and megapode bird mounds (*Megapodius
reinwardt*), which are common sights in the north Australian landscape. Their
soil presents no visually distinctive stratigraphy and often contains few if any
identifiable artifacts. While the makers of these mounds were accomplished
craftspeople, many of the tools, adornments, and implements they made would
have been composed of organic materials as a result of poor local utilitarian
stone sources. Such materials do not preserve well, if at all. This soil also pre-
serves few if any faunal remains, with the exception of shell deposits, which can
survive when the amount of shell is large enough to affect the pH of the immediate environment to a level that is conducive to preservation. The majority of
earth mounds are shallow sites that are difficult to identify and even photograph
(Figures 5.1a and 5.1b); few are prominent features in the landscape.

Even in these instances, large shell deposits close to the surface can lead to

Figure 5.1. An example of a prominent earth mound site in Kakadu National Park, NT: (*a*) unshaded; (*b*) shaded. Photos by author.

their miscategorization as shell mounds (Ó Foghlú 2017; see Roberts 1991). Shell mounds are a more prominent Australian archaeological site type that can occur in some of the same areas as earth mounds. In contrast to earth mounds, shell mounds have been a major focus of north Australian archaeological investigation for almost half a century (e.g., Bailey 1977, 1993, 1994, 1999; Brockwell et al. 2017; Holdaway et al. 2017; Larsen et al. 2015; Morrison 2013, 2014; Petchey et al. 2013; Shiner and Morrison 2009; Shiner et al. 2013; Stevenson et al. 2015; Stone 1992). The few anthropogenic signatures that can be detected within earth mounds are almost identical to those left by natural processes. For instance, bushfires, which can bring mature trees to the ground and smoulder within root systems for weeks, are seasonal in northern Australia. Many archaeological site types are burned along with their surrounding landscape on an almost yearly basis. The remains of anthropogenic fires therefore can be difficult to differentiate from those left by intense natural fires. Even one of the few artifact types that can survive in abundance is visually identical to the by-products of natural processes. Termite mound clay heat retainers, artifacts of human-engineered firing, can occur all throughout earth mound matrices. However, so, too, can the remains of naturally baked termite mound clay, which can result when an infested tree burns to the ground and smoulders for a number of weeks (Ó Foghlú 2017).

The second problem is that it is difficult to understand and interpret the information that is obtained from these sites. Even when it is possible to obtain interpretable data, earth mounding behavior can be difficult to understand and quantify from the biased lens of Western (i.e., nonlocal) perspectives. Earth mounds do not fit within the Western concept of a complex construction and yet they are not the result of careless, unplanned discard. The past and present landscapes that they are a component of would not meet the criteria of an urban area, although many of these places would have been complex, cosmopolitan hubs of interaction and exchange (see Ó Foghlú et al. 2016).

These two problems lie at the heart of a research project (Ó Foghlú 2019), now nearing completion, investigating the nature of earth mound sites in two important regions in northern Australia: in Weipa, Queensland, and Kakadu National Park, Northern Territory (Map 5.1). This chapter attempts to highlight

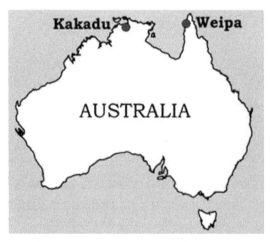

Map 5.1. Australia, showing the locations of the two study areas.
With permission of Australian National University, © CartoGis CAP.

the important role that archaeologies of listening played in this project: they were imperative in addressing how information from earth mound sites could be obtained, interpreted, and understood.

The Emergence of Earth Mounds in Weipa, Cape York

Wathayn Country is the first focus of this project. Wathayn Country, an estuarine landscape of mangrove-lined environments, tidal mudflats, and wooded, gently sloping laterite plains, is situated on the northern bank of the Embley River on the Weipa peninsula, Cape York (Map 5.2). To the Aboriginal communities who live here (referred to in the text as Traditional Owners), Wathayn holds deep importance, both as a cultural landscape of deep and long-held meaning and as a place of valued ecological resources (Ó Foghlú 2017; Ó Foghlú et al. 2016).

Wathayn is a rich archaeological landscape. Aboriginal society and presence had established itself as an integral component of this landscape long before the

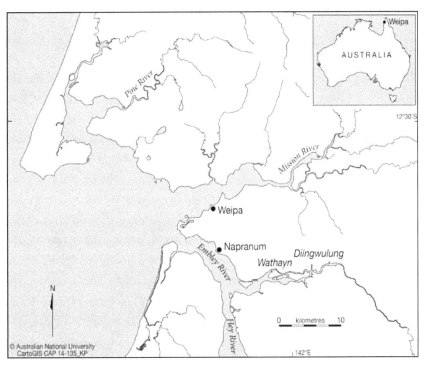

Map 5.2. The Weipa Region of Northern Australia. With permission of Australian University, © CartoGis CAP.

emergence of earth mound sites (e.g., Brockwell et al. 2017; Holdaway et al. 2017; Ó Foghlú et al. 2016; Petchey et al. 2013; Shiner et al. 2013; Stevenson et al. 2015). One of the most heavily investigated archaeological site types in both Wathayn and the greater Weipa area consists of distinctive shell mound sites, the largest of which can be over 10 m high and contain over 10,000 metric tons of shell (Bailey 1999:105). Shell mounds are a persistent site type throughout the late Holocene, emerging out of a period of sea-level stabilization and coastal progradation, possibly as early as 4,000–5,000 years ago (Bailey 1977, 1993, 1994, 1999; Holdaway et al. 2017; Larsen et al. 2015; Morrison 2013, 2014; Petchey et al. 2013; Shiner et al. 2013; Stevenson et al. 2015; Stone 1992), clearly dated archaeological evidence also supports "ongoing mound construction" as recently as post 200 cal. BP (Morrison 2014:10).

However, specifically in the Wathayn locality, new work is starting to reveal that the most intensive period of shell mounding clusters around 2,700–2,100 cal. BP (Holdaway et al. 2017; Petchey et al. 2013; Stevenson et al. 2015:17). It is only after this period (i.e., ca. 2100 BP onward) that earth mounds start to appear in Wathayn, in partial response to environmental change (Brockwell et al. 2017; Ó Foghlú 2017; Stevenson et al. 2015).

The Emergence of Earth Mounds in Kakadu National Park

The second area investigated as part of this project is located in Kakadu National Park (declared in 1979; Jones 1985:v–vii) where the Nourlangie Creek floodplains meet those of the winding South Alligator River in the Northern Territory (Map 5.3). This junction, extending up from Ki'na (Giina) in the south to the Goose Camp headland in the northeast, is made up of gently sloping laterite margins that border the floodplains, vast plains of black cracking clays that extend out into the tidal river channel. Again, as at Weipa, Aboriginal society and presence had long established itself as an integral component of this landscape before earth mounds began to emerge from it (e.g., Jones 1985). However, unlike Wathayn Country, here we learn that hypersaline conditions, which would not have supported substantial vegetation, existed from ca. 6000 BP to sometime before ca. 1400 BP in this locality (Hope, Hughes, and Russel-Smith 1985). Close to the latter end of this period, these conditions ceased; clays were stabilized by grasses, salt began to leach from the upper soil horizons, and rich black clay, the product of surface wash and organic decay, started to accumulate. Lagoons became substantial freshwater bodies, which brought large popula-

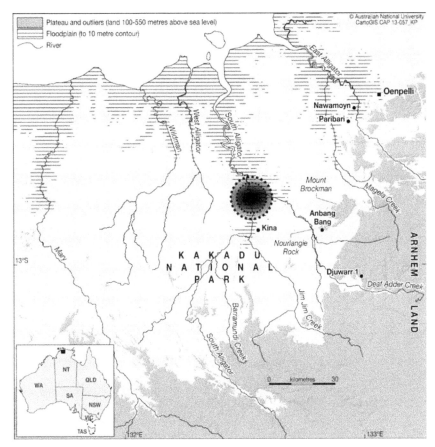

Map 5.3. The Kakadu National Park Region, with the study area highlighted. Map by author.

tions of water birds and vegetation. It is only after this point that conditions for sustained anthropogenic settlement became more favorable. Many earth mounds have been recorded in this rich archaeological landscape (see Hope, Hughes, and Russel-Smith 1985; Meehan et al. 1985).

Listening

To learn about people and communities who were once deeply connected to a landscape, it is helpful to listen to the people and communities who are now deeply connected to that landscape. For this research, it was imperative to consult with Traditional Owners in both regions, people and communities who are the custodians of living bodies of traditional knowledge that have been carried down through periods of immense conflict and change. This knowledge is in many cases firmly supported by each region's ethnographic corpus (Ó Foghlú 2017; Ó Foghlú et al. 2016). By consulting with local Traditional Owners, it was possible to obtain the necessary education about what could be investigated, confirmed, or discounted as evidence. Listening introduces us to informed reasoning backed by expert opinions from people who experience these landscapes and their traditions every day. Traditional knowledge is not just extensive in its scope; it comes from a completely different but equally valid place of learning and understanding. Listening does not provide a blueprint of the past; it highlights the questions that need to be asked about the past.

Listening to Experts in Wathayn Country

In Wathayn Country, for instance, it was possible to learn about some of the intricacies of termite mound clay heat retainers from experts who knew how to craft and use them and for whom they held important meaning (Beatrice Gordon, personal communication 2012, 2013; Elisabeth Coconut, personal communication 2013; Graham Peinkina, personal communication 2012, 2013; Rocky Madua, personal communication 2013).

This education enabled an experimental study of local termite mound clay types to be conducted through the adaptation of an existing X-ray diffraction technique (applied in Coutts, Henderson, and Fullagar 1979). This analysis, carried out under the advice and guidance of Dr. Ulrike Troitzsch (Research School of Earth Sciences, Australian National University), demonstrated that, despite being similar on a visual level, termite mound clay heat retainer artifacts are distinct from naturally baked termite mound clay on a crystalline level. As a result of this distinction, it became clear that instead of yielding minimal assemblages of identifiable artifacts, earth mounds in Wathayn can contain many thousands of cultural artifacts (Ó Foghlú 2017, 2019).

Many aspects of material culture do not survive to the present day in artifactual form. It was possible to learn from experts in Wathayn about the manufacture and use of organic compound implements and adornments, such as fishing spears, seed necklaces, artworks painted on living tree bark, and shell tools. Being able to cross-reference this information with information recorded by some of the region's first colonial populations over a century before (i.e., the ethnographic corpus) also allowed for a far greater understanding of how great the absence of evidence could be in this region (Ó Foghlú 2017, 2019; Ó Foghlú et al. 2016).

Listening to Experts in the South Alligator Floodplains

In November 2012, on the South Alligator floodplains, in Kakadu National Park, a number of modern earth mound sites were identified during a field-work trip that sought to identify and survey archaeological earth mounds for future excavation and analysis. These sites were still in active use but remarkably similar to archaeological earth mound sites. The sites are maintained and used by Patsy "Raichiwanga" Raglar. Patsy is an Aboriginal teacher and guide who shares her Traditional Knowledge with guests and tourists through the ecotourism company Animal Tracks. Some of these mound sites are used privately and others are no longer used as a result of environmental changes in those areas. Patsy provided extensive guidance and education about the multifaceted aspects of these sites and all of the activities instrumental in their formation. It was possible to monitor and survey the formation of two sites over the course of three years, with detailed knowledge from Patsy about firing durations, the number of uses, and the number of attendants that contributed to site development (Ó Foghlú 2017, 2019). Patsy uses tools like firesticks that are identical to artifacts uncovered in nearby archaeological investigations (e.g., Clarke 1985) and recorded in the ethnographic corpus (Ó Foghlú 2017). She provided new understanding and experience of what was now understood to be one of the fundamental processes of earth mound formation: human-engineered firing.

Existing analytical techniques were tailored as a result of what was learned and applied in an attempt to understand how soil burned in this complex way was different from soil that had burned naturally in bushfires. An in-depth archaeomagnetic analysis, adapted from groundbreaking techniques applied in Oldfield and Crowther (2007), was conducted under the advice and guidance of Dr. Dave Heslop (Research School of Earth Sciences, Australian National University [ANU] College of Physical & Mathematical Sciences). χ_{lf}, χ_{fd}, and χ_{ARM} readings were taken from soil samples collected on, within, and off earth mound sites and natural features and bilogarithmically plotted χ_{ARM}/χ_{fd} versus χ_{ARM}/χ_{lf}. In combination with this, an in-depth soil chemistry analysis was also conducted in which Munsell coloration, total organic content, pH, particle size analysis, total phosphorus, and total Kjeldahl nitrogen were carefully measured under the advice and guidance of Andrew Higgins (Fenner School, ANU).

The results of these analyses corroborated one another: anthropogenic signatures on and within earth mound sites can be detected and even quantified (Ó Foghlú 2017, 2019). It was only through listening and learning that many of the complexities of earth mound formation could be truly appreciated and questioned. Listening highlighted the questions that needed to be asked.

Information from Earth Mounds

A more comprehensive model of earth mound formation can be put forward as a result of obtaining more interpretable data from these sites. Formation commences when people gather in an area to construct an earth oven site with the intention of reusing it many times after the event. Earth oven cooking involves firing heat retainers in an intense open fire within a small hole, until most of the fuel has combusted. Heat retainers can be made from stone, tempered clay, termite mound clay, or other heat-retentive materials (e.g., shell). Layers of protective organic material, like paperbark and/or aromatic vegetation, are laid over these heat retainers and glowing embers, along with the food that is to be baked, followed by more layers of organic material. The oven is then completely covered and sealed with soil and left to bake until the food is ready to eat (Ó Foghlú 2019; Beatrice Gordon, personal communication 2012, 2013; Elisabeth Coconut, personal communication 2013; Graham Peinkina, personal communication 2012, 2013; Patsy "Raichiwanga" Raglar, personal communication 2012, 2013, 2014; Rocky Madua, personal communication 2013).

Using this site over and over instigates the mass buildup of dark charcoal-rich soil, which both surrounds and becomes the site. This buildup makes the soil softer to dig and more heat retentive after every use. Multiple earth ovens can be employed on the mound as it develops, and surface fires become easier to ignite and manage in this charcoal-rich environment. The active site becomes a raised clearing in a landscape often dominated by concealing bushland, with a surface ideal for erecting complex shelters. The more an earth mound is used, the more efficient it becomes, through mindful curation and mounding of the charcoal as it forms. The site becomes an activity place in the landscape.

These are just the fundamental processes of earth mound formation. Listening to local Traditional Owners is not just imperative in increasing the scope of how information can be obtained, it is also imperative in increasing the scope of how this information can be interpreted and understood so that the best explanation can be reached.

Interpreting the Past through Local Realities

Many aspects of earth-mounding activities can be difficult to understand and appreciate through the constrained lens of Western perspectives. Interpreting these sites, their landscapes, and the societies that they are a product of through local realties can increase the interpreters' scope of understanding and explanatory standards as they work toward the inference to the best explanation. To Peter Lipton (2004:124), philosopher of science and epistemology, "some possible worlds make more sense than others." Therefore, to draw from Lipton (2004:56, 209), the explanatory considerations and standards of the interpreters must be malleable if they are to evolve to track the truth. A number of concepts can be put forward to illustrate this.

Country

Monchamp (2014:3) explains how the word "Country" is a proper noun in Aboriginal English, a collective of human and nonhuman actors "acting in the world with will and intention" (Monchamp 2014:120). Country is a landscape concept that "is not a static, bounded parcel of space but rather a lived-in place within which one has a relationship with (rather than to) the land" (Monchamp 2014:3). Relationships with Country must be maintained and "are manifold and intrinsic to people's identities and ways of being in the world" (Monchamp 2014:127, 135).

Understanding Country as a concept is key to understanding the sites, people, and places that make up some of its components.

Movements throughout and off Country can be dictated by many factors that can range from utilitarian to deeply important, including violent weather seasons, management and curation of resources, important rites and rituals, and special events. Sometimes movement can occur as part of a greater collective or in smaller familial groups. Country as a concept does not fit squarely within the Western conceptions of territories, borders, and boundaries; it comes from a different but equally valid place of understanding. When trying to assess whether an earth mound's position and purpose in the landscape was dictated by everyday considerations or by deeply significant events, there is much to consider.

Similarly, when attempting to interpret dates obtained from earth mound matrices and understand why certain sites have been abandoned at a time when other sites nearby have not, interpreting the past through local realities can provide deeper understanding. The landscapes and societies from which earth mounds developed would not meet any Western criteria of an urban area or indeed fit squarely anywhere along a spectrum that set Western culture as the standard against which to make judgments about other cultures.

Yet many of these places would have been cosmopolitan and multilingual hubs of interaction and exchange and centers of innovative craft production, art, music, and established seasonally specialist harvesting (Ó Foghlú 2017, 2019; Ó Foghlú et al. 2016). Even if definitive explanations cannot be reached, it is important as archaeologists that we know how little we know to better appreciate the complexity of what we are trying to investigate and interpret.

Constructions

Many types of traditional structures documented in the research areas of this project (e.g., Leichhardt 1845–1846:399–422; Roth 1900:1–63) and throughout Australia (e.g., Memmott 2007) would fit into the Western concept of a complex construction. Earth mounds do not easily fit within this concept. They are not the result of unplanned, careless discard; they are the product of mindful, long-term site curation and development. Earth mounds become more efficient and sustainable after every use and are complex, in spite of an apparent minimalism that masks their complexity (Ó Foghlú 2017, 2019). It can be difficult to understand this type of multifaceted, long-term, allocentric development if every construction in interpreters' (nonlocal) reality is the product of a direct, sought-out objective. Understanding these sites through local realities can demonstrate that they are an alternate but equally valid and important class of complex construction.

Mnemohistory, Weaving Multiple Realities to Form a Coherent Narrative

The difference between collective memory and history can be viewed as a difference based on the relevance of the past to the present (Olick 1999, 2007, 2008; Olick and Robbins 1998). History is an inscribed past with which we no longer have an organic connection, whereas collective memory is "an active past that forms our identities," to which we are connected in the present (Olick and Robbins 1998:111). Collective or social memory is a connective structure involving forms and processes such as tradition, myth, commemoration, and monument building where remembering individuals remember together (Olick and Robbins 1998:105–106).

Assmann (1997:9) uses the term "mnemohistory" to describe this active process of meaning-making through time. Unlike history, mnemohistory is concerned not with the factuality and original significance of the past (which in history is highly important) but with the actuality of the past as it is remembered in the present (Assmann 1997:8–9). We position ourselves and are positioned by the narratives of this past (Olick and Robbins 1998:122), and our communities are constituted by this past—a real community is a community of memory (Olick 2007:20). Different communities remember different things. As an archaeologist, I have found that interpreting the past through one's own mnemohistory, through one's own reality, is not enough. Local mnemohistories must be drawn on by listening to local communities.

The colonial conquest of the Alligator Rivers region in the nineteenth century caused local populations to crash to approximately 4 percent compared to the population at the time of colonial contact (Keen 1981; Reid 1990). In Cape York, the invasion of colonial populations in Queensland claimed over 90 percent of the Aboriginal population by the beginning of the twentieth century (Bottoms 2013; Loos 1982). Enslavement, kidnapping, mass deportations, autocratic control, theocratic control, and the spread of numerous introduced diseases brought these cataclysms to Aboriginal communities in these regions. Many of these occurred well into the twentieth century (Blake 1998; Bottoms 2013; Frankland 1994; Gillet 1986; Keen 1981; Loos 1982; Meston 1895, 1896; Ó Foghlú et al. 2016; Reid 1990; Scambary 2013; Sharp 1992; Taylor 2003).

Nonlocal interpreters often find it difficult to escape their own mnemohistories, when they must also interpret the past through local mnemohistories. There are great disparities in many nonlocal mnemohistories that can be very detrimental to the interpretation of the local past. Bottoms (2013) describes Queensland's killing times as a "conspiracy of silence," a collective consciousness for which the Aboriginal past is not part of an active past for the non-Aboriginal community. Yet for the Aboriginal communities in these regions, these times are very much a part of collective memory, an active past and mnemohistory: different but equally valid and important parts of the past inform the present.

Country is an archive of material memory in the form of archaeological sites and artifacts. Archaeological discoveries and interpretations can affect the mnemohistories of places being investigated, how communities perceive the places they live in, how they connect with the past. So, too, must nonlocal archaeologists be affected by local mnemohistories, so that multiple realties can be woven together to form an interconnected, coherent narrative. This begins through listening.

What Is Important? Why Is It Important?

Archaeologists do not get to decide what is and what is not archaeologically important for the communities connected to archaeological sites or what contributes to collective histories and identities. Archaeologists need to listen to what is important and understand why it is important. Archaeology has often, in its antiquarian past, been dominated by an obsession with artifacts and sites that are perhaps the oldest or the most aesthetically pleasing (and perhaps understandable) from a Western perspective (e.g., Hammerich 1893; Walker 1786; Wilde 1857, 1861). The terms "Stone Age," "Bronze Age," and "Iron Age" originally developed from disproportionate fascinations with particular artifact types and are now recognized as unsuitable terms (see Bradley 2007, 25).

In Wathayn Country, despite the local paucity of utilitarian stone sources and the correspondingly small role of stone materials in local material culture, stone tools dot the landscape. Some are quite large, like adze/axe heads, and some can even be found in datable earth mound contexts, although this is rare (Ó Foghlú 2017, 2019). These pieces are highly technical in their artisanship and are, of course, highly important in the interpretation of Wathayn's past material culture. Furthermore, it is reasonable to assume that the oldest artifact types that can survive in Wathayn's archaeological record are those rare examples made from stone. Conventionally, archaeologists have always focused on such artifact types, holding them to be, perhaps, the most archaeologically important. Traditional Owners in Wathayn know a lot about many of these stone pieces from their oral history, and much of this is reinforced by ethnographic accounts recorded over 120 years. Locally, however, these artifacts represent important relics of a somewhat distant past. In contrast, the discovery of a postcolonial contact glass artifact, on an earth mound site in Wathayn, meant a great deal to Traditional Owners. Glass tools are seen as a relic of more recent generations. These artifacts represent a connection to living memories, an active past, and a more immediate time (see Ó Foghlú et al. 2016). The discovery of this artifact in Wathayn in an earth mound context demonstrated that these sites and the practices from which they developed were still being utilized (or reutilized) after colonial populations arrived in Weipa. Being able to confirm this archaeologically was important for Traditional Owners in Wathayn. Archaeologists must listen and understand why this is important.

Interpretation of archaeological sites in general has, in the past, also been subject to disproportionate focus. Conventionally, archaeologists have often focused on the original uses and purposes of sites, again holding them to be perhaps the most archaeologically important. This has often overshadowed the interpretation of later uses or reuses of sites. To draw from Bradley (1993) and Holtorf (1998), later use or reuse of an archaeological site can be as important as its original function in interpreting the entire life history of a site and the culture that shaped it. In Wathayn and the Alligator River floodplains, it meant a great deal to Traditional Owners to know that archaeological evidence confirmed that many of the practices and traditions that are part of their cultural identity today have been part of these landscapes for millennia (Beatrice Gordon, personal communication 2012, 2013; Elisabeth Coconut, personal communication 2013; Graham Peinkina, personal communication 2012, 2013; Ó Foghlú 2017, 2019; Ó Foghlú et al. 2016; Patsy "Raichiwanga" Raglar, personal communication 2012, 2013, 2014; Rocky Madua, personal communication 2013).

While the initial uses of earth mound sites are important, so, too, is their utilization (or possible reutilization) after colonial contact. Again, it is the connection to living memories, an active past, and a more immediate time. Being able to understand not just the history but the mnemohistory of Country means that archaeologists can help contribute to a recent past with which the Traditional Owners still have an organic connection, a past that is a shaper of cultural identity and collective memory today. Archaeologists alone cannot decide what is archaeologically important, but they can listen and understand why something is archaeologically important to the communities connected to archaeological sites.

Conclusion

Listening is imperative from both strategic and moral standpoints. Listening made it possible to obtain interpretable information from archaeological earth mound sites and gain the necessary education about how to interpret and understand this information. Many parts of this research project would not have been achievable without an archaeology of listening (Ó Foghlú 2019).

Archaeologists will find it advantageous to recognize and draw from local knowledge as well as their own realities to work toward inference to the best explanation. To learn about people who were once deeply connected to a landscape, archaeologists should listen to the living people who are deeply connected to that landscape. Listening can introduce us to informed reasoning backed by expert opinions from people who experience these landscapes and their traditions every day. Archaeologists will also find it beneficial to draw from local mnemohistories, because different parts of the past inform the present for different communities. These multiple realties can be woven together to form an interconnected, coherent narrative. Archaeologists do not get to decide what is archaeologically important for communities connected to archaeological sites; they must listen and understand why something is important.

Listening cannot provide a blueprint of the past; rather, it highlights the questions that need to be asked about the past.

Acknowledgments

I would like to give utmost thanks to the Traditional Owners of Wathayn and Kakadu for granting access to their Country, and in particular to Beatrice Gordon, Elisabeth Coconut, Graham Peinkina, and Patsy "Raichiwanga" Raglar for all of their invaluable assistance, guidance, advice, and education. I would also like to give heartfelt thanks to Rocky Madua, Jason Wipa, Dave Lindner, and Sean Arnold for their invaluable assistance, guidance, advice, and education. Heartfelt thanks, too, to Dr. Sally Brockwell and Dr. Janelle Stevenson for their continuing supervision, guidance, and help. And to Andrew Higgins, Fenner School, ANU, for his tireless help; to Dr. Dave Heslop, Research School of Earth Sciences, ANU College of Physical and Mathematical Sciences; and to Dr. Ulrike Troitzsch, Research School of Earth Sciences, ANU. Industry Partner Rio Tinto Alcan (RTA) gave generous financial support in Weipa; thanks to the RTA staff—Siobhan Walker and Eloise Hoffman. Fieldwork was supported by Australian Research Council (ARC)–funded Linkage Project: Enhancing Cultural Heritage Management for Mining Operations: A Multi-Disciplinary Approach (LP110100180) with Industry Partner Rio Tinto Alcan; ARC-funded Discovery Project: Earth Mounds in Northern Australia: Archaeological and Environmental Archives of the Mid to Late Holocene (DP120100512); ARC Linkage project From Prehistory to History: Landscape and Cultural Change on the South Alligator River Kakadu National Park (LP110201128); and the Australian National University. Dr. Jack Fenner (ANU) contributed significantly with mapping, surveying, guidance, and help. Dr. Justin Shiner and Rio Tinto Alcan, cultural heritage management staff, and Gabrielle O'Loughlin and Mary Blyth (Cultural Programs, Kakadu National Park) supported me greatly. Many thanks also to Kristie Martin and Haylee Martin for proofreading the manuscript.

References Cited

Assmann, J.

1997   *Moses the Egyptian: The Memory of Egypt in Western Monotheism.* Harvard University Press, Cambridge, MA.

Bailey, G.

1977   Shell Mounds, Shell Middens and Raised Beaches in the Cape York Peninsula. *Mankind* 11(2):132–143.

1993   Shell Mounds in 1972 and 1992: Reflections on Recent Controversies at Ballina and Weipa. *Australian Archaeology* 37:1–17.

1994   The Weipa Shell Mounds: Natural or Cultural. In *Australian Archaeological Association Conference*, edited by M. Sullivan, S. Brockwell and A. Webb, pp. 107–129. Australian National Parks and Wildlife Service, Canberra.

1999   Shell Mounds and Coastal Archaeology in Northern Queensland. In *Australian Coastal Archaeology*, edited by J. Hall and I. J. McNiven, pp. 105–113. ANH Publications, Department of Archaeology and Natural History, Research School of Pacific and Asian Studies, Australian National University, Canberra.

Blake, T.

1998   Deported . . . At the Sweet Will of the Government: The Removal of Aborigines to Reserves in Queensland 1897–1939. *Aboriginal History* 22:51–61.

Bottoms, T.

2013   *Conspiracy of Silence: Queensland's Frontier Killing Times.* Allen and Unwin, Sydney.

Bradley, R.

1993   *Altering the Earth: The Origins of Monuments in Britain and Continental Europe.* Society of Antiquaries of Scotland, Edinburgh.

2007   *The Prehistory of Britain and Ireland.* Cambridge University Press, Cambridge.

Brockwell, S.

2006   Earth Mounds in Northern Australia. *Australian Archaeology* 63:47–56.

Brockwell, S., B. Ó Foghlú, J. Fenner, J. Stevenson, U. Proske, and J. Shiner

2017   New Dates for Earth Mounds at Weipa, North Queensland, Australia. *Archaeology in Oceania* 52:127–134.

Clarke, A.

1985   A Preliminary Archaeological Analysis of the Anbangbang I Site. In *Archaeological Research in Kakadu National Park*, edited by R. Jones, pp. 77–102. Australian National Parks and Wildlife Service, Canberra.

Coutts, P., P. Henderson, and R. Fullagar

1979   *Records of the Victorian Archaeological Survey Number 9: A Preliminary Investigation of Aboriginal Mounds in North-Western Victoria.* Ministry for Conservation, Melbourne.

Frankland, K.

1994   *A Guide to Queensland Government Records Relating to Aboriginal and Torres Strait Islander People.* Records Guide 1. Queensland State Archives and Department of Family Services and Aboriginal Islander Affairs, Brisbane.

Gillet, A.

1986   Opium-Smoking in Australia 1850–1915. Unpublished B.A. (Honors) thesis, University of Queensland, Brisbane.

Hammerich, A.

1893   *Studier over Bronzelurerne i Nationalmuseet I Kobenhavn. Aarbøger for nordisk oldkyndighed og historie*, Række II, Bind 8, pp. 141–190. Udgivne af det kongelige Nordiske oldskrift-selskab, Copenhagen.

Holdaway, S., P. C. Fanning, F. Petchey, K. Allely, J. I. Shiner, and G. Bailey

2017   Temporal Variability in Shell Mound Formation at Albatross Bay, Northern Australia. PLoS ONE 12(8):e0183863.

Holtorf, C.

1998   The Life-histories of Megaliths in Mecklenburg-Vorpomern (Germany). *World Archaeology* 30(1):23–38.

Hope, G., P. Hughes, and J. Russel-Smith

1985   Geomorphological Fieldwork and the Evolution of the Landscape of Kakadu National Park. In *Archaeological Research in Kakadu National Park*, edited by R. Jones, pp. 229–240. Australian National Parks and Wildlife Service, Canberra.

Jones, R. (editor)

1985   *Archaeological Research in Kakadu National Park*. Australian National Parks and Wildlife Service, Canberra.

Keen, I.

1981   *Alligator Rivers Stage II Land Claim*. Australia Government Publishing Service, Canberra.

Larsen, B., S. Holdaway, P. Fanning, T. Mackrell, and J. Shiner

2015   Shape as an Outcome of Formation History: Terrestrial Laser Scanning of Shell Mounds from Far North Queensland, Australia. *Quaternary International* 2015:1–8.

Leichhardt, L.

1845–1846 Continuation of My Log from the Abel Tasman to Pt Essington, the 8 September 1845. Manuscript C 155, Safe 1/292, Mitchell Library, Sydney, New South Wales.

Lipton, P.

2004   *Inference to the Best Explanation*. 2nd ed. Routledge, London.

Loos, N.

1982   *Invasion and Resistance: Aboriginal-European Relations on the North Queensland Frontier, 1861–1897*. Australian National University Press, Canberra.

Meehan, B., S. Brockwell, J. Allen, and R. Jones

1985   The Wetland Sites. In *Archaeological Research in Kakadu National Park*, edited by R. Jones, pp. 103–154, Australian National Parks and Wildlife Service, Canberra.

Memmott, P.

2007   *Gunyah Goondie + Wurley: The Aboriginal Architecture of Australia*. University of Queensland Press, St. Lucia.

Meston, A.

1895   *Queensland Aboriginals: Proposed System for Their Improvement and Preservation*. Government Printer, Brisbane.

1896   *Report on the Aboriginals of Queensland*. Government Printer, Brisbane.

Monchamp, A. M.

2014   *Autobiographical Memory in an Aboriginal Australian Community: Culture, Place and Narrative*. Palgrave Macmillan, New York.

Morrison, M.

2013   Niche Production Strategies and Shell Matrix Site Variability at Albatross Bay, Cape York Peninsula. *Archaeology in Oceania* 48:78–91.

2014   Chronological Trends in Late Holocene Shell Mound Construction across Northern Australia: Insights from Albatross Bay, Cape York Peninsula. *Australian Archaeology* 79:1–13.

Ó Foghlú, B.

2017   Sustaining Cultural Identity through Environmental Sustainability: Earth Mounds in Northern Australia, c. 2200 BP to Present. In *Shallow Pasts, Endless Horizons: Sustainability and Archaeology*, Proceedings of the 48th Annual Chacmool Archaeological Conference, edited by J. Favreau and R. Patalano, pp. 51–73. Chacmool Archaeological Association of the University of Calgary, Alberta, Canada.

2019   Mounds of the North: Discerning the nature of Earth Mounds in Northern Australia. Unpublished Ph.D. dissertation, Department of Archaeological and Natural History, Australian National University, Canberra.

Ó Foghlú, B. D. Wesley, S. Brockwell, and H. Cooke

2016   Implications for Culture Contact History from a Glass Artifact on a Diingwulung Earth Mound in Weipa. *qar [Queensland Archaeological Research]* 19:1–22.

Oldfield, F., and J. Crowther

2007   Establishing Fire Incidence in Temperate Soils Using Magnetic Measurements. *Palaeogeography, Palaeoclimatology, Palaeoecology* 249:362–369.

Olick, J.

1999   Collective Memory: The Two Cultures. *Sociological Theory* 17(3):333–348.

2007   From Usable Pasts to the Return of the Repressed. *Hedgehog Review* Summer:19–31.

2008   Collective Memory. In *International Encyclopaedia of the Social Science,* vol. 3, edited by W. Darity, pp. 7–8. 2nd ed. Macmillan Reference, Detroit.

Olick, J., and J. Robbins

1998   Social Memory Studies: From "Collective Memory" to the Historical Sociology of Mnemonic Practices. *Annual Review of Sociology* 24:105–140.

Petchey, F., P. Fanning, S. Holdaway, J. Shiner, and C. Beresford

2013   Preliminary Radiocarbon Dates from the Weipa Archaeological Research Program (WARP) 2010–2012 Field Seasons. Unpublished paper presented at the AAA Conference, December 1–4, Coffs Harbour, New South Wales.

Reid, G.

1990   *A Picnic with the Natives: Aboriginal-European Relations in the Northern Territory to 1910*. Melbourne University Press, Melbourne.

Roberts, A.

1991   An Analysis of Mound Formation at Milingimbi, Northern Territory. Unpublished M.Litt. thesis, Department of Archaeology and Palaeoanthropology, University of New England, Armidale, Australia.

Roth, W.

1900   Report [to the Commissioner of Police, Queensland] on the Aboriginals of the Pennefather (Coen) River District and Other Coastal Tribes Occupying the Country between the Batavia and Embley Rivers [Visited by the Minister during His Last Trip]; with Vocabularies and Anthropometric Charts. Cooktown, 8 January 1900. Manuscript [Microfilm CY 208], Mitchell Library, Sydney, New South Wales.

Scambary, B.

2013   *My Country, Mine Country: Indigenous People, Mining and Development Contestation in Remote Australia.* Australian National University Press, Canberra.

Sharp, N.

1992   *Footprints along the Cape York Sandbeaches.* Aboriginal Studies Press, Canberra.

Shiner, J., P. Fanning, S. Holdaway, F. Petchey, C. Beresford, E. Hoffman and B. Larson.

2013   Shell Mounds as the Basis for Understanding Human-Environment Interaction in Far North Queensland, Australia. *Queensland Archaeological Research* 16:65–92.

Shiner, J., and M. Morrison

2009   The Contribution of Heritage Surveys toward Understanding the Cultural Landscape of the Weipa Bauxite Plateau. *Australian Archaeology* 68:52–55.

Stevenson, J., S. Brockwell, C., Rowe, U., Proske, and J. Shiner

2015   The Palaeoenvironmental History of Big Willum Swamp, Weipa: An Environmental Context for the Archaeological Record. *Australian Archaeology* 80:17–31.

Stone, T.

1992   Origins of the Weipa Shell Mounds. Unpublished M.Sc. thesis, Department of Geography, Australian National University, Canberra.

Taylor, C.

2003   Constructing Aboriginality: Archibald Meston's Literary Journalism, 1870–1924. *Journal of the Association for the Study of Australian Literature* 2:121–139.

Walker, J.

1786   *Historical Memoirs of the Irish Bards.* T. Payne and Son, London.

Wilde, W.

1857   *A Descriptive Catalogue of the Antiquities of Stone, Earthen and Vegetable Materials in the Museum of the Royal Irish Academy.* Printed by M. H. Gill, printer to the academy, Dublin.

1861   *A Descriptive Catalogue of the Antiquities of the Animal Materials and Bronze in the Museum of the Royal Irish Academy.* Hodges and Smith, Dublin.

6

Listening to History Performed in Pilgrimage

JONATHAN WALZ

People employ objects and performances to make meaning. Understanding a community's things, practices, and words from their situated perspectives can motivate alternative histories. I explore the opportunities that material and other expressions offer humanists and social scientists for writing transformed histories not reliant on documents. How might an archaeologist's practice shift or grow in new directions in such circumstances where observing and listening are necessities? In this chapter I employ diverse sources—objects, ritual acts of healing, and the spoken words of healers—to remake aspects of a regional past for people who live between Mount Kilimanjaro and the Indian Ocean coast of East Africa.

This chapter further grapples with scholars' relationships and interactions with people and traces of the past. While imperialism, slaving, colonial authority, and capitalism are undeniably important topics in later African history, archaeologists and other scholars who write about East Africa's late precolonial and colonial pasts tend to approach material culture through the lenses of capitalism and consumer culture. In other words, they treat objects almost exclusively as commodities, a recipe for reiterating conventional wisdom about Eurasian agency and power in the region and for diminishing Africans' roles in and perspectives on their own histories. This skewed arrangement invites revisions to practice.

If attended to, traces—residues of past experiences that linger and resonate in the present—can provide clues to history absent in documents penned by outsiders. Archaeologists and historians also employ essential tools drawn from ethnography. Moreover, they are fluent in African languages, strive to live with and listen to people on the ground, and take the time to walk landscapes. A keen awareness of material culture, landscapes, and ritual behavior evident in documents, maps, and photographs can also inspire new questions and challenge standard interpretations.

I draw from my experiences during three years of living among Zigua communities: mixed subsistence farmers who occupy the unique but risky environs of lowland northeastern Tanzania. There I practiced experiential and medical archaeology and listened. I engaged the Zigua, their material culture, and intangible aspects of their contemporary healing practices. Much can be gained by archaeologists who reorient their attention to people's daily lives and beyond commonly reiterated topics and sources that emphasize Eurasian rather than African histories in Africa. Knowing the meanings of Zigua expressions and objects creates an intellectual space for Zigua history within global history.

Setting the Stage

As so often happens with field research, the people I encountered and personal experiences changed my approach. I first visited northeastern Tanzania in 1999. Based on a preliminary landscape reconnaissance, I planned a regional scale archaeology project that sought to identify early African settlement and interactions during the last 1,500 years (Walz 2010, 2013). The primary field strategy was to employ nineteenth-century caravan routes and nodes (stopping places) known from documents and oral traditions to help identify through archaeology more ancient evidence of interaction between the coast and hinterland of Tanzania. For a variety of reasons, this was challenging.

Then, one night, I suffered abdominal pains. Away from the city, I inquired about medical treatment among Tanzanians living in the area. They suggested I visit Mzee Rashidi (Rajabu) Ali Janja. I came to learn that he was a Zigua healer of renown. Janja treated my illness with medicines composed of artifacts and incantations about nature spirits and ancestors. He motivated me to change my practice: to root the project's research in local knowledge and the traces of Zigua experience (Walz 2009, 2015a). Shortly thereafter, I took steps to engage Zigua ways of knowing the world. I resolved to learn from the healers and others in the community who kept, expressed, and treated Zigua historical experience. I intended to gain understanding by attending to traces and practices that originated, as far as possible, within the community itself and their mediation of evidence as they understood it.

Thus, I began to integrate medical and experiential archaeology as primary aspects of my larger historical project. Medical archaeology examines the way in which material culture and society relate to and are influenced by issues of health, illness, and healing, broadly construed. Such an approach is appropriate for northeastern Tanzania because of its layered history of social trauma and because of its risky environments, both physical and political, at the outskirts of regional power along the coast and in the highlands. In the intermediate landscape, people like the Zigua view their world through practices and symbols couched in terms of healing and harm (Feierman 1990; Walz 2015b). My experiences with healers and with the ancestral landscapes of northeastern Tanzania helped me understand how Zigua "being in the world" carries implications for how archaeologists might also understand and interpret them and their beliefs, actions, and words.

The Zigua live on a landscape lying between the Eastern Arc Mountains, particularly the West and East Usambara Mountains, and the Indian Ocean coast of Tanzania (Beidelman 1986; Giblin 1992). This region is defined by uncertainty and social flux. Zigualand sits at an intersection of multiple, often unstable, environments and people with different lifeways (agricultural, pastoral, urban). In addition, incursions from outside people and influences have exploited them and their land. The most striking events have compounded suffering during the last 150 years or more: a pronounced nineteenth-century slave and ivory trade, the violence of first German and then British colonization (late 1880s through mainland independence in 1961), and a cash-crop plantation production system based on migratory labor. Since independence, environmental exploitation, "villagization" (forced relocation for cooperative living and labor, beginning in the 1970s), and distancing by the postcolonial state have further degraded and displaced Zigua and other peripheral communities (Giblin 1992; Håkansson 2008; Huijzendveld 2008; Kimambo 1996).

Zigua healers mediate these tumultuous experiences, making something new through their performances, collected objects, and words. For healers, medical practice uses objects and acts to heal Zigua experience and to make a bearable future for villagers. This framing is underscored by an awareness that material culture in this and other cases is not just material. Rather, material and immaterial aspects are strongly allied as they are used to effect by healers. Performances, landscapes, healing objects, and the words that authorize healing are bound to the Zigua spiritual universe. Objects and acts help bridge and resolve experiences across space and time (e.g., Ogundiran 2002; Zedeño 2008).

In this chapter I discuss Zigua healers and their assembly of objects during medical performances, ritual events that transform traumatic landscapes to meaningful being. Healers throughout eastern Africa are well placed to negotiate and remake their communities' experiences. Contemporary healers traverse segments of historic caravan routes and gather items from a dispersed area along these corridors. Such practices begin to transform and repurpose retrieved objects to restore social balance in a tumultuous era and area. Highlighting the Zigua and their epistemology (way of knowing the world) diversifies historical narratives about the social practices that accurately situate Zigua historical experience and generate insights into the deeper history of this region of Tanzania.

In part, this account is motivated by a desire to attend to how historians rematerialize the past through our actions. We gather traces not of isolated objects, moments, or events but of human gestures: practices and performances (e.g., de Certeau 1984; Inomata and Coben 2006; Joyce 2105). If historians treat objects as means to an end, and not as ends in themselves, we had better avoid artificially fragmenting and fossilizing pasts. In this view, humans shape and interpret objects as objects influence human thoughts and actions. An approach to history that makes intellectual space for the disciplinary practices of history, anthropology, and archaeology and that integrates local knowledge drawn from meaningful collaborations with community members best addresses the Zigua scenario.

Immaterial and Material Traces

As close as 20 km from the Indian Ocean, the dramatic mountains of northeastern Tanzania present upsetting disaster scenarios. I have memories of one terrible day in Mombo, a town positioned along the skirt of the West Usambara Mountains in Korogwe District. A rush of coffee-colored water—a literal waterfall, where none previously cascaded—appeared ominously along a precipice uphill and rushed into town along roadways and paths as it hurtled down, following the course of least resistance. Plastic basins and chickens swirled past our guest house. Our anxiety heightened as the water and mud swelled around us. Houses dissolved. After the flood, we found bodies exposed at the graveyard just downhill. The local landscape lay ravaged, and the stench of human feces filled the air. Shortly thereafter, villagers scattered to check on their families and neighbors. That moment of trauma, alongside Janja's previous healing treatment of me (noted earlier), reoriented and extended my archaeological project to account for human vulnerabilities and the story-performing and objects that the Zigua deem meaningful.

In the days after the disaster, community discussions about serpents as nature spirits and ancestors became profuse. For the Zigua farmers who also keep some cattle and small stock in the arid lowlands between the West Usambara Mountains and the Indian Ocean coastline, such snakes are central to the semantic domain (domain of meaning). For the Zigua, serpents are both real and mythical. As symbols, snakes deployed in healers' stories, healing practices, and community conversation bring together tradition and modern change. The snake is a good example of how healing objects (discussed later) also operate to address and resolve profound but uneven social changes linked to local exigencies, global influence, and state policy. By listening to local stories, I came to understand that serpents as ancestral spirits have been influential in the Zigua worldview into antiquity (e.g., Dannholz 1989 [1912–1918]; see Walz 2010).

These days, stories about snakes address environmental and social changes felt to be negative by most villagers. An already risky (arid) climate exacerbates the uncertainty of compounded change. Communities negotiate these tensions by sharing their vulnerabilities and working to rebalance their eco-social world. Symbols, such as water (that makes the land fertile in this precariously arid space) and serpents (nature spirits and ancestors that stabilize the social world), found in traditional myths and shared rituals serve as healing and stabilizing influences that reassure communities:

> The snake inhabiting Tongwe [a sacred mountain] is Kimondo [a serpent name] and cannot be seen. The snake rises when there are clouds at the mountain top. . . . This occurs during the rainy season [*masika* (Swahili)] but not the summer [*kiangazi* (Swahili)]. When elders need rain they climb to the top [of the mountain] and perform ancestral rites [*matambiko* (pl., Swahili)]. . . . On their [the men's] descent and when they reach the base of the mountain, it rains. There is another snake that resides in the ocean. The ocean swallows everything. Nothing escapes it. All the trash from floods [the foreignness that is washed away] is eaten there. But the ocean returns and those things are gone. (Rashidi Kigoto, personal communication, January 30, 2006)

Zigua healers tell their communities that their current difficulties derive, in part, from villagers' failures to attend to traditions: the veneration and propitiation of nature spirits and ancestors (represented as snakes) and honoring, through ritual performance, the preservation of sacred places. Mentioning serpents and honoring them by attending to the places they inhabit—such as Mount Tongwe—help counter stresses and manage the negotiated social outcomes of tradition and change. As Gonzales (2009:94) notes, people in the coastal hinterland "[pay] homage to antecedent generations [ancestors] because antecedent generations [hold] the power to affect the lives of their corporeal descendants."

Natural, constructed, and conceptualized landscapes anchor and legitimize—in fact, naturalize—stories about nature spirits and ancestors that take snakes as their form (Walz 2013; also see Schmidt 2017). Landscape features (including mountain pinnacles, sacred forests, caves, whirlpools, and waterfalls) that house nature spirits and ancestors and the material traces of important pasts, including historical traumas, offer a means to balance tradition (familiarity) and change (uncertainty). Thus, serpents mark unique geographical features and eco-social intersections relevant to long-term regional contests over power: places where intensive connectivity and external impacts, especially with the Indian Ocean, have had and continue to have a disproportionate influence.

We can observe a similar coexistence of tradition and change in the healing objects employed by Zigua healers. To address community experience, healers unite ritual acts, words, and the pasts embodied in objects. Zigua healers' excursions along historic caravan routes and their assembly of items (artifacts to an archaeologist) gathered from unique loci (tied to foreign influences as well as ancestors and nature spirits) forge something new from places and objects in northeastern Tanzania to prevent future harm. Healers (in the most general terms, diviner-doctors, or *waganga* [pl., Swahili]) reference places that shelter ancestors and nature spirits (e.g., serpents), by collecting clippings of certain trees and other plants (often with pharmacological properties) as well as material traces mnemonic of past traumas (e.g., the slave trade). They deploy medicines (a type of object where material and belief meaningfully intersect) in ceremonies where their words enact treatment. These performances are understood both by observation and by listening closely to healers.

Humanmade objects (artifacts) and/or natural objects (clippings of certain trees and other plants said to house ancestors and nature spirits and/or to cure illnesses) from these and other localities are essential components of healers' medicines. Thus, healers' collections of objects coalesce from multiple past episodes of experience, facilitating treatments of "one period [of change] . . . through the lens of another [more traditional and familiar]" (Basu 2007); this ritual transformation is enabled by the complex palimpsest of time in landscapes and by careful selection of material objects. Such traces, repurposed for healing, address the reverberations of traumatic pasts in Africans' lives today.

The Zigua use such places and objects to make and debate their collective experience, including how they represent Zigua historicity, negotiate and resolve contemporary tensions, and intervene against the anticipated future. To do so, healers draw from a reservoir of community experiences that integrates the entire region and all episodes—ancient, colonial, and modern—to produce meaning that radiates across space and through time. For the Zigua, in this construction, there is neither an isolated place nor a prehistory (Walz 2015a). Healers' practices make possible a medical archaeology that engages African and Indian Ocean links.

Healing Rituals and Objects

For healers, three acts initiate a process of social rebalancing in Zigua communities. In the healers' view and in my interpretation, the purpose of performance is to domesticate (Prestholdt 2008) experience and to create the possibility of an alternative future, as opposed to an anticipated future of additional alienation. Thus, one of the goals of healing is to familiarize what seems foreign (corrosive to tradition). These acts by healers include, first, retracing historical caravan routes during annual pilgrimages to the Indian Ocean coast. Second, healers collect objects from historical caravan nodes, old marketplaces, and other locales while retracing and improvising routes. Last, healers articulate route itineraries during healing rituals that use the assembled and transformed objects (often ground into smaller bits or powders) as medical treatments. Performance and materials mutually constitute Zigua healing treatments. The embedded histories of the objects used are a principal source of their healing potential. A healer's skill and the appropriate accompanying words during treatment authorize the potency of the medicine, as people's participation in (private and public) healing rituals confirms their faith.

As healers interact with the landscape and its features and objects, they determine the materials that will later be made into medicines. Rashidi Janja serves as an example. A healer-historian of renown from the village of Lewa in Muheza District, Janja retrieved surface objects along a route that he traced from a Zigua sacred mountain, Mount Tongwe, to the coralline shore of the Indian Ocean about 15 km away. Janja's pilgrimage to the coast and back is an annual circuit. He returned home following the first (excursion) and second (collection) acts of this medicine-making ritual, empowered with the ingredients for his treatments. Janja's trajectory mimics a primary corridor of interaction known from nineteenth-century European documents and Zigua and other oral traditions (e.g., Farler 1882). Beginning in 1999, my ethnographic research, interviews with residents, and systematic archaeological assessments reidentified residues of this general corridor at multiple sites in the vicinity (Biginagwa 2012; Walz 2005, 2013).

I recount here an annual round with Janja. During his excursion and collection, Janja ambles ahead of me. With purpose, he navigates the winding dirt path that intermittently marks the landscape or disappears beneath our feet. At more than 70 years of age, he brushes aside grass that laps against his trouser legs. After a few moments, he diverts to a nearby clearing and bends slowly to the damp ground. Among the debris at this abandoned marketplace, he identifies a glass bead. The weather is somewhat wet, and the iron-rich clay gathers at his fingertips as he brushes it back from the small white object. We are standing at the edge of a thin pathway that connects two hamlets set on a gently undulating landscape with panoramic views. The glint of the Indian Ocean and the distant river escarpment sparkle on the eastern horizon.

After a kilometer or so, Janja collects another small item along the pathway. In this manner, he assembles the objects metonymic of the historic route and its associations. All the while, as he proceeds, Janja navigates the shifting terrain, the uneven surfaces of eroded or obscured trails, and the characteristic vegetation that frequently slows his progress. On occasion, he halts, usually within sight of a sacred mountain (Mount Tongwe or its male-gendered twin, Mount Gendagenda) or a prominent ridge that flanks the nearby river. From my perspective as an accompanying observer, landscape features and historical sites foster his manner of negotiating the landscape. The healer himself maintains and establishes relationships among places with somewhat different temporalities linked by paths constitutive of the landscape.

On rare occasions, Janja briefly spoke about certain scents or the sounds of a distant body of water (whether the ocean or a waterfall along the proximal river). These sensory revelations assemble *and* make the region's landscape for him. As Cuelenaere (2011:128–129) emphasizes, recalling the observations of de Certeau (1984):

> [M]otion itself grounds speech. Moreover, for de Certeau a walker actualizes a wide range of possibilities. . . ."In that way," says de Certeau, "[the walker] makes them exist as well as emerge." In other words, the body in motion frames possible paths and segments a field of action. . . . Thus, the walker not only engages possible paths, but also creates a path as she walks.

In this manner, movement signifies and emplaces meaning, even more so than "speech acts," which occur infrequently in Janja's excursion. As Fabian (1991:188) remarks when discussing performance, "[T]he closer the process gets to actual performance the less 'talk' there is to record, transcribe, and make into 'texts.' Even the talking that can still be recorded is now all acting."

During the first day of Janja's progress, his walking and halts seem to address the landscape in fragments. However, as his itinerary continues, the outline of a more holistic rendering emerges. An unfamiliar outsider needs experience, as an apprentice, to grasp the underneath meanings. It is noteworthy that in certain stretches segments of "the" way vanish completely, due in part to the effects of the short rains that sponsor lush vegetation. When the exact path cannot be identified, Janja employs his knowledge of landscape features, memories of his past pilgrimages, and improvisation in areas where the way is futile. For three days, Janja makes a path, just as any *bricoleur*—someone who draws from what is available to achieve a task—manages uncertainties. Often Janja is within clear view during his journey, although he is frequently without any audience.

In the third ritual act, back at his home, a medicine gourd (*bahari* [Swahili], meaning "ocean") is enacted as Janja's principal ritual paraphernalia (Giles 1989; Figure 6.1). It already contains, among other additives, components of 40 plants

Figure 6.1. Rashidi Janja's healing gourd (*bottom right*) and other ritual healing paraphernalia. Photo by author.

(a number of significance in Islam; the identities of plants were verified using multiple sources: Sangai 1963) and other items (used to treat physical ailments) that he gathers from the wider landscape throughout the year. The *bahari* is particularly empowered by clippings from certain trees species (e.g., baobabs, *mibuyu* [pl., Swahili]), preferably situated atop seven mountains sacred to the Zigua: Tongwe, Potwe, Kizara, Gare, Sambani, Kimbe, and Kwa Lagulu.

Janja explains the rationale for his preference to gather plants from high spaces (vertical axes):

> Mountains cure. The elders go to mountains because they see everything there. The ocean is visible. It [the ocean] takes and collects everything, coming and going. This gourd is like an *mzimu* [(Swahili) meaning "spirit dwelling"]. It collects [-*sanya* (Swahili)] and cools [-*poza* (Swahili)] foreign things. (Rashidi Janja, personal communication, September 11, 2002)

According to Janja, at mountain apexes the total landscape—*all of time*—is manifest and therefore can be contemplated and treated.

Critical are the origins of the healing objects already in Janja's healing calabash. Objects from unique places (features and sites) or spatial intersections empower the *bahari* and its medicine (*dawa* [Swahili]), including plants collected from *misitu saba* [Swahili, meaning "seven forests," a type of place that for the Zigua typically embodies and shelters ancestors and nature spirits], *masoko saba* [Swahili, meaning "seven market centers," always located in the lowlands], and *njiapanda saba* [Swahili, meaning "seven intersections of paths"]. *Maji ya bahari* [Swahili, meaning "salt water" or "ocean water" from the coast] is a final additive of significance. This is the order in which Janja mentions these items/places. The *sequencing* is critical. The first localities Janja voices are "local"/ancestral (i.e., sacred forests). Next, he denotes foreign-influenced places [markets, with *wagonjwa wa mbalimbali*, meaning "sick people from far away"]. Third, he marks intersections (meeting points of paths). Last, Janja highlights the locale of resolution (ocean) (Rashidi Janja, personal communication, September 11, 2002).

Janja then handles the previously referenced foreign objects: glass beads or (much less frequently) Eurasian shards of glass or ceramic fragments collected from caravan route nodes during his annual pilgrimage, frequently marketplaces with historic origins or sites of foreign impact during the early (German) colonial period (representative of circulation and metonymic of routes). Janja located these alien objects (signs of change) during hot months (dry seasons), a period during which much of the countryside is more easily accessed because of diminished tropical vegetation. As in many societies in coastal eastern Africa, the descriptor "hot" associates with "harm" and "chaos" (or illness), in this case the impacts of imperial and colonial outsiders during a previous period.

Janja adds these artifacts (now made into a powder) to the *bahari*, which already contains a mix of remains, including pulverized plant parts. Simultaneously, he articulates, in the *reverse order* of his passage along the route, the objects' points of origin (from the coast to the interior). Again, notice the sequencing: from the Indian Ocean coast (from whence many foreign influences, including Islam and capitalism, came) to the interior, a place more insulated and familiar.

From my perspective, Janja's retracing (commemoration) of caravan routes and figurative collapsing of the landscape—fixed terrain features and associated circulating objects—into a healing container enables the contemplation of all of time, the familiarization of the foreign, and a reconciliation of prominent cultural intersections in Zigua experience. The power of the medicine in the *bahari*, then, partially derives from *performances of collection*. The *bahari* rebalances tradition and change by referencing terrain features that shelter ancestors and nature spirits as well as the traditions imbued in such places, which are critical for restoring order. This process is a materialization through which healers and their communities envision and come to terms with social and environmental ruptures and resilience. Therapeutics like that found in this type of healing ameliorate change and the anxiety of uncertainty by what I see as a "cooling" of tensions at places and through items that capture the full extent of the temporality of the landscape (Walz 2015b).

In fact, these rural Tanzanians work hard not to reconcile tradition and modernity but to make something *new* from the two. In such circumstances, tradition (the familiar past) is represented as legitimate, while the future is represented skeptically as change (uncertainty). The interlacing of these themes, for example, in the materials collected in the medicine calabash, produces a metonymy that transforms each onto the other through relationships of contiguity and identity, resulting in an imagination that change is ancient and that continued tradition is inevitable. In other words, on the grand landscape (via special features) and in objects (e.g., healing calabashes), social cosmologies rooted in metonymies bind together space-time categories. In this form and through ritual enactments informed by recounting object itineraries (emplacements, motion, and objects' repurposing), experience is more easily negotiated (Joyce and Gillespie 2015).

Zigua practices and their view of reality has other implications for remaking regional history. Medical practice in East Africa seems to serve distinct social purposes. It helps Zigua and other communities to familiarize the foreign (including influences and impacts originating in the western Indian Ocean), initiate therapeutics, and reassert their power in the face of social and environmental changes (e.g., Feierman 1974; Schoenbrun 2006). To domesticate foreign residues is to enfold them into a system of signs to process deeper histories. Treating traces like Eurasian glass beads from caravan stations strictly as "of the past" misses the significance of how African healers domesticate alien items and, in the process, repurpose them to meet internal needs. Understanding the material culture, rituals, and oral traditions that surround Zigua healing also helps challenge other historical interpretations of lowland northeastern Tanzania. Up to this point, regional histories rely almost exclusively on written European sources. I briefly review two cases in which a renewed comprehension of Zigua practices, initiated through listening, affects scholarly interpretations of the region's past: one instance of a more recent history and the other of a more ancient past.

The first case concerns Mount Tongwe, a locality sacred to lowland Zigua speakers. In the early 1850s, Kimweri ye Nyumbai, ruler of the (highland) Shambaa Kingdom, suggested to the German missionary Johann Krapf that he should construct a mission station atop Tongwe. It has been argued in secondary literature (Lane 1993) that two Shambaa officials and a lowland trader familiar with Tongwe (who were apt to benefit from such an arrangement) induced Kimweri to tender the missionary a place at the kingdom's periphery. In exchange, Kimweri sought to attain guns and powder that might be employed to regain his shrinking authority over the surrounding landscape. It was in this context that Sultan Seyyid Said of Zanzibar, learning of Krapf's potential influence, commissioned a fort to be built on Tongwe, circa 1853 (Figure 6.2). Historians have tended to argue that Said hoped to limit Krapf's hinterland influence (e.g., Lane 1993), deter Kimweri's designs on lowland expansion, and prevent interference with the booming slave and ivory trade between Zanzibari merchants and mainland raiders.

Given that the Zigua disrupted the Shambaa king's lowland dominion, Kimweri's curious selection of Tongwe for the placement of the fort can be interpreted differently, as an indirect attempt to squelch or usurp the sacred space atop the mountain (Walz 2009). It appears that Kimweri duped the sultan (although he

Figure 6.2. The remains of Tongwe Hill Fort, an outpost of the nineteenth-century Zanzibari state in inland northeastern Tanzania. Photo by author.

originally attempted to dupe Krapf) into doing something that Kimweri himself could not do or did not want to do at the time: occupy a mythical center of power (snakes and all) from which the Zigua drew inspiration. In effect, the Shambaa leader, lacking the weapons to challenge gun-wielding lowlanders, hoped to fuel angst among his political competitors (the sultan and the Zigua).

The continued residence of nature spirits and ancestors in the form of serpents on Tongwe today—a place occupied and impacted by the sultan's garrison—speaks to the resiliency of the Zigua. From this African rendering, informed by the Zigua worldview (the presence of snakes and the significance of certain landscape features) and the material treatments, oral histories and traditions, and ritual performances that bolster it, the Zigua and a hinterland space are highlighted while integrating new sources. The extant narrative is thereby challenged and a new history with African actors and perspectives suggested.

Zigua materials and acts pertinent to the inland histories also confront conventional history up to a millennium ago. The East Africa coast and its immediate hinterland tend to be dominated by interest in and research on coastal Swahili communities, towns, and city-states and the cosmopolitan linkages of Swahili people to maritime contexts and developments. The Swahili and their creole culture (of mixed African and Asian cultural tendencies) developed from opportunities to direct and transport people, ideas, and materials among multiple invested communities in Africa and overseas. But other Africans who occupied the region in antiquity *also* engaged the Indian Ocean's influences to varying degrees. Based on ancient traces recovered through archaeology in the hinterland of northeastern Tanzania, we can see that people in this region have long engaged with oceanic influences (Walz 2010, 2013).

The regional scale project (begun in 1999) that I alluded to earlier sought to assess the long-term archaeology of lowland northeastern Tanzania using a caravan route strategy. I examined the vicinities of nineteenth-century caravan routes but also engaged them as potential hubs of production and human interaction in antiquity. By listening to and following healers during their ritual excursions on the landscape, I was influenced to discover long-term settlement in the same locations as more recent caravan nodes. There is copious evidence for interior African connections to the Indian Ocean at places such as Mombo (the site of the flood previously recounted) and 150 km inland at Gonja Maore in Kilimanjaro Region (Walz 2013; Walz and Dussubieux 2016). These findings generate a new and revised past for the ancient hinterland that draws it into relationships beyond Africa. Traces found through ethnography, oral history, and now archaeology (glass and carnelian beads, marine shells, and ceramics with coastal or oceanic origins) indicate substantial ties among residents in northeastern Tanzania and beyond their borders into the larger oceanic world.

Rather than serving as an economic and cultural periphery, this hinterland space served as a point of intersection critical to the regional flow of people, raw materials, goods, and, putatively, ideas. A number of characteristics of the area motivated this remarkable history: the varied landscape of northeastern Tanzania, which incorporates prominent mountains and a steppe that approach the oceanic coastline, and diverse languages among communities who practice a range of productive lifeways. Communities depended on and competed against others in the region. Competition amplified during the tension-filled periods of imperialism, colonialism, and resistance.

Contemporary rituals that employ the immaterial and material traces outlined above address many such factors, including oceanic ties. Aspects of Zigua medical practice—Islamic numerology, the lunar scheduling of healers' annual pilgrimages to the coast, and the use of artifacts of foreign origin—integrate Africa-derived practices and oceanic objects of more ancient origin. However, objects from overseas reached the interior in the late first millennium AD, marking influences to the local areas that also inevitably required community management, especially at points of concentrated impact.

These cases illustrate what can be gained by engaging the contemporary Zigua. By listening and understanding their space-time, social geography, and chronology of discourses, we come to historical insights impossible to gain through archaeology and documentary sources only. By reflecting on our scholarly practice and adopting methods deeply embedded in the history of anthropology, we can generate alternative pasts and inspire new representations where some aspects of African history have tended to remain subaltern (Schmidt and Patterson 1995; Schmidt and Walz 2007). This approach overcomes the limitations of atemporal scientific study and dematerialized humanistic study. For me, listening and becoming articulate in the pleats of culture and history that, when enfolded, reveal the material and immaterial traces developed out of a set of experiences and relationships that I fostered in Tanzania.

Concluding Thoughts

Objects, performances, and oral stories offer a means to know people and how they wrestle with and reformulate their social condition across space and through time. Janja's performances and the objects that he and other Zigua healers gather help make connective webs of meaning that motivate and enable Zigua communities to process their experiences. In due course, a type of order is reestablished in changing times through the actions and articulations of powerful healers enacting ritual acts that repurpose along with the participation of supplicants and a discerning public at ceremonies.

A critical approach to archaeology—one invested in being present and listening closely—transformed and enriched my comprehension of the Zigua and their experiences in lowland northeastern Tanzania. I am closer to such awareness because of Janja and my time living among the Zigua and knowing their stories, objects, and landscapes. Janja and the villagers with whom I interacted on a daily basis wrested the conditions of research from me, changing my scholarly practice. They redirected me to a deeper engagement: their historical approach and their societal condition and experiences rendered through meaningfully constituted material culture, landscapes, acts, and words.

The result of this collaborative research suggests that healing ameliorates Zigua alienation from their recent historical experience as they navigate the impacts and obligations of a changing world. This process began in antiquity, when the first entanglements between Africans and Indian Ocean influences began to emerge. The words and practices of Zigua healers are outcomes of this legacy, significant in part because they accommodate aspects of both ancient and contemporary influences. The trustees of community heritage, like healers, continue to find ways to process pasts and to make something new in changed times. Landscape performances, oral expressions, and interactions with ancestral places and mnemonic objects in effect make healing *about* treating and debating societal change through debris as healers *domesticate the future* and forge new possibilities. This pathway integrates community perspectives and knowledge. Like healers, archaeologists can locate meaning and possibility in both the tangible and immaterial traces that arise from how Zigua healers listen to the hinterland. Such awareness, found in the experiences we make and the community collaborations that we forge, inspires new questions, histories, and futures. As the Zigua case shows, an approach to science that values people *first* is most transformative to African history.

References Cited

Basu, P.

2007   Palimpsest Memoryscapes: Materializing and Mediating War in Sierra Leone. In *Reclaiming Heritage: Alternative Imaginaries of Memory in West Africa*, edited by F. de Jong and M. Rowlands, pp. 231–259. Left Coast Press, Walnut Creek, CA.

Beidelman, T.

1986   *Moral Imagination in Kaguru Modes of Thought.* Indiana University Press, Bloomington.

Biginagwa, T.

2012   Historical Archaeology of the 19th Century Caravan Trade in Northeastern Tanzania: A Zooarchaeological Perspective. Unpublished Ph.D. dissertation, Department of Archaeology, University of York, York, UK.

Cuelenaere, L.

2011   Aymara Forms of Walking: A Linguistic Anthropological Reflection on the Relation between Language and Motion. *Language Sciences* 33:126–137.

Dannholz, J.

1989   [1912–1918] *Lute: The Curse and the Blessing.* Steigerdruck, Axams, Austria.

de Certeau, M.

1984   *The Practice of Everyday Life.* University of California Press, Berkeley.

Fabian, J.

1991   Of Dogs Alive, Birds Dead, and Time to Tell a Story. *In Chronotypes: The Construction of Time*, edited by J. Bender and D. Wellbery, pp. 185–204. Stanford University Press, Palo Alto, CA.

Farler, J.

1882   Native Routes in East Africa from Pangani to the Masai Country and the Victoria Nyanza, *Proceedings of the Royal Geographical Society* (new series) 4:730–746.

Feierman, S.

1974 *The Shambaa Kingdom: A History.* University of Wisconsin Press, Madison.

1990 *Peasant Intellectuals: Anthropology and History in Tanzania.* University of Wisconsin Press, Madison.

Giblin, J.

1992 *The Politics of Environmental Control in Northeastern Tanzania, 1840–1940.* University of Pennsylvania Press, Philadelphia.

Giles, L.

1989 Spirit Possession on the Swahili Coast: Peripheral Cults or Primary Texts? Unpublished Ph.D. dissertation, Department of History, University of Texas, Austin.

Gonzales, R.

2009 *Societies, Religion, and History: Central-East Tanzanians and the World They Created, c. 200 BCE to 1800 CE.* Columbia University Press, New York.

Håkansson, N. T.

2008 The Decentralized Landscape: Regional Wealth and the Expansion of Production in Northern Tanzania before the Eve of Colonialism. In *Economies and the Transformation of Landscape*, edited by L. Cliggett and C. Pool, pp. 239–265. AltaMira, Lanham, MD.

Huijzendveld, F.

2008 Changes in Political Economy and Ecology in West-Usambara, Tanzania, ca. 1850–1950. *International Journal of African Historical Studies* 41:383–409.

Inomata, T., and L. Coben

2006 *Archaeology of Performance: Theaters of Power, Community, and Politics.* AltaMira, Lanham, MD.

Joyce, R.

2015 Transforming Archaeology, Transforming Materiality. *Archaeological Papers of the American Anthropological Association* 26:181–191.

Joyce, R., and S. Gillespie (editors)

2015 *Things in Motion: Object Itineraries in Anthropological Practice.* School for Advanced Research Press, Santa Fe, NM.

Kimambo, I.

1996 Environmental Control & Hunger: In the Mountains & Plains of Nineteenth-Century Northeastern Tanzania. In *Custodians of the Land: Ecology & Culture in the History of Tanzania*, edited by G. Maddox, J. Giblin, and I. Kimambo, pp. 71–95. James Currey, London.

Lane, P.

1993 Tongwe Hill Fort. *Azania* 28:133–141.

Ogundiran, A.

2002 Of Small Things Remembered: Beads, Cowries, and Cultural Translations of the Atlantic Experience in Yorubaland. *International Journal of African Historical Studies* 35(2/3):427–457.

Prestholdt, J.

2008 *Domesticating the World: African Consumerism and the Genealogies of Globalization.* University of California Press, Berkeley.

Sangai, G.

1963   *Dictionary of Native Plant Names in the Bondei, Shambaa, and Zigua Languages with the English Equivalents.* East African Herbarium, Nairobi, Kenya.

Schmidt, P.

2017   *Community-Based Heritage in Africa: Unveiling Local Research and Development Initiatives.* Routledge, New York.

Schmidt, P., and T. Patterson (editors)

1995   *Making Alternative Histories: The Practice of Archaeology and History in Non-Western Settings.* School for American Research Press, Santa Fe, NM.

Schmidt, P., and J. Walz

2007   Re-representing African Pasts through Historical Archaeology. *American Antiquity* 72(1):53–70.

Schoenbrun, D.

2006   Conjuring the Modern in Africa: Durability and Rupture in Histories of Public Healing between the Great Lakes of East Africa. *American Historical Review* 111:1403–1439.

Walz, J.

2005   Mombo and the Mkomazi Corridor. In *Salvaging Tanzania's Cultural Heritage*, edited by B. Mapunda and P. Msemwa, pp. 198–213. Dar es Salaam University Press, Dar es Salaam, Tanzania.

2009   Archaeologies of Disenchantment. In *Postcolonial Archaeologies in Africa*, edited by P. Schmidt, pp. 21–38. School for Advanced Research Press, Santa Fe, NM.

2010   Route to a Regional Past: An Archaeology of the Lower Pangani (Ruvu) River Basin, Tanzania, 500–1900 C.E. Unpublished Ph.D. dissertation, Department of Anthropology, University of Florida, Gainesville.

2013   Routes to History: Archaeology and Being Articulate in Eastern Africa. In *The Death of Prehistory*, edited by P. Schmidt and S. Mrozowski, pp. 69–91. Oxford University Press, Oxford.

2015a   Healing Space-Time: Medical Performance and Object Itineraries on a Tanzanian Landscape. In *Things in Motion: Object Itineraries in Anthropological Practice*, edited by R. Joyce and S. Gillespie, pp. 161–177. School for Advanced Research Press, Santa Fe, NM.

2015b   Zigua Medicine, between Mountains and Ocean: People, Practices, and Objects in Healing Motion. In *Histories of Medicine and Healing in the Indian Ocean World*, vol. 2, edited by A. Winterbottom and F. Tesfaye, pp. 197–218. Palgrave Macmillan, New York.

Walz, J., and L. Dussubieux

2016   Zhizo Series Glass Beads at Kwa Mgogo, Inland NE Tanzania. *Journal of African Archaeology* 14(1):199–201.

Zedeño, M.

2008   Bundled Worlds: The Roles and Interactions of Complex Objects from the North American Plains. *Journal of Archaeological Method and Theory* 15(4):362–378.

7

Local Narratives, Regional Histories, and the Demise of Great Zimbabwe

INNOCENT PIKIRAYI

The only written account of Great Zimbabwe, a complex of stone-walled structures located in south-central Zimbabwe (20° 16' 23" S, 30° 56' 04" E), dating from the early second millennium AD, is by the chronicler João de Barros (Beach 1980; Mudenge 1988; Pikirayi 2001).[1] Many scholars regard this as the only window into Great Zimbabwe's past, since the site was apparently unknown until its rediscovery by the Europeans in the late nineteenth century (Burke 1969)—a process that would unleash destructive antiquarian investigations (Bent 1893; Hall 1905; Hall and Neal 1902) and settler appropriation of the site.

A reevaluation of Barros's account opens up Great Zimbabwe to developments associated with recent histories, not only within its immediate landscape but also in the broader context of the expansion of its culture to distant regions of the Zimbabwe plateau. The document mentions a prince called Burrom, ruler of a state called Butua, based at a site identified as Great Zimbabwe. During a survey of Great Zimbabwe's water resources conducted by a team from the University of Pretoria and local research institutions, we became fascinated by a landform called Boroma by the local communities (Pikirayi et al. 2016).

Furthermore, a historical archaeological study of other cultural landscapes some distance from Great Zimbabwe reveals interesting local dynamics that connect the site with developments in distant parts of the Zimbabwe plateau. Local histories from the Zimuto Communal Lands where the site of Chizhou is located point to Zimbabwe Culture communities migrating into south-central sections of the Zimbabwe plateau from the north. Such histories have remained subaltern due to lack of interrogation of the archaeological record. These, if fully exploited, have considerable potential for understanding cultural and sociopolitical developments of the last four centuries or so. The histories of Great Zimbabwe are inscribed on the various landscapes of south-central Zimbabwe and beyond, showing how transformations that took place within Zimbabwe Culture after the sixteenth century may have occurred. I present both of the sites, highlighting the alternative histories that they tell about Great Zimbabwe and the spread of its culture on the basis of listening to local histories and traditions.

Zimbabwe in Recent History

This chapter reports work in progress, based on current research investigating the last half millennium of cultural developments following the end of occupation of Great Zimbabwe (Pikirayi 2013). Entitled "Great Zimbabwe in Recent History: Historical Archaeologies of South-Central Zimbabwe,"[2] the project attempts to address the origins of later Karanga and other regional histories that are connected with the last four centuries of Great Zimbabwe's existence. These histories are not only vital in understanding what could have happened to Great Zimbabwe but also critical in telling the story of its development from much earlier times. Archaeology, in collaboration with other disciplines, plays a useful role in writing the story of Great Zimbabwe and relating it to other transformative global developments of the early modern era, when the site was clearly experiencing decline and loss of complexity. Local histories are extremely useful in understanding sociopolitical dynamics on the Zimbabwe plateau, especially for the most recent periods. However, not many of these have been used to study Great Zimbabwe from the sixteenth to the nineteenth century, when the site became known to the European world (Mazarire 2013). Some of these local histories tell stories of decline or collapse of a sociopolitical system once based at Great Zimbabwe, which may not be evident from its stratigraphy or material culture remains (see, e.g., Pikirayi 2013).

The key research question is to characterize developments associated with post-sixteenth-century Great Zimbabwe and the associated human population dynamics in south-central Zimbabwe plateau that account for the abandonment or the processes associated with the people leaving the site and its immediate landscape. The project addresses several specific research questions:

1. What were the characteristics of the landscape in which Great Zimbabwe is located and how did it influence historical developments during the period 1500–1900 AD?

2. What local histories directly relate to the landscapes of south-central Zimbabwe, and what do these say about Great Zimbabwe after the sixteenth century?

3. Great Zimbabwe was not in its prime when Portuguese accounts refer to it in the middle of the sixteenth century and certainly seems to have lost its significance considerably by the late nineteenth century when Europeans first set sight on it (Bent 1893; Burke 1969). How do we explain abandonment and demise in the context of Great Zimbabwe?

4. The repopulation of south-central Zimbabwe since the seventeenth century seems to have targeted particular ecological and related niches. How do we explain this dynamic and the impact on Great Zimbabwe?

5. Only parts of Great Zimbabwe were inhabited when the first European antiquarians commenced investigations on the site. How do we explain this?

The primary objective of this project is to structure a formal approach to investigating the history of Great Zimbabwe (Figure 7.1), whose earlier past is largely known from archaeology. Such an approach would move the focus of in-

Figure 7.1. The landscape around Great Zimbabwe, south-central Zimbabwe plateau. Photo by author.

vestigation from the core parts of the site to the peripheral settlements and be-yond—the immediate granite landscape and territorial hinterland. The broader objective is to interrogate the landscapes of south-central Zimbabwe to provide new and more recent histories of Great Zimbabwe.

To date, archival research aimed at compiling a local history digital archive of south-central Zimbabwe, to be correlated with the environmental and archaeo-logical record generated from planned future landscape surveys and excavations, has been conducted. Oral history surveys aimed at collecting additional local and regional histories of south-central Zimbabwe that may be linked with Great Zim-babwe have been sampled geographically, following preliminary consultations with traditional and local leaders and some reading of available local histories.

The Conceptual Frame

This chapter focuses on two issues related to the treatment of recent histories of the southern Zimbabwe plateau. First, it provides a response to the anthro-pological critique by Joost Fontein (2006) on archaeologists and interpretation of Great Zimbabwe. Second, it provides a new critique of the "Refuge" phe-nomenon, used by earlier archaeologists and historians in characterizing the terminal periods of the Zimbabwe Culture (Pikirayi 1993, 2000, 2001, 2004). I discuss each of these in turn.

An anthropological critique of the archaeology and cultural heritage man-agement of Great Zimbabwe refers to "the silence of unheard voices and un-told stories," "the unrepresented pasts of local communities," and "the silence of anger—the alienation—and desecration of Great Zimbabwe" (Fontein 2006: 12–13). Fontein sees a lack of representation of local histories, not only in the literature but also in museum displays and in archaeological narratives (Pikirayi 2001), including heritage management reports (Ndoro 2005).

From a scholarly perspective, Great Zimbabwe's "silence" (Fontein 2006) comes, first, from the interpretation of the site's chronology, dominated by ra-diocarbon dating, which presents it essentially as a product of prehistory; sec-ond, the failure to understand post-1500 Portuguese accounts, although some of these accounts make references to the site; and third, the meaning of the spread of the Zimbabwe tradition elsewhere on the Zimbabwe plateau.

The second broader context, which is intricately linked to the first, is the contested ownership of Great Zimbabwe, which brings to the fore both commu-nity and local histories. Because scholars have presented a monolithic account of Great Zimbabwe largely based on the interpretation of the site's stratigraphy and material culture, the dominance of archaeological narratives over other narratives in presenting the story of the site is obvious. Local and regional histories remain marginalized, yet they provide complex stories of human movements and interactions within the broader cultural landscape in which Great Zimbabwe is situated, where alternative and richer histories are located (see, e.g., Fontein 2006; Mazarire 2013; Ndoro 2005). These landscapes tell the story of Great Zimbabwe, which the stone structures and the poor stratigraphic context may no longer be able to reveal.

Our engagement with local communities around Great Zimbabwe required that we listen to their narratives of the places. Listening became an exercise in absorption of cultural meanings, including readings of the landscapes, the stories, narratives, and histories that they tell us. Listening to narratives about water, we realized, has to do with exploring the concept of place, sense of place, spirit of place, place-making, placelessness and nonplace, and almost everything to do with place (see Harvey 1996; Hayden 1988; Relph 1976, 1981).

Given the coincidence between "Burrom" in Portuguese accounts and the Boroma hills adjacent to Great Zimbabwe, I decided to investigate the history behind this term, however vague and patchy it appeared to be. The conclusions presented here are only tentative. Given that clan leaders living nearby have a vested interest in the landscape, they may or may not divulge much, as they sometimes frugally referred to Boroma merely as "one of the hills, alongside Sviba, and Mavazhe" (Simbarashe Munyimo, personal communication March 2016).

This chapter also offers a critique of the characterizations of the period in Zimbabwean history, which normally coincides with the spread of Europeans worldwide and the reporting of local events in Western texts (see Pikirayi 1993). The period from the sixteenth to the nineteenth century on the Zimbabwe plateau remains poorly understood, often subsumed under the term "Refuge Period," in reference to sites connected with nineteenth-century Nguni raids (Huffman 1971, 1974a, 1974b; Summers 1958) or to interethnic fighting, where different groups defended themselves against hostile neighbors. Stone structures, mostly rough in construction and often located on a hilltop, are attributed to this period and interpreted as refuge settlements or fortifications. The conditions generated by these events are often regarded as marking an end to the Zimbabwe Culture. This has become the general archaeological as well as historical characterization of the period in the Zimbabwe plateau since the sixteenth century.

This period is largely covered by detailed oral histories and traditions for most parts of the Zimbabwe plateau, especially in areas not reported in European accounts (Beach 1980, 1988; Pikirayi 1993, 2004) until the end of the nineteenth century. Despite the rich oral sources, historical narratives are dominated by events connected with Nguni migrations (*mfecane*) from southeastern Africa during the early to mid-nineteenth century. Thus, nineteenth-century European settlers reported on the impoverished state of indigenous Zimbabwe plateau communities, often living in refuge or fortified settlements (see, e.g., Bent 1893), and interpret these as a "decadent" development from the classical Zimbabwe Culture states. This biased view of Zimbabwe's recent history is largely shaped by European perceptions of how both local and regional developments were perceived as an impediment to the colonial project.

To understand the demise of the Zimbabwe Culture, it is necessary to address the nature of transition from Great Zimbabwe to the Refuge Period. Research in northern Zimbabwe (Pikirayi 1993, 2009) has shown that the Zimbabwe Culture and Refuge communities clearly represented mutually exclusive entities, which has implications for other areas of the Zimbabwe plateau (Pikirayi 2004). In this chapter I use local knowledge around Chizhou Hill to reinterrogate the Refuge concept among the Karanga (southern Shona speakers) and attempt to understand the complex nature of the long-neglected historical archaeology of Zimbabwe in relation to recent developments in historical analysis.

The late historian David Beach wrote extensively about Shona history and made considerable use of oral traditions, particularly in areas of the Zimbabwe plateau not covered by Portuguese or English written sources (e.g., Beach 1980, 1983, 1984). A scholarly critique of these traditions suggests that richer historical textures can be realized when investigating sites of the recent past. Carefully treated, oral narratives or local histories can serve much the same purpose as written texts, as useful sources of historical and to a considerable extent archaeological information (e.g., Schmidt 1978, 2006, 2013). While it has long been acknowledged in African history that the major limitations of oral accounts are time depth, loss of memory, and strategic adaptation in the process of transmission, they are extremely useful sources of historical and archaeological information (see, e.g., Andah and Okpoko 1979; Jones and Russell 2012; Schmidt 2006; Vansina 1965, 1985; Whiteley 2002). Critical analysis shows that a much closer symmetry between these oral accounts and archaeology is possible than previously thought. The area in which Chizhou Hill is situated is rich in local histories about Karanga movements since at least the eighteenth century, and there are hilltop sites dated to this period. Moreover, the German traveler

Karl Mauch passed through the area in the early 1870s and made useful observations about the Karanga groups living in the area (Burke 1969, Mazarire 2013).

Case Studies

Two case studies, Boroma hills and Chizhou Hill, both in south-central Zimbabwe and connected in one way or the other with Great Zimbabwe, illustrate how listening to local histories and narratives shed completely different views on post-sixteenth/seventeenth-century developments on the south-central Zimbabwe Plateau.

Boroma Hills

Boroma, a granite batholith some five to six km southeast of Great Zimbabwe, is a place-name and has a history (Figure 7.2). However, it is apparently contested in local narratives (Fontein 2015). Interest in investigating this landform was circumstantial, triggered by our research on the water resources of Great Zimbabwe (Pikirayi et al. 2016). Its proximity to Great Zimbabwe raised considerable interest, given the sixteenth-century Portuguese accounts.

Figure 7.2. Water flowing from the Boroma hills, shown in the background. Photo by author.

The Boroma hills are a sacred landscape, where chiefs of the Duma clans are buried (Fontein 2015). Fontein conducted extensive ethnographic fieldwork in 2005/2006 around Lake Mutirikwi and east of Great Zimbabwe and succeeded in highlighting the importance that local clans and communities attach to their ancestral lands. The chiefs in the area, especially those of the Mugabe clan, are buried in caves in Boroma, where sacred *mapa* (ancestral graves) are sited. The hills also lie at the boundary of the Murinye and Mugabe clans and are thus an intensely contested domain, especially in terms of claims to ancestral authority over land, knowledge of the sacred hills, caves, and springs, and particularly graves and burial practices. Around Boroma are other hills and rock shelters that contain numerous much older graves, including the dried remains of pre-Duma chiefs. Some of these remains were disturbed at Sviba Hill, when a cell-phone company erected a network booster on its summit.

The Boroma hills are an important source of spring water, which irrigates fields in the eastern part of Great Zimbabwe and is now also used by the town of Nemwana, immediately west of Great Zimbabwe (Pikirayi et al. 2016). According to Fontein (2015:134), citing a traditional leader from the area, in the springs on Boroma hills "'mysterious things happen,' and 'strange sounds' of 'heavy rain,' or 'raging torrents,' or 'of cattle bellowing' and other animals." All this points toward the existence of water spirits. According to oral historical sources, Boroma was a ruler, a political dynasty, and a ruling house or family with claims to royalty (Beach 1980; Mudenge 1988).

The first references to Boroma relate to the Torwa or Butua state during the sixteenth century. According to secondhand Portuguese written accounts, Boroma is the only Torwa ruler we know by name ruling at Great Zimbabwe during that time (Beach 1980:200). According to these accounts, he was a subruler of the Monomotapa or Mutapa state, which we know was based in northern Zimbabwe and was a successor to Great Zimbabwe (Pikirayi 1993).

Another Boroma is mentioned as a subruler in Rozvi oral traditions dating to 1800, west of the upper Tugwi River, in south-central Zimbabwe. The Rozvi, who established a state in this region dating from the mid-seventeenth century and succeeded the Torwa, are reported to have defeated him. There are suggestions that this Boroma was linked to the one mentioned by the Portuguese in connection with Great Zimbabwe. Ndarikure, a stone-walled site located in the upper Shashe, is mentioned in connection with the Rozvi. The site resembles Great Zimbabwe in terms of architectural style. It has not been investigated archaeologically, so it is probable that it may even date earlier than the seventeenth century, coinciding with the expansion of the Zimbabwe culture northward.

In northern Zimbabwe, Boroma is mentioned in connection with a ruling house of the Mutapa State, between 1704 and 1868. This house contested for the throne with another house, Nyamhandu. According to Mudenge (1988), the Mutapa state was a confederacy during that period and had lost control of the Zimbabwe plateau. Using oral traditions and Portuguese written sources, Beach (1980:144, 146) locates the state in the Zambezi lowlands, farther north. What is interesting is that the name "Boroma" is imprinted not only around Great Zimbabwe but also within the region(s) dominated by the culture once based at Great Zimbabwe. It is therefore not just a place-name but a name whose significance resonates around the site and landscape of Great Zimbabwe and apparently beyond it.

Chizhou Hill

Located in south-central Zimbabwe, some 80 km north of Great Zimbabwe in the Zimuto Communal Lands, Chizhou Hill is an example of a site that can be used to interrogate narratives about local responses to Karanga and other group expansion in the region in the period leading to the nineteenth century (Figure 7.3).

Figure 7.3. View of Chizhou Hill. Photo by author.

In early 2000 preliminary archaeological surveys were conducted around and on the hill to determine the nature of settlement and the cultural identity of the site (Pikirayi 2004). Associated oral information and local histories were collected from the nearby Gurajena village. Ceramic typology tentatively dates Chizhou from the eighteenth century onward. Literally meaning "small elephant," Chizhou is linked to the Nemarundwi dynasty, which claims origin from the Mount Fura region, in northern Zimbabwe. This region is part of Mukaranga, the heartland of the Mutapa state during the fifteenth and sixteenth centuries (Beach 1980). The Mutapa state represents the northern expansion of the culture once based at Great Zimbabwe, in the southern portions of the Zimbabwe plateau (Beach 1980; Mudenge 1988). The Nemarundwi dynasty's links with Chizhou and claims of northern origins suggest migrations connected with the demise of the Mutapa state since the seventeenth century (Pikirayi 1993). So far this is the only known hill in south-central Zimbabwe with oral accounts claiming direct connections with a state entity.

Archaeological remains are concentrated in three areas: the base of the hill to the west, the hill summit, and the hilltop area on the north-facing side. The foot of the hill features a scatter of potsherds and lumps of house plaster (*dhaka*), stretching more than 100 m along the hill and more or less the same distance from the hill. Once thickly covered by acacia trees, this area has been cleared for modern settlements and cultivation. The extent of archaeological remains suggests that this was a village, stretching up the hill slope toward the summit.

The settlement on the hilltop is on the northern end, just off the summit, easily accessible from the western side. Some open space, about 80 m² in size, is demarcated in the south, east, and north by massive boulders in a roughly circular to oval formation. Poorly coursed and largely collapsed stone walling, about 1 m high and 1 m thick, blocks spaces between the boulders, leaving only an opening to the north. This probably served as an entrance, where poorly coursed, freestanding, short lengths of walling lean onto the boulders on either side (Figure 7.4). There are at least four house mounds inside, each about 1.5 m across, as well as another stone wall, about 3 m long and apparently coursed in Great Zimbabwe architectural style (Pikirayi 2004). This was clearly a residential area.

Archaeological remains from the summit of the hill are indicative of functions related to defense. The summit, located immediately to the south, contains massive interlocking boulders with a cave-tunnel underneath. Rough, collapsed stone walling blocks the western entrance to the cave. The cave-tunnel, more

Figure 7.4. Poorly coursed stone walls close to the summit of Chizhou Hill, blocking entrance to a cave. Photo by author.

than 20 m long and over 2 m wide in places, opens again in the east, where it was once blocked around the entrance by untrimmed stones, now collapsed. Its roof is at least 1.5 m high. Archaeological remains inside and outside the cave are insubstantial. The potsherds and iron slag found in the interior and immediately outside both entrances suggest limited use of the site. Two short lengths of stone walls running north-south and abutting boulders on either side seem to have blocked access to the uppermost part of the hill, where there is a circular *dhaka* feature about 1 m in diameter—possibly a lookout point. Elders from the nearby Gurajena village say that the area was used as a refuge during the nineteenth century. Associated pottery described in Pikirayi (2004) is very variable, with the type closest to the Zimbabwe Culture displaying a reddish brown exterior and grayish black interior, decorated on the neck region with alternate triangular panels of red ochre and graphite burnish.

Several hills in the vicinity of Chizhou have roughly coursed stone walls, associated with defensive settlements or refuges used during the nineteenth century. These are the more substantial Mazambara Hills, about 15–20 km southwest of Chizhou, traditionally associated with the Zimuto dynasty. The Zimuto people are reported to have lived in these hills during the turbulent times connected with the Ndebele raids in the nineteenth century (Mr Jacob Matikiti, personal communication, February 28, 2000).

Interpretation and Discussion

Oral accounts collected by Beach (1980) suggest the settlement at Chizhou Hill dates from 1760. The open area immediately north of the summit offered less defensive advantages than the summit itself. It contained substantial housing in an enclosure-like formation with some of the walls neatly coursed, which would suggest the presence of an important person and his or her family. Although this area can be accessed fairly easily from the western side, stone walling on the southern side serves as a barrier, limiting access to two narrow passages. Its location also took into account security considerations. The summit, which is difficult to access, undoubtedly served defensive functions, including the blocking walls, the limited artifactual evidence, and the presence of large ceramic vessels in one of the caves, which would be ideal utensils for storage under conditions of siege. While caves are sometimes used for religious and other ritual activities such as rainmaking and ancestral veneration, the location of these structures and features makes such functions less likely.

While the use of hilltops in southern African goes back to be late first millennium (see, e.g., Huffman 1986), it is necessary to determine the nature of transformations that occurred after 1500 AD among the Karanga that generated conditions characteristic of the Refuge Period (Summers 1958), as not all these sites are products of Nguni migrations or more specifically Ndebele raids during the nineteenth century.

The situation in northern Zimbabwe after 1600 AD shows a clear break from the earlier Zimbabwe Culture and the local Mahonje tradition, associated with political instability in the Mutapa state during the seventeenth century (Pikirayi 1993:70). On the contrary, while an apparent break with the pasts exists in southern Zimbabwe, there is also evidence of cultural continuity to the present, based on similarities in material culture and, in some contexts, continuation of stone-building traditions. However, when the historical experiences of recent Karanga in south-central Zimbabwe are considered, we also notice some subtle changes within the Zimbabwe Culture that eventually led to its demise. The links with the Mutapa state in northern Zimbabwe are of particular interest. These are to be found in local dynastic histories and oral traditions.

Local Histories and Group Origins

Three Karanga dynasties—the Gurajena, Nemarundwi, and Zimuto—arrived in the Zimuto area in the middle of the eighteenth century (Beach 1980; Pikirayi 2004). Prior to their arrival, this area was occupied and controlled by the Rozvi, whose remnants are identified as the Chademana people (Beach 1980:274). Beach (1980:300) provides a detailed treatment of the oral histories, suggesting that the Gurajena people initially settled in the southern part, near the Mazambara Hills, when they arrived. This would soon change with the subsequent arrival of the Zimuto and Nemarundwi, triggering group dispersal. Beach (1980:291, 1994a:145, 168, 1994b) dates these developments to the second half the eighteenth century.

The dynastic histories of these groups point to initial intergroup fighting, which means that some of their early settlements could have been used as refuges. There is also a link between some dynasties and certain hills; for example, the Zimuto people are said to have lived within and around the Mazambara Hills. According to the traditions collected by Beach (1980, 1994a, 1994b), as well oral accounts that I collected in the late 1990s and during the current fieldwork, the Nemarundwi people are said to have arrived from the northern Zimbabwe plateau. Informants mention Mount Fura, some 500 km to the north, suggesting a migration from an area occupied by the Mutapa state (Pikirayi 1993), a successor to Great Zimbabwe. The Nemarundwi are said to have lived on and around the Chizhou Hill, in south-central Zimbabwe. They were soon joined by the Gurajena people from the east, who intermarried with them and were given a place to settle near the hill (Isaac Makombe, personal communication, March 1988).

In 1872 Karl Mauch passed through the area "between N and NNE to Makurudsena [Gurajena], rather to one of his small kraals nestling close to a granite kopje, which has a white appearance when seen from a distance" (Burke 1969:207). The only hill in the area with such prominence is Chizhou. The remains associated with nineteenth-century Gurajena villages, located by traditional elders about 1 km southwest of Chizhou Hill, are not easy to identify: grain bins are continuously built and rebuilt on these surfaces to such an extent that it is difficult to isolate modern sherds and house structures from earlier structures and other cultural material. The present location of the village is less than a kilometer away, on the upper edges of a small stream flowing south and on the western side of a smaller range (Biravira/Musosi). This range also has traces of potsherds in places, suggesting the existence of past settlement. Thus, by 1890 small villages in the Zimuto area were sited on hilltops and hill slopes (see Beach 1980:picture opposite 210). Although the Ndebele, one of the Nguni groups who migrated from Zululand and settled on the Zimbabwe plateau, were raiding the area south of Great Zimbabwe in 1872 (see Burke 1969:21l ff.), the Gurajena people were worried about a different problem. In 1871 their settlements were destroyed and their cattle were driven off by the Bengulu (Burke 1969:208). This generally explains why traditions of Ndebele raiding are rather uncommon in the area and why settlements are not exclusively located on hilltops.

The Broader Context

Although there is close similarity between the archaeology from Chizhou and other contemporary sites in the region, site variability is explicitly brought out by the historical contexts, which are particular to each site. The historical evidence suggests that we are looking at shifting settlement systems in response to political and security considerations. It is in this milieu that we must understand the demise of the Zimbabwe Culture after the sixteenth century, when the Portuguese refer to Great Zimbabwe and the prince Burrom.

From available evidence, it appears that the transformation of the Zimbabwe Culture since the sixteenth and seventeenth centuries AD was a gradual process. It is possible to interpret the relevant archaeological evidence with the assistance of historical sources, especially written records and oral traditions. Some historical events may provide clues such as changes in the nature and form of material culture items and aspects connected to the use of space at some archaeological sites. Following the demise of the Mutapa and Torwa states (which represented the Zimbabwe Culture in both material culture and settlement pattern), the Zimbabwe plateau witnessed the emergence of comparatively smaller polities defined along totemic lines (Beach 1980). These nucleated around the ruling dynasty and controlled small territories. A territory always belonged to the dominant totem. The demise of the Mutapa and Rozvi states resulted in small to major migrations of population, from the areas formerly under their control to the southern and the northern edges of the Zimbabwe plateau. Very few of these migrating groups would claim to have found the land that they eventually occupied empty. The more powerful groups often displaced smaller, weaker ones, who in turn, moved some distance away. Other groups were simply absorbed through marriage or allowed to settle nearby. This movement is a complex process that has only been documented on a very general scale (Beach 1980:279–317).

How and when did the elite stone buildings decline and what replaced them? Why do most settlements appear to have been located on the hilltops during this time? What happened to the typical Great Zimbabwe–style pottery? The decline of the Zimbabwe Culture is initially inferred from the disappearance of the tradition of building neat stone walling. In the area of the Mutapa state this occurred during the sixteenth century. However, Great Zimbabwe material culture is seen there in contexts from the seventeenth century and later, suggesting that the stone-building tradition might have been replaced by new forms of settlement construction (Pikirayi 1993). With the decline of state authority, capital and provincial centers may have declined accordingly, as they lost some of their administrative and political functions. In fact, it was no longer necessary for people to generate the wealth required to build such centers once central authority had declined.

This decline might have been accelerated by a decrease in population, especially in the heart of the Mutapa state, during the seventeenth century. This also meant a loss of territory and a reduction in the court size of the Mutapa rulers. With the movement of Zimbabwe Culture communities away from the core of the state, political organization may have assumed a three-level form, such as petty chief (small territorial chief), village head, and family head. This is difficult to see archaeologically, however, as these levels are represented by settlements that are generally of the same size (Huffman 1986:295). The founding of new settlements elsewhere reflects a sociopolitical organization that was not synonymous with a state-level organization. Political control was probably based on the family unit. Thus, in terms of the internal arrangement of such settlements, a ruler's residence was situated close to those of his immediate relatives (wives and sisters). The ruler's residence was surrounded by commoner habitation, constituting a village, usually based around an extended family and incorporating members of the same totem. Political control was vested in the families who had previously been connected to the ruling houses and who, because of leadership and seniority, had led the dynasty or group away from the core of the state. This movement was necessitated either by defeat in a conflict over leadership or by the desire to settle in new peaceful lands. The Nemarundwi dynasty discussed above is a case in point.

The preferences for settlement location of such migrants are difficult to judge, given the limited studies connected with historical period sites, but one would expect a continued association between the elite and hilltops and the commoners and the base or foot of hills. This symbolic link between hills/mountains and rulers was still regarded as important during the more recent historical period, but it is important to bear in mind other factors.

Hills also served additional functional roles as refuges, especially in times of war. Prominent hills could be used for ordinary settlements or for defensive purposes. Intergroup fighting during this time surely dictated that some settlements be sited on hilltops rather than on low ground. In addition, hills were often associated with rainmaking and other religious activities.

Another problem is what happened to Great Zimbabwe–tradition material culture, as exemplified by its pottery, with well-burnished/painted designs. One would expect remnants of this style among the smaller groups that were once part of the tradition. However, this is not the case. The reasons for this absence may be because pottery has been associated with a high level of sociopolitical and economic organization since the twelfth century, so its appearance was synonymous with state-level organization. Loss of sociopolitical and economic authority probably meant that some of the pottery no longer served the same functions. The late historical period pottery might therefore be expected to be much simpler, reflecting only the basic traits inherited from earlier periods.

Beach appropriately summarizes some of the major issues discussed here:

> The migrations in the centre and south of the plateau do indeed show a movement towards a less complex way of life than had been offered by the states. Nevertheless, this was not a new development, nor were these small unities a debased or fragmented form of the state. On the contrary, they were in the same tradition not only of those small territories that had co-existed with the states in their heyday, but . . . with the original Shona settlements in the beginning of the Later Iron Age, or even with the political formations of the Early Iron Age. Seen in this light, therefore, the new settlers were reverting to the mainstream of Shona politics and society from which the state forming period had been a diversion. (Beach 1984:50)

The availability of oral historical data presents a platform to ask more meaningful questions pertaining to a particular archaeological site than a prehistoric site would allow. It is inappropriate to categorize sites like Chizhou as simply Refuge Period settlements, as they served for more than defensive functions.

The historical archaeologies connected with more recent events are less implicit, especially in the absence of written texts. However, this apparent constraint can be minimized by careful handling of the oral texts, some of which refer to archaeological data. If Chizhou Hill represents the processes of settlement connected with the movements of the Karanga from the Mutapa state to south-central Zimbabwe and in the process leading to the reestablishment of the Zimbabwe Culture, what do the Boroma hills tell us about Great Zimbabwe? In my view, there is too much coincidence between the Boroma hills and Boroma the ruler based at Great Zimbabwe and thus a strong possibility that a connection exists between these two.

Fontein's (2015) central theme is immanence of the past and materiality of belonging. He identified remains of pottery, stone walling, and pre-Duma graves when he visited the sacred hills of Boroma in 2006. This points to not only the immanence of many pasts in the materialities of place but also to the continuation in meaning, practice, and rule that these can engender and make possible. The study of Boroma is about place-making and community identity (see, e.g., Hayden 1988 on suppressed cultural histories of ethnic minorities and women in Los Angeles). Places make memories cohere in complex ways. Further, according to Relph (1976), memories also make places cohere: the formal recognition of these places through restoration and preservation can be a powerful way to reinforce community identity. According to Jones and Russell (2012), memory is a transient product of the activities of remembering and reminiscing, which take place in the context of social interaction and interactions between people and their environments (see also Halbwachs 1992; Mills and Walker 2008). Furthermore, the extent to which social memory is mediated by mnemonic devices such as images, objects, oral histories, stories, folklore, myths, events, and places or sites depends to some degree on how far removed people are from direct experience of the events, people, and places concerned (Jones and Russell 2012).

From the mid-1990s onward, scholars have increasingly paid attention to the complex relationship of people to places following acute global conditions of exile, displacement, tight immigration controls, and struggles by indigenous peoples and cultural minorities for ancestral homelands, land rights, and retention of sacred places. However, not much work has been done on the ethnography and archaeology of place to understand how people actually live in, perceive, and invest with meaning the places they identify as home. Feld and Basso (1996) demonstrate the ways in which people experience, express, imagine, and know the places in which they live. When we refer to intergroup fighting or conflicts in precolonial African history, we often talk about movement to another place as one the outcomes but always forget about the negative impact of such displacement. This also produces memory in relation to specific forms of experience, such as war, trauma, political oppression, loss of places, and so on (see, e.g., Schmidt 2010).

In archaeological contexts, place-making is about the context of built form and environment and the production of architecture and settlement. The interest was in the generative forces and purposes of ordinary building activity in abandoned settlements in Cappadocia in Turkey and of the Anasazi in New Mexico (see Stea and Turan 1993). It is also a process that has meaning and sociopolitical and economic implications. It involves creating permanences that are nevertheless always subject to change, dissolution, and replacement. Because they are made and remade, they do not have fixed identities (see Harvey 1996). This is perhaps what we are missing in understanding the recent histories of Great Zimbabwe and the landscape immediately around it.

I have considered both the archaeological and historical evidence from Great Zimbabwe and discussed the site in the context of both local and regional histories on the Zimbabwe plateau. It is the dynamics of these histories that tell of Great Zimbabwe's declining regional role and its eventual demise as a center of considerable political and economic power. During the fourteenth and fifteenth centuries, the story of Great Zimbabwe can only be gleaned by examining external written accounts and by extracting historical information from datable ceramics and glass beads found there. From this perspective, the work of Randall-MacIver (1906) is significant, especially his "Medieval Period" dating of Great Zimbabwe (which should be contrasted with Hall 1909, primarily a futile rejection of Randall-MacIver's groundbreaking work on the site). There is also a need to consider seriously post-fifteenth-century migrations by the Karanga and other groups, reported from oral sources as a process of expansion from south-central Zimbabwe northward toward the Zambezi basin (Beach 1980). However, during the seventeenth century the Karanga are reported in both oral traditions (Beach 1980) and Portuguese written accounts (Pikirayi 1993) as migrating southward, leaving much of northern Zimbabwe under a Mutapa state but increasingly under siege from the Portuguese. While these traditions show a reversal of earlier expansion or migration and a subsequent reconnection with the landscape of Great Zimbabwe, the events also underline how Great Zimbabwe lost its significance in relation to other centers in the region.

Conclusion

In studying Great Zimbabwe, I have been listening to the anthropological critique, foregrounding "the silence of unheard voices and untold stories" (Fontein 2006:12–13). Listening also to local people and their own historians, I hear the toponyms of Great Zimbabwe's immediate and broader cultural and natural landscape. Hydronyms and oronyms locate the still marginalized local and regional histories that provide complex stories of human movements and interactions within the broader landscape in which Great Zimbabwe is situated. These histories not only tell us about the dynamics within Great Zimbabwe's immediate landscape but also provide a broader context for the expansion of the site's culture and influence to distant regions of the Zimbabwe Plateau. Although the stone-built monumental structures of Great Zimbabwe excited Europeans' interest, they are only a point in the system of mountains and rivers that marked and nourished the state. These landscapes tell the story of Great Zimbabwe, which the stone structures and the poor stratigraphic context may no longer provide.

Understanding the demise of Great Zimbabwe after the sixteenth century not only requires examining the processes of leaving the settlement (see Pikirayi 2006, 2013), but also the subsequent return (Pikirayi 2004). Local histories from the Zimuto Communal Lands illustrate complex group movements, while material culture from the site of Chizhou suggests how these groups adjusted to less complex, less monumental ways of living.

Notes

1. The account reads:

> There are other mines in a district called Toroa, which by another name is known as the kingdom of Butua, which is ruled by a prince called Burrom, a vassal of Benomotapa, which land adjoins the aforesaid consisting of vast plains, and these mines are the most ancient known in the country, and they are all in the plain, in the midst of which there is a square fortress of masonry within and without, built of stones of marvellous size, and there appears to be no mortar joining them. The wall is more than twenty-five spans in width, and the height is not so great considering the width. This edifice is almost surrounded by hills, upon which are others resembling it in the fashioning of the stone and the absence of mortar, and one of them is a tower more than twelve fathoms high.

> The natives of the country call these edifices Symbaoe, which according to their language signifies court, for every place where Benomotapa may be is so called; and they say that being royal; property all the king's other dwellings have this

name. . . . When and by whom these edifices were raised, as the people of the land are ignorant of the art of writing, there is no record, but they say they are the work of the devil, for in comparison to their power and knowledge it does not seem possible to them that they should be the work of men. . . . The distance of this edifice from Sofala in a direct line to the west is a hundred and seventy leagues, or thereabouts and it is between 20° and 21° south latitude . . .

In the opinion of the Moors who saw it, it is very ancient, and was built there to keep possessions of the mines, which are very old, and no gold has been extracted from them for years, because of the wars . . .

It is guarded by a nobleman, who has charge of it after the manner of a chief alcaide, and they call this officer Symbacayo, as we should say keeper of the Symbaoe, and there are always some of Benomotapa's wives therein, of whom this Symbacayo takes care. (Theal 1898–1903:6:267–268)

2. The project is funded by the South African National Research Foundation (NRF) as Grant Number 98833 and within the framework of the African Origins Platform.

References Cited

Andah, B, W., and A. I. Okpoko
1979   Oral Traditions and West African Culture History: A New Direction. *West African Journal of Archaeology* 9:201–224.
Beach, D. N.
1980   *The Shona and Zimbabwe, 900–1850.* Mambo Press, Gweru, Zimbabwe.
1983   Oral History and Archaeology in Zimbabwe. *Zimbabwe Prehistory* 20:8–11.
1984   *Zimbabwe before 1900.* Mambo Press, Gweru, Zimbabwe.
1988   "Refuge" Archaeology, Trade and Gold in Nineteenth Century Zimbabwe: Izidoro Correia Pereira's List of 1859. *Zimbabwean Prehistory* 20:1–8.
1994a   *A Zimbabwean Past: Shona Dynastic Histories and Oral Traditions.* Mambo Press, Gweru, Zimbabwe.
1994b   *The Shona and Their Neighbours.* Blackwell, Oxford.
Bent, T. J.
1893   *The Ruined Cities of Mashonaland.* Bulawayo, Rhodesia.
Burke, E. E. (editor)
1969   *The Journals of Carl Mauch.* National Archives of Rhodesia, Salisbury.
Feld, S., and K. Basso (editors)
1996   *Senses of Place.* SAR Press, Santa Fe, NM.
Fontein, J.
2006   *The Silence of Great Zimbabwe: Contested Landscapes and the Power of Heritage.* UCL Press, London.
2015   *Remaking Mutirikwi: Landscape, Water and Belonging in Southern Zimbabwe.* James Currey, New York.
Halbwachs, M.
1992   *On Collective Memory.* Edited and translated by L. A. Coser. University of Chicago Press, Chicago.

Hall, R. N.

1905   *Great Zimbabwe*. Methuen, London.

1909   *Prehistoric Rhodesia*. F. T. Unwin, London.

Hall, R. N., and W. G. Neal

1902   *The Ancient Ruins of Rhodesia*. Methuen, London.

Harvey, D.

1996   *Justice, Nature and the Geography of Difference*. Blackwell Publishers, Oxford.

Hayden, D.

1988   Placemaking, Preservation, and Urban History. *Journal of Architectural Education* 41(3):45–51.

Huffman, T. N.

1971   A Guide to the Iron Age of Northern Mashonaland. *Occasional Papers of the National Museums of Rhodesia* 4(1):21–44.

1974a   *The Leopard's Kopje Tradition*. Museum Memoir 6. National Museums and Monuments of Rhodesia, Salisbury.

1974b   The Linguistic Affinities of the Iron Age in Rhodesia. *Arnoldia* 7(7):1–12.

1986   Iron Age Settlement Patterns and the Origins of Class Distinction in Southern Africa. *Advances in World Archaeology* 5:291–338.

Jones, S., and L. Russell

2012   Archaeology, Memory and Oral Tradition: An Introduction. *International Journal for Historical Archaeology* 16(2):267–283.

Mazarire, G. C.

2013   Carl Mauch and Some Karanga Chiefs around Great Zimbabwe 1871–1872: Re-Considering the Evidence. *South African Historical Journal* 65(3):337–364.

Mills, B., and W. Walker

2008   *Memory Work: Archaeologies of Material Practice*. SAR Press, Santa Fe, NM.

Mudenge, S.I.G.

1988   *A Political History of Munhumutapa*. Zimbabwe Publishing House, Harare, Zimbabwe.

Ndoro, W.

2005   *The Preservation of Great Zimbabwe: Your Monument, Our Shrine*. Conservation Studies 4. ICCROM, Rome.

Pikirayi, I.

1993   *The Archaeological Identity of the Mutapa State: Towards an Historical Archaeology of Northern Zimbabwe*. Studies in African Archaeology 6. Societas Archaeologica Upsaliensis, Uppsala, Sweden.

2000   Wars, Violence and Strongholds: An Overview of Fortified Settlements in Northern Zimbabwe. *Journal of Peace, Conflict and Military Studies* 1(1):1–12.

2001   *The Zimbabwe Culture: Origins and Decline in Southern Zambezian States*. AltaMira Press, Walnut Creek, CA.

2004   Less Implicit Historical Archaeologies: Oral Traditions and Later Karanga Settlements in South-Central Zimbabwe. In *African Historical Archaeologies*, edited by A. M. Reid, and P. J. Lane, pp. 243–267. Kluwer Academic/Plenum Publishers, New York.

2006   The Demise of Great Zimbabwe, AD 1420–1550: An Environmental Reappraisal.

In *Cities in the World, 1500–2000*, edited by A. Green and R. Leech, pp. 31–47. Society for Post-medieval Archaeology Monograph 3, Leeds, UK.

2009   Palaces, Feiras and Prazos: An Historical Archaeological Perspective of African-Portuguese Contact in Northern Zimbabwe. *African Archaeological Review* 26(3):163–185.

2013   Great Zimbabwe in Historical Archaeology: Re-conceptualizing Decline, Abandonment, and Reoccupation of an Ancient Polity, A.D. 1450–1900. *Historical Archaeology* 47(1):26–37.

Pikirayi, I., F. Sulas, T. T. Musindo, A. Chimwanda, J. Chikumbirike, E. Mtetwa, and E. M. Sagiya

2016   Great Zimbabwe's Water. *Wires Water* 3(2):95–210.

Randall-MacIver, D.

1906   *Medieval Rhodesia*. Macmillan, London.

Relph, E.

1976   *Place and Placelessness*. Pion, London.

1981   *Rational Landscapes*. Barnes and Noble, New York.

Schmidt, P. R.

1978   *Historical Archaeology: A Structural Approach in an African Culture*. Greenwood Press, Westport, CT.

2006   *Historical Archaeology in Africa: Representation, Social Memory, Oral Traditions*. AltaMira, Lanham, MD.

2010   Social Memory and Trauma in Northwestern Tanzania: Organic Spontaneous Community Collaboration. *Journal of Social Archaeology* 10:255–279.

2013   Oral History, Oral Traditions and Archaeology: Application of Structural Analysis. In *Oxford Handbook of African Archaeology*, edited by P. Mitchell and P. Lane, pp. 37–47. Oxford University Press, Oxford.

Stea, D. and Turan, M.

1993   *Placemaking: Production of Built Environment in Two Cultures*. Aldershot, Avebury, UK.

Summers, R.

1958   *Inyanga: Prehistoric Settlements in Southern Rhodesia*. Cambridge University Press, Cambridge.

Theal, G. M.

1898–1903 *Records of South-Eastern Africa*. 9 vols. C. Struik Publishers, Cape Town, South Africa.

Vansina, J.

1965   *Oral Tradition: A Study in Historical Methodology*. Routledge and Kegan Paul, London.

1985   *Oral Tradition as History*. University of Wisconsin Press, Madison.

Whiteley, P. M.

2002   Archaeology and Oral Tradition: The Scientific Importance of Dialogue. *American Antiquity* 67(3):405–415.

PART II

Reaching for Epistemic Humility

8

"Listening to Whom and for Whose Benefit?"

Promoting and Protecting Local Heritage Values

GEORGE NICHOLAS

At a community event some years ago on an Indian Reserve in British Columbia, I overheard a Secwepemc elder say to a young man who was fooling around, "You can't listen when your mouth is moving. So be quiet and learn." He was suitably embarrassed in front of his peers and thanked her for the important lesson. This chapter is about what can be learned when we, as archaeologists, stop talking and listen—advice I have long taken to heart.

Over the course of 30 years of working with and for Indigenous peoples, my view of archaeology has changed in significant ways. Steeped in an archaeological orientation that combined culture history with processualism, my research was (and is) strongly oriented to early postglacial land use and the human ecology of wetland-rich environments. However, I soon found my worldview changing as I taught archaeology in a post-secondary institution on an Indian Reserve in Canada for 15 years. That formative experience led me to a second avenue by which to engage with archaeological questions and heritage values. The interplay between these two distinct ways of approaching and engaging with the past has subsequently strongly influenced the archaeology that I do and the heritage research and activism that I engage in, providing a sometimes uncomfortable but always productive tension.[1] This has instilled a degree of pragmatism about the nature of archaeology and its often-privileged position but also a sense of optimism that it can be made more relevant and representative while still maintaining scientific rigor.

I have spent much time considering the challenges that both descendant communities and archaeologists are confronted with in trying to reach common ground. When asked to speak at the Ḭ̀àà katì Traditional Knowledge gathering in Yellowknife, Northwest Territories, several years ago, I distilled what I have learned in a presentation entitled "Why Heritage Is Not Just about 'Things.'" Namely, heritage is not just about things; it is not limited to the past; it permeates the fabric of indigenous societies; it is largely intangible; heritage research may have unintended consequences; and heritage objects and places are best managed by the heritage holders (Nicholas 2014a).

Each of these six points reflects conceptions, values, and uses of heritage that transcend the familiar cultural historical and neoevolutionary dimensions of contemporary archaeology. Descendant communities, especially indigenous ones, have long had concerns about how their heritage has been treated by archaeologists and others, especially when used in inappropriate, unwelcome, or harmful ways. Areas of concern include the consequences of modern and ancient DNA research; the question of control over, benefits from, access to, and protection of heritage objects, places, and information; efforts to repatriate cultural patrimony and human remains and the information derived from those; the inappropriate display of sacred objects; and the selective acceptance of traditional knowledge by archaeologists, climatologists, and others (Nicholas 2018). What is important is that understanding how and why these issues emerge at the intersection of archaeological goals and heritage values is not a unilateral process but requires listening to community members (see Cusack-McVeigh 2016).

In this chapter I describe the value of what can be learned from indigenous community members as well as how ethnographic archaeological studies contribute to a fuller understanding of heritage, directly benefit community needs and interests, and make substantial contributions to archaeology and heritage preservation. I focus on efforts undertaken by the Intellectual Property Issues in Cultural Heritage (IPinCH) project, an international initiative that I directed from 2008 to 2016. I begin by addressing the familiar concept of heritage and why it is problematic.

Why "Heritage" Is Problematic

Archaeology is how we learn what happened in the past, while heritage is that set of values given to or possessed by objects, places, and information derived from archaeology and other means. We are most familiar with these scientific and historic meanings but less so with local values and specific needs of descendant communities, especially in the case of Indigenous peoples, whose knowledge of how things were or came to be may be rooted in different epistemologies and ontologies. Without talking with and listening to community members, both archaeological inquiry and heritage management policies remain incomplete, if not skewed to outsider interests. This tends to perpetuate Western perspectives and expectations rather than provide opportunities to learn about decidedly non-Western ways of life, both past and present, via local heritage values. In British Columbia, for example, Hul'qumi'num elder Arvid Charlie referred to this difference:

> When new sites are a few years old they're called heritage. Our sites have been here thousands of years. Their sites, if they're old, may be a hundred and fifty years. They say it's old, but to us that was yesterday. Our ancient sites—since time immemorial. They value their places that have a few years old. To us, our old, much older sites are very important to us. Many of these places have our old people buried in them. So it's not only a heritage site, it's a graveyard. . . . If they [white people] can have important places that are only few years old, why not? Why can't we say our places are important to us? Because they are our culture, our heritage. It's about our past and it's our future. (McLay et al. 2008:17)

One challenge here is to discern how Western and indigenous conceptions of heritage actually are different. To put it simplistically, the former tends to emphasize the tangible, while the latter is defined not just by the intangible (Nicholas 2017) but also by relationships and responsibilities aligned with knowledge, objects, and places (Noble 2008). Even when acknowledging that one's engagement with the world may be grounded through material culture, it is always filtered through the society's collective knowledge, experiences, traditions, social obligations, and origin stories that both shape and reflect what people do and why they do it. A distinct concept of "heritage" may also be absent in many indigenous societies, since what it represents is entwined with all other facets of people's lives. As one Yukon elder said, heritage is "everything that makes us who we are" (Carcross-Tagish First Nation et al. 2016:30).

The knowledge that shapes and guides each person's life is learned, earned, shared, cared for, and embedded in objects or places (Figure 8.1). This means that fundamentally there is no difference between the place and the stories and knowledge that location holds, nor between an object and the historical continuity it may exude or the social obligations it may convey. Under such conditions, the archaeological (or other) analysis of cultural property and the management of such heritage (including determination of significance)

Figure 8.1. Madeline Karkagie (Sahtú Nation) preparing moose sinew thread for sewing a moose-skin boat, Punk Mountain base camp, Mackenzie Mountain region, Northwest Territories. NWT Archives N-2007–002: 00328.1.

impose great responsibility on those who not only engage with but often make decisions about other people's heritage.

It is essential that we as outsiders commit to engaging with indigenous knowledge systems if we are to understand a community's needs and concerns. But this is challenging. As Bell and Napoleon (2008:6–7) note:

> The very terms "culture," "property," and "ownership" are Western legal, social, economic, and political constructs that are imposed on First Nations . . . [to many] . . . these terms are still incomprehensible (i.e., no equivalent concept in First Nations languages), inappropriate (i.e., disrespectful of First Nations concepts), or inadequate (i.e., too narrow).

The archaeological corollary of this concerns the problematic nature of some terms (e.g., "abandoned," "ruins," "prehistory": Zimmerman 2010:474–475), for example, compared to the use of more respectful terms such as "belongings" (vs. "artifacts") and "person" or "ancestor" (vs. "skeletal remains"). This extends to the practices of labeling important heritage sites by terms (or numbers) of convenience, rather than by local names, such as the Marpole Midden site vs. čəsnaʔəm (Wilson 2016) in Vancouver, British Columbia. In non-Western contexts, we must not only become familiar with another syntax but ultimately learn another way of thinking. This is where listening becomes critical, too, if we are to understand other ways of thinking and being.

Adjusting the Ethnographic Lens

Archaeologists and anthropologists have long depended on living peoples as a means to make sense of the cultural world, past and present.[2] Ethnography in its many guises has provided a means to suggest modern analogs for ancient peoples (e.g., Wilson 1851) or to observe objects in action to identify the function of a particular artifact type (e.g., Kroeber 1961) or to correlate house structure with residence patterns (Porcic 2010). A major field of archaeological research, ethnoarchaeology,[3] emerged in response to the growing use of ethnographic data and the opportunities to illuminate aspects of past human behavior—but also in recognition of the need to develop appropriate strategies for collecting and using (or not) the information obtained (see David and Kramer 2001).

What characterizes these approaches is the use of local knowledge to address *archaeological goals*. Lewis Binford's Nunamiut land-use studies in Alaska (1982) contributed a suite of new ideas and data about technological organization and annual/lifetime range, while his work with the Alywara of Australia (1986) sought insights into tool-manufacture strategies. Notably, these particular studies were based more on observation than conversation. Indeed, Binford privileged his views over local ideas, thus virtually ignoring his community "partners"—an example of how not to do ethnoarchaeology.[4] While this strategy did not arguably limit his land-use study, some types of information require direct community input, as illustrated by the example of Richard Gould's (1980:154) "righteous rocks." In seeking to interpret the lithic assemblages at Puntutjarpa rockshelter, Western Australia, Gould learned from Ngatatjara men that they collected for tool manufacture a particular chert not for its flaking properties (technically inferior to more readily available chert) but for its association with a Dreaming place. Such ethnoarchaeological projects, whether situated in the neoevolutionary goals of processual archaeology or the direct historic methods of culture history, are aimed at obtaining local information *for the benefit of archaeological inquiry*. In the examples above, it was the need to address archaeological questions that led to seeking local information. Such projects may nonetheless yield insights (to outsiders) into local values or world-views that are not directly evident in material culture alone if the right questions are asked (as in Gould's case).[5]

What has generally gone unremarked is that ethnoarchaeology and similar uses of ethnoarchaeological information have too often been a one-way ex-change of information (Hollowell and Nicholas 2008).[6] For many archaeologists, ethnographic opportunities are simply an additional and often unique source of information, but Indigenous peoples may respond differently. As Deloria (1969:81) stated in his inimitable tongue-in-check but very serious critique, *Custer Died for Your Sins: An Indian Manifesto*:

> The fundamental thesis of the anthropologist is that people are objects for observation, people are then considered objects for experimentation, for manipulation, and for eventual extinction. The anthropologist thus furnishes the justification for treating Indian people like so many chess-men available for anyone to play with.
>
> The massive volume of useless knowledge produced by anthropologists attempting to capture real Indians in a network of theories has contributed to the invisibility of Indian people today.

Such a perspective, shaped by decades (if not centuries) of suffering un-der state colonialist and assimilationist policies, disenfranchisement, or worse, portrays archaeological and anthropological research continuing the legacy of scientific colonialism. That observation is not unwarranted: archaeologists have contributed to this by controlling flows of information, extracting cultural capital as raw data, claiming right of access to data and property rights over the knowledge produced, and otherwise transforming data into social and eco-nomic capital, with benefits rarely shared with the source communities (Hol-lowell and Nicholas 2007).

Concerted efforts have been made to redress this situation, as well as the un-derlying power imbalance, through a variety of approaches that include commu-nity-based participatory research (e.g., Atalay 2012; Schmidt and Pikirayi 2016), critical discourse (e.g., Lydon and Rizvi 2010), activist archaeology (e.g., Atalay et al. 2014), indigenous archaeology (e.g., Nicholas 2014b), and public archaeol-ogy (e.g., Skeates, McDavid, and Carman 2012). These provide opportunities for communities to benefit directly from research on their heritage but also identify and challenge inequities in decision-making, site significance assessment, and other elements of archaeological practice and heritage management. Another approach is archaeological ethnography, which is described as "an emerging space of thinking, engagement, dialogue, collaboration, and intervention, rather than merely a scholarly practice at the interface between archaeology and anthropology" (Hamilakis and Anagnostopoulos 2009:83; see also Castañeda and Matthews 2008). Taking a more reflexive, self-critical, and community-driven orientation transforms ethnographic research from an extractive process to one that enriches. This is illustrated by a growing number of examples in which heritage research is done by the community, for the community (e.g., Ferguson and Colwell-Chanthaphonh 2006; Lyons 2013; Schmidt 2017; Schmidt and Pikirayi 2016). I add to these a set of community projects funded by the IPinCH Project.

Heritage Is Living

The Intellectual Property Issues in Cultural Heritage (IPinCH) Project (www. sfu.ca/ipinch) was an international, multidisciplinary research project (2008–2016) that examined intellectual property-related issues emerging within the realm of heritage, especially those affecting Indigenous peoples. These included complex and often difficult questions about who has rights and responsibilities relating to the use of and benefits from tangible and intangible cultural heritage, including artifacts, archaeological sites, and associated traditional knowledge and values. To address these issues, IPinCH was designed to assist scholars, institutions, descendant communities, policymakers, and other stakeholders to negotiate equitable, appropriate, and successful research policies and practices involving cultural heritage, including archaeology.

To help develop a fuller understanding of local conceptions of heritage ownership and rights, the IPinCH project funded a series of community-directed projects and special initiatives in Canada, the United States, Australia, New Zealand, Kyrgyzstan, and elsewhere, addressing pressing cultural heritage challenges in specific contexts (http://www.sfu.ca/ipinch/project-components/community-based-initiatives/). In each case, community values and needs were foregrounded by research where the community was in the driver's seat. Each study was developed with the community. Community members determined research goals, identified the most appropriate methods to employ, reviewed research products and data to determine what information could be shared, and retained full control of project from start to finish. Most importantly, the community was the primary beneficiary of the research. I offer four examples below of projects seeking new understandings of heritage, not by digging but by listening.

This initiative was developed to identify the nature of heritage from the perspectives of four participating Yukon First Nations (YFN): the Champagne and Aishihik First Nations, the Carcross-Tagish First Nation, the Ta'an Kwäch'än Council, and the Tr'ondek Hwëch'in First Nation. It had four goals:

1. document how "heritage value" is defined by Yukon First Nations Elders, heritage workers, youth, and other members; and to characterize the different aspects or categories recognized by our community as having heritage value (e.g., peoples, places, stories, ways, and things);
2. learn about who (individuals, families, clans, governments, organizations) has stewardship responsibility for the different aspects of Yukon First Nations heritage;
3. learn what constitutes stewardship of the different aspects of Yukon First Nations heritage; and
4. learn about other values, norms, laws, or practices that may affect heritage resources; and management practices by self-governing Yukon First Nations. (Carcross-Tagish First Nation et al. 2016:2)

Information was obtained through interviews, small focus-group discussions, and a workshop with individuals and cultural workers within the Yukon First Nation communities. Both youth and elders were included in these sessions. Although participants identified various archaeological or heritage objects and places as culturally important, what was most highly valued were the relationships—the experiences and the stories attached to them—that established their significance (Figure 8.2). As the report authors note:

[U]nderstandings of what constitutes a "direct relationship" between YFN and an item for the purpose of establishing YFN ownership and management may vary with the nature of an item, spiritual powers or practice, or stewardship responsibilities derived from YFN laws; the latter may or may not place emphasis on the age of an item, geographical location, or ancestral connection through acts of creation or prior physical possession. (Carcross-Tagish First Nation et al. 2016:29)

Community members noted that the process of sharing traditional knowledge derived from or associated with objects, and the aggregate of experience shared between people, was often given greater significance than the objects

Figure 8.2. Champagne and Aishihik First Nations elder Paddy Jim points out landmarks to staff member Paula Banks on the floor map at Da Kų, the CAFN Cultural Centre, Whitehorse, Yukon, June 2013. Photo by Amy MacKinnon, courtesy of the Champagne & Aishihik First Nations.

or places themselves. Here significance is based not on the type, age, or rarity of objects, as so often measured in archaeological site evaluations, but in the "foundational concepts of YFN heritage (e.g., responsibility, community, spirituality, sharing, and its holistic nature)" (Carcross-Tagish First Nation et al. 2016:53). Thus, when one Yukon elder stated that there is a "real sense of spiritual connection. . . . Our ancestors are here, you know. You look up the hill there at the gravesite, those are all our ancestors up there. They are here with us today" (Carcross-Tagish First Nation et al. 2016:45), he was referring to a profound connection between past and present.

Moriori Cultural Database

The Moriori of the Chatham Islands, New Zealand, developed a cultural database for traditional knowledge, a management plan based on Moriori aspirations and *tikane* (cultural protocols and obligations) to protect a sacred grove of *rakau momori* (living tree carvings), and ethical protocols and guidelines for research and fieldwork. This project was led by Maui Solomon and Susan Thorpe, of the Hokotehi Moriori Trust. For this community, traditional knowledge research is ethical and appropriate only when: (1) it is carried out "in country"; (2) there is an intergenerational component (i.e., youth and elders); and (3) the work is centered on a premise of reciprocity (Thorpe and Solomon 2014:21).

Moriori heritage management is situated at the nexus of reconciliation, respect, and responsibility, as exemplified in the proper course of action for caring for the *rakau momori*. From an archaeological perspective, these are culturally modified trees; for the Moriori, those images constitute living beings. Within the sacred groves, some of the trees are diseased, so the images on them were laser scanned to record and preserve information important to the community. The team also developed a cultural knowledge database for recording elders' traditional knowledge in an indigenous methodological and ethical framework to better make land-use decisions. In this process, the project also helped reconnect youth to elders through their participation (Figure 8.3). Indeed, as project

Figure 8.3. Moriori youth and family members used digital recording of laser scanning work at the Manukau *urupā* (cemetery) to sensitively preserve valued information, Chatham Islands, New Zealand. Photo courtesy of the Hokoteki Moriori Trust.

member Victor Steffensen noted, "when the young ones are behind the cameras recording elders they are listening and listening without interruption or distraction" (Thorpe and Solomon 2014:24).

Material culture retains a significant role in Moriori society. As Thorpe and Solomon note (2014:48), "If we think of the carvings as signifiers and accept that archaeology is a study that gives meaning to material evidence, then we are better informed if we understand those signifiers. We learn about culture through understanding its signifiers—the means by which we understand concepts." An important priority that developed out of this work is to obtain and preserve oral records. Solomon and Thorpe (2012:254) write:

> Hokotehi's recording work is now centred on the words, names and memories of our elders. Naming and knowledge of place is known to be strongly connected to retention of guardianship roles and duties—"a sense of place." Despite problems caused by poor or inappropriate research in the past, Hokotehi has also consciously adopted an approach in line with its core values of "sharing, unity and listening."

The Journey Home

For many Stó:lō (People of the River) of southwestern British Columbia, the process of repatriating their ancestors from the Laboratory of Archaeology (LOA) at the University of British Columbia is informed by a desire to learn as much as possible about the lives of those individuals, and to respectfully bring them home. A collaboration between Stó:lō Nation's Stó:lō Research and Resource Management Centre (SRRMC) and the LOA led by David Schaepe, Susan Rowley, and the Stó:lō House of Respect Caretaking Committee provided an opportunity to determine the types of anthropological research and scientific analyses that may be applied to answer community-based questions (Figure 8.4): Who decides which questions to ask and which means of research to implement? Who interprets the results? Who owns those data? How do "scientific" and "cultural" ways of knowing interrelate? And who is allowed to share in and benefit from this knowledge? Engaging these questions through long-term dialogue is central to the Stó:lō's relationships within and between their communities, their ancestors, and the LOA.

Participants in the House of Respect Caretaking Committee include Stó:lō community-based researchers, cultural leaders, cultural practitioners, and *shxwlá:m* (Indian doctors) who advise on repatriation and museum-related is-

Figure 8.4. Ancestors in boxes. Photo by David Campion. Courtesy of the Stó:lō Research and Resource Management Centre.

sues. Discussions between the committee members, and LOA archaeologists and bioarchaeologists facilitated the SRRMC's development of culturally appropriate guidelines for research on Stó:lō ancestors' remains. These guidelines address the community's control over processes of analysis and repatriation, including knowledge produced from such research, supporting outcomes developed "in a good way." Committee members and project partners engaged in dialogue for over six years, sharing knowledge, listening carefully, and building on each other's knowledge as they worked through framing repatriation and research processes in a Stó:lō way.

Speaking of what has been learned through the authorized studies of his ancestors, Herb Joe, a member of the Stó:lō House of Respect Caretaking Committee, stated:

What comes to mind for me is the gift of knowledge [and] awareness that is happening for use [in working] with the ancestors. The amount of knowledge that we're acquiring and will continue to acquire with the DNA samples and all that, that's going to be a gift to the Stó:lō people . . . our children, grandchildren, and great grandchildren, they're going to be healthier people with the gift of this knowledge about who they are and where they came from. (Schaepe et al. 2015:32)

Grassroots Resource Preservation and Management in Kyrgyzstan

The Kyrgyz people are passionate about their heritage and eager to share it with visitors, but their knowledge of the rich archaeological record of Kyrgyzstan is limited. The collapse of the Soviet Union in 1991 resulted in economic challenges and ethnic divisions that have affected how their history has been told and by whom. As Kubatbek Tabaldiev notes, "since Soviet Time people did not have a full understanding of the meaning and values of the cultural heritage objects. Usually, researchers came and conducted their own research, published outcomes, but did not work with local communities. . . . In general, local people know nothing about them" (Abdykanova et al. 2016:44).

The goal of the "Grassroots Resource Preservation and Management in Kyrgyzstan: Ethnicity, Nationalism and Heritage on a Human Scale" project was to develop, promote, document, and evaluate a set of small-scale heritage and cultural property preservation/education projects designed by citizens of the Kyrgyz Republic (Abdykanova et al. 2016) (Figure 8.5). Initiatives developed by the Kyrgz team included: (1) developing a management plan for an internationally significant heritage site that is an ancient architectural masterpiece with local spiritual significance; (2) preserving oral traditions unknown to younger Kyrgyz generations by reconnecting young people to their heritage and their country's resources, inspiring them to be better stewards of their material and spiritual heritage; and (3) developing plans to develop and promote cultural tourism in ways that promote but also protect important heritage places (http://www.sfu.ca/ipinch/project-components/community-based-initiatives/grassroots-resource-preservation-and-management-kyrgy/). These projects emerged from local interests and desires, with assistance provided by Kyrgyz and American team members. Reflecting on what was accomplished, team co-leader Aida Abdykanova noted that "the process of communication with local communities is one of the essential values. Another is an ideology. I have to value and understand the concept of cultural heritage in order to share your knowledge and conviction" (Abdykanova et al. 2016:46).

. . .

What is evident from these and the other community initiatives is that what we call heritage is linked to multifaceted and often complex notions of stewardship, responsibility, spirituality, and identity. Yet none of these are evident or accessible

Figure 8.5. Anne Pyburn and members of the Kyrgyzstan project meeting to share information and learn about archaeological ethics, heritage museums, and cultural centers. Photo courtesy of Caroline Beebe.

without talking with and listening to elders and other knowledge holders, and that is true even for community members. Indeed, for Yukon First Nations, "the heritage value of an object is not necessarily related to its age, rarity, or uniqueness, but rather it is determined largely on the basis of connection to community" (Carcross-Tagish First Nation et al. 2016:68).

There are also great responsibilities for both those caring for and studying heritage objects and places. The Stó:lō are enriched when ancestral human remains are studied respectfully and refer to these studies also as biographies and artifacts as belongings[7]—two seemingly simple word substitutions that make a world of difference to them.

The need to work with and for communities must be based on respect, including respect for other sets of values. Anne Pyburn notes:

[L]ocal people and Indigenous scholars live with archaeological materials throughout their lives and know what issues are related to their past that could be addressed or undermined by archaeological interpretations. Genuine respect for local people and their traditions and their human rights to use and interpret their heritage resources means that foreigners, such as me, should begin with the idea that they are working *for* the community, not *with* the community, and certainly not as project directors. (Abdykanova et al. 2016:46)

As these four examples illustrate, learning is inseparable from both the intergenerational transmission of knowledge and the cross-cultural understanding of heritage values. Being able and willing to consider unfamiliar types or conceptions of heritage leads to more effective and meaningful management or care, at least at the level of individual archaeologists and their community partners. In North America, however, heritage management decisions are generally made by government agencies implementing policies that foreground Western science-based notions of significance. The long-standing challenge for Native Americans, First Nations, Métis, and Inuit is to get the government(s) to take their fingers out of their ears and confront the legacy of colonialism.

Moving from Talking to Doing

At a 2014 workshop in British Columbia for the IPinCH-funded Secwepemc Territorial Authority (STA) initiative (http://www.sfu.ca/ipinch/project-components/community-based-initiatives/secwepemc-territorial-authority-honoring-ownership-ta/), our community partners spoke of their commitment to regain control of their heritage sites and much more—a struggle that had lasted 150 years. Chief Wayne Christian stated: "We are tired of talking; we want action." To them, heritage sites are historical, spiritual, and political points of reference and now figure prominently in their efforts to assert jurisdiction over their traditional lands, in part by forcing the provincial government to acknowledge a landmark shift from consultation to consent to usher in a long-awaited government-to-government relationship. In November 2014 several of the scholars and grassroots people associated with the STA collaborating community were invited to work with the Tsilhqot'in Nation leadership not long after the Supreme Court of Canada's landmark Williams Decision and declaration on

Aboriginal Title.[8] The court's decision in favor of the Tsilhqot'in is monumental in Canadian legal history and has helped undergird the territorial authority of the Tsilhqot'in people, as it will for many First Nations in terms of land and heritage protection efforts.[9]

The granting of title also demonstrates that the First Nations' arguments were not only heard but understood.[10] Such changes in the legal landscape, coupled with the national Truth and Reconciliation Commission and Canada recently becoming a signatory to the United Nations Declaration on the Rights of Indigenous Peoples, are important steps in addressing the historic disenfranchisement of First Nations, Inuit, and Metis and the ensuing loss of culture, language, and sovereignty.[11]

For the most part, I have found that indigenous communities are genuinely interested in what archaeology and other research practices can reveal about ancestral lifeways, as well as what ethnographies have captured concerning traditional customs prior to the impact of colonialism. In Canada and elsewhere, many indigenous groups are actively involved in archaeology, traditional knowledge recording, and even studies of ancient human remains (Brownlee and Syms 1999; Hebda, Greer, and Mackie 2017; Syms 2014). However, serious concerns loom large when research results reveal or threaten information that is not meant to be shared or cause cultural, spiritual, or economic harm. I witnessed one striking example of this at the 2008 World Archaeological Congress in Dublin, Ireland, when an Aboriginal man from the Kimberlys in Western Australia stood up during a presentation on rock art in his territory and said to the presenter, "How dare you show that image; I could die for having seen it!" (referring to the most severe level of traditional punishment for breaking customary law and revealing secret-sacred knowledge).

More broadly, there is potentially much at stake regarding academic/scientific versus community access and ownership of knowledge, restrictive versus inclusive modes of resolution, the rights of knowledge holders versus knowledge users, and legal versus customary definitions of intellectual property, along with the legal and ethical challenges of new technologies (e.g., digital repositories, 3D scanning and printing) and research initiatives. It is thus our obligation as archaeologists, heritage managers, policy-makers, and members of the public to acknowledge that we have a great responsibility here. It is not an exaggeration to say that we should conduct our research "as if someone's life is on the line," for that is exactly the case when heritage research affects a person's or group's identity, well-being, and sense of history.

Conclusions: The Politics of Listening

Heritage research has typically been oriented toward scientific goals and/or the preservation of objects and places of historical or other significance. Archaeologists, ethnoarchaeologists, and ethnographers have long worked with local communities to observe activities, ask questions, and otherwise glean knowledge of that society's way of life, past or present. This has greatly enriched anthropology's understanding of the human condition in terms of generalizing trends but has also revealed much about diversity in lifeways, past and present. Yet these efforts, which are dependent on local knowledge, have done little to benefit the descendant communities. Even those approaches oriented to *meaning*, such as phenomenology, are primarily directed to an archaeological audience. One could argue that this dependency even represents yet another type of appropriation of indigenous knowledge.

Efforts have been made to turn this around, generally within the context of postcolonial, critical, Marxist, and indigenous archaeologies. These orientations acknowledge that descendant communities *should* have decision-making roles in how *their* heritage is cared for and that they should be the primary beneficiaries of such research (Hollowell and Nicholas 2009). Efforts to reformulate ethnographic research to foreground community needs (i.e., ethnographic archaeology, among other strategies) demonstrate that this can also yield fuller and more nuanced understandings of heritage—and the meaning(s) of cultural property—that benefit the community, outside researchers, policy-makers, and even the public.

Implicit in this discussion is the need for a fuller understanding of what heritage is in different cultural contexts and, importantly, for recognizing that, to heritage holders, the physical expressions of heritage may be less important than their intangible aspects. In a sense, this places anthropologically oriented archaeologists between the proverbial rock (i.e., artifacts) and a . . . soft place (i.e., the values that give objects and places their meaning). This has presented considerable challenges to protecting indigenous heritage objects and sites. Overcoming these is not an insurmountable task, but it does require a willingness to think outside of the box (of Western values). To develop effective, equitable, and meaningful ways to acknowledge and protect heritage objects, places, and information—whether our own or anyone else's—local values and understandings must be sought out. Whether we speak of "cultural property" or "heritage," ultimately we are dealing with the essence of who people are—and that is something that deserves great care and respect. This is what I have learned by listening.

Acknowledgments

I thank Peter Schmidt and Alice Kehoe for their invitation to prepare this chapter and the other members of our traveling workshop who have contributed feedback and friendship, especially Catherine Carlson, Audrey Horning, Innocent Pikirayi, Steve Mrozowski, Jonathan Walz, Kathryn Weedman Arthur, Jagath Weerasinghe, and Billy Ó Foghlú. I appreciate Holly Cusack-McVeigh's and Chelsea Meloche's review of the final draft. Aida Abdykanova, Anne Pyburn, Sheila Greer, Susan Thorpe, Maui Solomon, Dave Schaepe, and Sue Rowley reviewed the manuscript and kindly allowed use of their photographs.

Notes

1. After years of puzzling over what could possibly connect these two seemingly disparate research areas—processual approaches to hunter-gatherers and wetlands (Nicholas 2012) and indigenous archaeology (e.g., Nicholas 2008)—I realized that there were two distinct threads. The first is "cultural landscape and sense of place," a topic central both to archaeological research questions and to contemporary indigenous lifeways and ontology. The second is "representativeness," essential not only for doing good science (re sampling) but also for integrating multiple voices and perspectives in archaeology.

2. Indeed, because archaeologists can never directly observe the behaviors that they seek to understand (as is the case with astronomers and cosmologists), the discipline has long been dependent upon analogy to make bridging inferences and draw conclusions about the archaeological record (Hodder 1982; but see Wylie 2002).

3. Along with its progeny, especially behavioral archaeology (Schiffer 2010).

4. Compare this to Jarvenpa and Brumbach's (2006) more thoughtful approach.

5. For anthropological examples of unanticipated insights, see Bohannan (1966) and Lee (1969). Working at the interface of archaeology, ethnohistory, and oral traditions, Hall (1997) sought a new understanding of ancient ceremonialism informed by Native American beliefs, which provides a foundation for more recent studies of Hopewell ritual and belief.

6. There are notable exceptions. For example, Schmidt (1997) has shown that significant benefits accrued to the local community after ethnoarchaeological study of iron smelting, ranging from overcoming negative, "primitive" representations of African technology to enhancing psychological well-being.

7. See Wilson 2016 for a comparable Musqueam Nation (British Columbia) example.

8. Also known as the Tsilhqot'in Decision, this grants Aboriginal title to the Tsilhqot'in Nation to a portion of their traditional territory and shifts the standard from "consultation" to "consent" (https://scc-csc.lexum.com/scc-csc/scc-csc/en/item/14246/index.do; accessed July 17, 2017).

9. For a fuller account, see http://www.sfu.ca/ipinch/project-components/commu-nity-based-initiatives/secwepemc-territorial-authority-honoring-ownership-ta/; ac-cessed July 17, 2017.

10. This is in stark contrast to an earlier land claims case in British Columbia, *Del-gamuukw v. Regina* (1991), in which oral testimony of both the plaintiffs and their an-thropologist experts was clearly "not heard." In his closing remarks, Chief Justice Alan McEachern (incredibly channeling Thomas Hobbes) rejected the oral histories and stated that the Gitksan-Wet'suwet'en had no economy and that "pre-contact Aboriginal life in the area was 'nasty, brutish, and short'" (McEachern 1991:75). This was challenged in *Delgamuukw v. British* Columbia (1997), in which the court ruled that oral evidence was given equal if not greater weight than written evidence.

11. Yet only months after Canada officially removed its objector status in regard to the declaration, "Justice Minister Jody Wilson-Raybould called its adaptation into Ca-nadian law 'unworkable' in a statement to the Assembly of First Nations" (http://ipoli-tics.ca/2016/07/12/ottawa-wont-adopt-undrip-directly-into-canadian-law-wilson-ray-bould/; accessed July 17, 2017).

References Cited

Abdykanova, A., K. Tabaldiev, A. Zhumbaeva, and K. A. Pyburn
2016   Grassroots Resource Preservation and Management in Kyrgyzstan—Ethnic-ity, Nationalism and Heritage on a Human Scale: IPinCH Final Project Report. http://www.sfu.ca/ipinch/project-components/community-based-initiatives/grassroots-resource-preservation-and-management-kyrgy/; accessed July 17, 2017.

Atalay, S.
2012   *Community-Based Archaeology: Research with, by, and for Indigenous and Local Communities.* University of California Press, Berkeley.

Atalay, S., L. Clauss, R. McGuire, and J. Welch (editors)
2014   *Transforming Archaeology: Activist Practices and Prospects.* Left Coast Press, Wal-nut Creek, CA.

Bell, C., and V. Napoleon
2008   Introduction. In *First Nations Cultural Heritage and Law: Case Studies, Voices, and Perspectives*, edited by C. Bell and V. Napoleon, pp. 1–30. UBC Press, Van-couver.

Binford, L. R.
1982   The Archaeology of Place. *Journal of Anthropological Archaeology* 1:5–31.
1986   An Alyawara Day: Making Men's Knives and Beyond. *American Antiquity* 51(3):547–562.

Bohannan, L.
1966   Shakespeare in the Bush. *Natural History* 75(7):28–33.

Brownlee, K., and E. L. Syms
1999   *Kayasochi Kikawenow—Our Mother from Long Ago: An Early Cree Woman and Her Personal Belongings from Nagami Bay, Southern Indian Lake.* Manitoba Mu-seum of Man and Nature, Winnipeg.

Carcross-Tagish First Nation, Champagne and Aishihik First Nations, Ta'an Kwach'an Council, Tr'ondek Hwech'in First Nation, S. Greer, and C. Bell

2016 Yukon First Nations Heritage Values and Resource Management—Perspectives from Four Yukon First Nations: IPinCH Case Study Final Report. http://www.sfu.ca/ipinch/sites/default/files/resources/reports/yfn_ipinch_report_2016.pdf; accessed July 17, 2017.

Castañeda, Q., and C. Matthews (editors)

2008 *Ethnographic Archaeologies: Reflections on Stakeholders and Archaeological Practices.* AltaMira, Lanham, MD.

Cusack-McVeigh, H.

2016 Learning to Listen: Community Collaboration in an Alaskan Native Village. *Collaborative Anthropologies* 8(1–2):40–57.

David, N., and C. Kramer

2001 *Ethnoarchaeology in Action.* Cambridge University Press, Cambridge.

Deloria, V. Jr.

1969 *Custer Died for Your Sins: An Indian Manifesto.* University of Oklahoma Press, Norman.

Ferguson. T. J., and C. Colwell-Chanthaphonh

2006 *History Is in the Land: Multivocal Tribal Traditions in Arizona's San Pedro Valley.* University of Arizona Press, Tucson.

Gould, R. A.

1980 *Living Archaeology.* Cambridge University Press, Cambridge.

Hall, R.

1997 *An Archaeology of the Soul: North American Indian Belief and Ritual.* University of Illinois Press, Urbana.

Hamilakis, Y., and A. Anagnostopoulos (editors)

2009 Archaeological Ethnographies. *Public Archaeology* 8(2–3):63–322.

Hebda, R. J., S. Greer, and A. P. Mackie

2017 *Kwäday Dän Ts'ìnchį: Teachings from Long Ago Person Found.* Royal BC Museum, Victoria.

Hodder, I.

1982 The Use of Analogy. In *The Present Past: An Introduction to Anthropology for Archaeologists,* edited by I. A. Hodder, pp. 11–27. Pen and Sword Books, London.

Hollowell, J., and G. Nicholas

2007 Archaeological Capital as Cultural Knowledge. Paper presented at the 72nd Annual Meeting of the Society for American Archaeology, Austin, Texas.

2008 A Critical Assessment of Uses of Ethnography in Archaeology. In *Ethnographic Archaeologies: Reflections on Stakeholders and Archaeological Practices,* edited by Q. Castenada and C. Matthews, pp. 63–94. AltaMira, Walnut Creek, CA.

2009 Using Ethnographic Methods to Articulate Community-based Conceptions of Cultural Heritage Management. *Public Archaeology* 8 (2–3):141–160.

Jarvenpa, R., and H. J. Brumbach

2006 Revisiting the Sexual Division of Labor: Thoughts on Ethnoarchaeology and Gender. *Archeological Papers of the American Anthropological Association* 16:97–107.

Kroeber, T.

1961   *Ishi in Two Worlds*. University of California Press, Berkeley.

Lee, R.

1969   Eating Christmas in the Kalahari. *Natural History* 75(12):14–22, 60–63.

Lydon, J., and U. Rizvi

2010   *Handbook of Postcolonial Archaeology*. Left Coast Press, Walnut Creek, CA.

Lyons, N.

2013   *Where the Wind Blows Us: Practicing Critical Community Archaeology in the Canadian North*. University of Arizona Press, Tucson.

McEachern, Allan

1991   Reasons for Judgement: Delgamuukw v. B.C. Supreme Court of British Columbia, Smithers, British Columbia.

McLay, E., K. Bannister, L. Joe, B. Thom, and G. P. Nicholas

2008   A'lhut tu tet Sul'hweentst "Respecting the Ancestors": Understanding Hul'qumi'num Heritage Laws and Concerns for Protection of Archaeological Heritage. In *First Nations Cultural Heritage and Law: Case Studies, Voices and Perspectives*, edited by C. Bell and V. Napoleon, pp. 158–202. UBC Press, Vancouver.

Nicholas, G. P.

2008   Native Peoples and Archaeology (Indigenous Archaeology). In *The Encyclopedia of Archaeology*, vol. 3, edited by D. Pearsall, pp. 1660–1669. Elsevier, Oxford.

2012   Toward an Anthropology of Wetland Archaeology: Hunter-Gatherers and Wetlands in Practice and Theory. In *The Oxford Handbook of Wetland Archaeology*, edited by R. Menotti and A. O'Sullivan, pp. 761–778. Oxford University Press, Oxford.

2014a   Why Heritage Is Not Just About "Things." *TEDx Talk*. https://www.youtube.com/watch?v=HbPLXTJwVMY; accessed July 17, 2017.

2014b   Indigenous Archaeology (Archaeology, Indigenous). In *Oxford Bibliographies of Anthropology*, edited by J. L. Jackson. Oxford University Press, Oxford. http://www.oxfordbibliographies.com/view/document/obo-9780199766567/obo-9780199766567-0073.xml?rskey=oOVETa&result=83; accessed July 17, 2017.

2017   Touching the Intangible: Situating Material Culture in the Realm of Indigenous Heritage Research. In *The Routledge Companion to Cultural Property*, edited by H. Geismar and J. Anderson, pp. 212–231. Routledge, London.

2018   Converging or Contradictory Ways of Knowing: Assessing the Scientific Nature of Traditional Knowledge. *Traditional Ecological Knowledge*, U.S. National Parks Service. https://www.nps.gov/subjects/tek/george-nicholas.htm.

Noble, B.

2008   Owning as Belonging/Owning as Property: The Crisis of Power and Respect in First Nations Heritage Transactions with Canada. In *First Nations Cultural Heritage and Law: Case Studies, Voices, and Perspectives*, edited by C. Bell and V. Napoleon, pp. 465–488. UBC Press, Vancouver.

Porcic, M.

2010   House Floor Area as a Correlate of Marital Residence Pattern: A Logistic Regression Approach. *Cross-Cultural Research* 44:405–424.

Schaepe, D. M., S. Rowley, Stó:lō Xyolhmet S'olhetawtxw Sq'éq'ip (Stó:lō House of Respect Committee) Members, with D. Weston, and M. Richards

2015   The Journey Home—Guiding Intangible Knowledge Production in the Analysis of Ancestral Remains: IPinCH Final Project Report. http://www.sfu.ca/ipinch/resources/reports/journeyhome/; accessed July 17, 2017.

Schiffer, M. B.

2010   *Behavioral Archaeology: Principles and Practice.* Equinox, London.

Schmidt, P.

1997   *Iron Technology in East Africa: Symbolism, Science, and Archaeology.* University of Indiana Press, Bloomington.

2017   *Community-Based Heritage in Africa: Unveiling Local Research and Development Initiatives.* Routledge, New York.

Schmidt, P., and I. Pikirayi (editors)

2016   *Community Archaeology and Heritage in Africa: Decolonizing Practice.* Taylor and Francis, London.

Skeates, R., C. McDavid, and J. Carman (editors)

2012   *The Oxford Handbook of Public Archaeology.* Oxford University Press, Oxford.

Solomon, M., and S. Thorpe

2012   *Taonga Moriori*: Recording and Revival. *Journal of Material Culture* 17(3):245–263.

Syms, E. L.

2014   *Stories of the Old Ones from the Lee River, Southeastern Manitoba: The Owl Inini, Carver Inini, and Dancer Ikwe.* Manitoba Museum, Winnipeg.

Thorpe, S., and M. Solomon

2014   Moriori Cultural Database: Hokoteki Moriori Trust and IPinCH Project Final Report. http://www.sfu.ca/ipinch/project-components/community-based-initiatives/moriori-cultural-database/; accessed July 17, 2017.

Wilson, D.

1851   *The Archaeology and Prehistoric Annals of Scotland.* University of Edinburgh, Edinburgh.

Wilson, J.

2016   "Belongings" in "c̓əsnaʔəm: The City before the City." http://www.sfu.ca/ipinch/outputs/blog/citybeforecitybelongings/; accessed July 17, 2017.

Wylie, A.

2002   *Thinking from Things: Essays in the Philosophy of Archaeology.* University of California Press, Berkeley.

Zimmerman, L. J.

2010   Archaeology through the Lens of the Local. In *Archaeology in Situ: Local Perspectives on Archaeology, Archaeologists, and Sites in Greece*, edited by A. Stroulia and S. Buck Sutton, pp. 473–480. Lexington Books, Lanham, MD.

9

Listening and Waiting, Excavating Later

PETER R. SCHMIDT

"What is the magic in cranberries?" he asked the Indians again
and again. And they'd laugh at him. Or they'd say, "There's nothing
magical. It's just a good job, if you don't mind getting wet." . . . "But
I know these Indians think cranberries are magical," the director
said. "They just don't want to share the magic."

Blasphemy *by Sherman Alexie*

A novelist and social critic, Sherman Alexie is one of America's most accomplished Native American storytellers. His sentiment about white men and listening arises out of a short-story dialogue, but it wells up from deep inside a
long legacy of Native American experience with white settler colonialism and
domination. Alexie's pithy statement transcends geography or ethnicity to act
as a powerful proxy for marginalized people around the globe, those stripped
of identity and history by colonial experiences. The sentiment penetrates to the
core of how histories of the colonized have been written—with the white men
talking and writing and ignoring the voices of those whose land they have taken
and whose histories they have co-opted or erased. Sherman Alexie's Spokane
persona dances, universally, across other landscapes, constantly reminding us
that local identity is malleable, always subject to new manipulations and era-
sures, no matter what skin colors or nationalities are involved.

The failure to listen and learn from local knowledge systems is a hallmark
of colonialism. It has led to myriad policy and development failures in for-

mer colonized part of the world that ruined entire societies and left behind a wasteland of shredded identities. History is an integral part of the project of talking, not listening. African societies and their histories came out of rich oral literature that exhibited complex genres and ways of preservation. This was a very vulnerable way of maintaining historical records in the face of highly developed Western bureaucracy that demanded literacy as entre to power and privilege. Explicit expectations for literacy in writing colonial history excluded the nonliterate—a purposeful repression of oral literatures and a colonial determination *not to listen.* Simultaneously, colonial chroniclers wrote during conditions of imposition, repression, conflict, failed projects, and a host of other conflict-filled circumstances in which white Western perspectives prevailed. When colonial authorities occasionally listened to and accepted advice of local elites (usually on their payrolls), they did so at significant peril—finding that popular uprisings against elites often implicated the colonial government in awkward disputes with popular opposition groups in local society (Curtis 1989).

I was fortunate to begin my professional career in a superb setting for better understanding how colonial silencing and postcolonial listening unfolded over the colonial and postcolonial periods in Buhaya, a verdant hilly landscape west of Lake Victoria (Schmidt 1978). The Bantu-speaking Haya have a deep history attached to monumental landscape features, such as a 2,000-year-old memorial to the origins and significance of iron production in this region, between Rwanda and the lake. The stories I share about an archaeology of listening start in Buhaya, back to 1966, when, as a young postgraduate student at Makerere University in Uganda, I first visited this region with fellow students to observe the capital site of Karagwe Kingdom (once famous in Europe because the king hosted John Hanning Speke and James Grant), contiguous to eastern Rwanda. That visit provoked additional inquiry into the history of the region, a rich published literature that included a German ethnography (Rehse 1910) and extensive indigenous publications by F. X. Lwamgira (e.g., 1949a, 1949b), local administrator and historian.

Impressed by an extensive lineage of colonial observations and a surprisingly rich corpus of indigenous research into myth, oral traditions, folktales, and marriage customs, I returned to the region in early 1969 to continue research into how the Haya constructed their histories across social groups and time, using archaeology to enrich the tapestry of history. As I launched my research, I was keenly aware of my personal ignorance of how local people imagined their historical past, present, and future. It was patently clear that the practice of archaeology in such a setting required a thorough familiarity with the historical landscape—before an archaeology asking significant questions was possible. By necessity, my relationships with knowledge keepers in villages quickly developed to the point where I became an apprentice to a scattered group of key elders with extraordinary knowledge—elders who then passed me around to their circle of like-minded friends and relatives. Recognition of this relationship within the wider community carried the understanding that I was both a student and an apprentice who was learning the oral traditions and histories of the Haya (Schmidt 2017a).

Given this start to my field research, some have asked: "Why were you moving around Haya villages talking with elders and not excavating?" My response: I was learning history and landscape from local knowledge keepers with the anticipation that my hybrid perspectives could help unveil African histories heretofore hidden from view. My training came from anthropologists Stuart Struever and Frank Willett and historians John Rowe and Ivor Wilks, the latter two having worked and lived for decades in African communities, valorizing oral testimonies alongside archival and archaeological research.[1] This background, this way of seeing history, brought a perspective to the field that advocated settling in and understanding how local folks lived historically informed lives, how they played out historical knowledge in daily performances, and how the landscape was structured and given meaning by local cultural beliefs. It was critical to understand answers to these questions before I could be so bold as to put an archaeological shovel to the ground.

It was important to understand local ideas about the most important sites, the most significant ritual centers of great antiquity, and the most memorable places before I could make an informed decision about where I should or might excavate. If I succeeded in building the trust of local communities, then, with their guidance, I might be able to help explore historical questions of significance to them and to me—something that stuck out as a significant issue in their lives and in the way that their history was represented to others. In retrospect, this approach had strong affinities with the practice of participatory community research (see Atalay 2012; Colwell-Chanthaphonh and Ferguson 2008; Hollowell and Nicholas 2009; Pyburn 2003; Schmidt and Pikirayi 2016; Smith and Jackson 2008; and Smith and Waterton 2012 for examples of community-driven and participatory research that incorporates ethnographic methods and best ethical practice).

An Apprenticeship

For the first 10 months of a 20-month stay, I settled into three different villages in Buhaya to learn about local and religious myth and history (Map 9.1). Along the way, after scores of interviews and conversations, I came to see a natural intersection of perspectives: my awareness that a sacred site called Kaiija (Place of the Forge) was a central historical focus and interest of elders in central coastal Buhaya; and the encouragement by these same elders, excited by possible findings, that I (we) should undertake excavations at Kaiija. I remember thinking when the elders openly said that they wanted to see what was under the Kaiija tree shrine that they were deeply curious and committed historians. I followed their advice, because I, too, was tantalized by the legend of King Rugomora

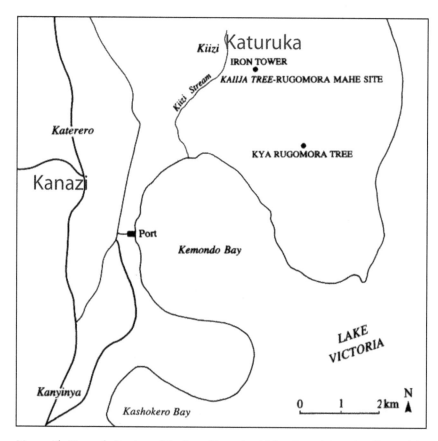

Map 9.1. The Kemondo Bay Area of Northwest Tanzania, with locations of Katuruka village and the sacred shrines of Kaiija and Kya Rugomora.

Mahe, who supposedly built an iron tower at Kaiija, with one of its legs at a distant shrine called Kya Rugomora. The royal capital compound of King Rugomora, who lived at the end of the seventeenth century, was built around this ancient local shrine as a means of co-opting its heritage power and legitimacy over the centuries (Schmidt 1978, 2006, 2013, 2017a).

Our first excavation, conducted by local villagers thoroughly trained in the methods of archaeology and overseen by elders (Schmidt 2014a), was placed precisely where the elders marked the location of an iron forge used to construct the iron tower (Schmidt 1978, 2006, 2013). As we worked as an integrated team with many from nearby residential units, I realized that we were engaged in testing an indigenous research hypothesis—that iron production evidence linked to the iron tower story was located in this zone beneath the Kaiija shrine (Map 9.2)—but only years later realized the implications of that engagement

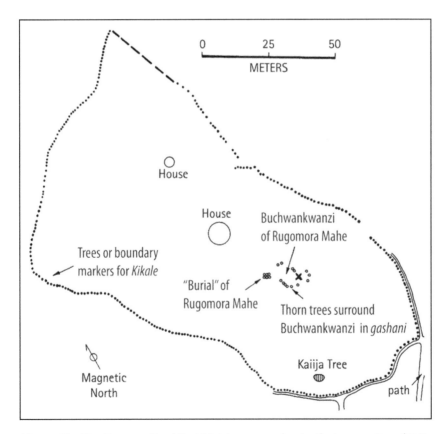

Map 9.2. The King Rugomora Royal Burial Estate, ca. 1970, showing the incorporation of Kaiija shrine within the core of the seventeenth-century palace compound.

vis-à-vis the principles of community-based participatory research. The research design arose from local knowledge, and its implementation was both participatory and collaborative.

As predicted by the elders, the first distinct feature to be uncovered was a pit with slag and charcoal. Upon exposing the boundaries of the pit and then setting this feature into broader spatial context, it proved to be a forge 2,000+ years old (Schmidt 1978, 1997), much older than King Rugomora's regime 300+ years ago. Additional examination of the oral texts showed clearly that woven into the legends of King Rugomora were ancient Cwezi (mythological) narratives (Schmidt 2006, 2013), showing a conscious attempt by the usurper Hinda clan to disguise its takeover of an ancient shrine by creating an identity with Cwezi myths and thus creating the illusion of a regime of great antiquity (see Kaindoa 2013 and Schmidt 1978 for the original text). Initial scholarly reactions from the most influential historian of Africa deeply betrayed a profound misunderstanding of the role of local participants: "It would be becoming to acknowledge that there had been an element of luck as well as of judgment in his discovery" (Oliver 1979:290). This perspective ignores local knowledge and leadership—no surprise for the era when this was written. Agency from the perspective of this outside observer/reader was through my activities, as if I was isolated from, separated from, and unaware of my intimate relationships.

The iron forge (and its associated structural remains) beneath the Kaiija shrine tree came to be recognized as the most ancient iron working in eastern Africa, remembered and affirmed by the monumental attributes of the shrine. Given the presence of late first millennium BCE dates in the Early Iron Age assemblage (Clist 1987; Schmidt and Childs 1985), the Kaiija phenomenon dates to the latter first millennium BCE, a remarkable time depth for oral traditions about the specific function of archaeological features to remain viable, but not so remarkable when juxtaposed to Mesopotamian oral accounts of exceptional complexity preserved over hundreds of years (Schmidt 2006).

An ensuing debate arose over dating of oral traditions linked to iron production. An age of 2,000+ years for oral traditions seemed much too old and apparently inconsistent with three occupational periods for some to accept—a heresy against the scripture of literacy (Oliver 1979).[2] This notion was put to rest with the recognition that conditions of continuity prevailed at neighboring sites with more detailed dating (Clist 1987; Schmidt and Childs 1985) and with the recognition of Kaiija's use as a sacred site through deep time and through the control of several religious cults (Schmidt 2017a).[3]

We came to learn that frequent and long-lived ritual performances by different but interrelated cults over 2,000 years ensured continuity in the core meaning of the Kaiija shrine (Schmidt 2013, 2017a). For anthropology and history, this recognition introduces a new understanding of the capacity for longevity of oral accounts, a deep-time antiquity at odds with Western refusal to listen, living within a colonial paradigm (e.g., Mason 2000). No matter how little Euro-centric historians dislike dating oral genres to such deep antiquity, the association will not go away. It is a critical insight into the antiquity of oral accounts on landscapes deeply configured by local cultures over deep time. The Kaiija tree shrine marks a major shift away from the Western paradigm about oral traditions incapable of deep antiquity (Schmidt 2006).

As a young apprentice of Haya history, I was often lost in the detail and troubled by not seeing historical problems of high value that might merit archaeological inquiry. As I was wrapping up my initial oral tradition inquiries, my focus was also pulled to documenting huge iron smelting sites on the landscape while I was trying simultaneously to understand the historical importance of ritual sites that repeatedly appeared in local discourses (Schmidt 1978). My elderly guides helped me regain a focus on significant historical problems when they encouraged me to stop listening to their stories and start listening to their advice as to where it was important to expand knowledge about the past (for additional insights into the genesis of mutuality in community engagements, see Pikirayi and Schmidt 2016; Pyburn 2003; Smith and Waterton 2012; Tully 2007). Once I began to follow their path, a surprisingly rich array of insights and contributions unfolded over the next decade. What if I had listened to only their narratives rather than to the tellers of the narratives? Had I continued to examine just the narrative forms or had I continued to devote significant attention to survey and test excavations without the intervention of elders, then this paradigm shift in the antiquity of oral traditions and the role of ritual performance in maintaining threads of continuity would have been lost to our scholarly discourse.

Listening with Interruptions, Awakening to Female Knowledge Keepers

My next narrative about the value of an archaeology of listening has its origins during the same period—the beginning of my career as an archaeologist and my collection of oral testimonies in the same subregion south of Bukoba town. As I listened to scores of oral testimonies years ago, my ear was attuned to oral traditions linked to sacred sites and other physical places of cultural importance, foremost among them the Kaiija shrine. As I now reflect on this experience, I see, again, that it fits closely with today's participatory community approach. What I did was congruent with local cultural sensibilities; it was also in keeping with my apprenticeship to the most knowledgeable keepers of oral accounts to follow the lead and advice of local collaborators; and I was able to reach a deeper understanding of Haya history based on mutual respect (Schmidt 1978, 1997, 2010, 2017a). Yet participatory approaches of this era also carried with them entrenched androcentric ideas about who could and who could not be trusted to provide reliable testimonies.

This issue first arose when I interviewed a female spirit medium in northern Buhaya in 1969. My male counterparts in Kiziba Kingdom quickly and pointedly questioned me as to why I was engaged in such an interaction and warned that I had best pay attention to my relationships in their circle (Schmidt 2017a). As disquieting as it was at the time, this experience captured a norm in Haya culture—suppression of female voices in matters pertaining to history and culture, a perspective that was amplified by a discipline-wide and colonial proclivity to filter local testimonies through male points of view. I was captured as much by my own background as I was by local values.

Moving Forward

When I first started inquiries into the history of Rugomora Mahe and the Kaiija shrine tree, my focus with local counterparts was to collect multiple accounts of many different genres of oral traditions, including royal Hinda clan history, Cwezi oral traditions, and the relationship of King Rugomora to the Kaiija shrine in Katuruka village (Schmidt 2006, 2013, 2017a). During my initial study, collaborating elders told me that a "caretaker" once lived in the palace house in the burial estate of King Rugomora where the Kaiija shrine tree was also situated. Each time I inquired about this person, I was told only that she or he had abandoned the site in the early 1960s. Beyond such comments, silence prevailed; I failed to elicit specific answers about where the caretaker had decamped to and why. Reflecting on this now, I wonder: if I had pressed harder, would I have learned more about this individual and her or his role at the shrine and burial estate? Yet such reflexivity is overwhelmed by the values that then inhibited free inquiry into histories held by women (Schmidt 2017a). When testimonies were conveyed by privileged voices of powerful males, I was powerless to interdict such practice (especially in my role as apprentice), so female histories remained subaltern, out of circulation, outside of discourse. I have also learned over more than four decades that my restricted ability to listen to female voices within collaborative settings of the late 1960s and 1970s was as subject to change as other cultural practices that developed vulnerability with the coming of HIV/AIDS in Buhaya (Schmidt 2010).

Culture Change and HIV/AIDS

After an absence of more than two decades from Buhaya, I returned in 2008 to find communities living under the pall of HIV/AIDS (e.g., Lwihula et al. 1993; Mutembei 2001; Ndamugoba et al. 2000; Rugalema 1999). The people of Katuruka village, the location of the Kaiija shrine and the burial estate of King Rugomora, were living without hope and with a deeply eroded sense of identity (Schmidt 2010, 2014a, 2014b, 2017a). Out of my social visit came an invitation to participate in an initiative by village elders to inquire into their oral traditions and sacred sites, to preserve their heritage knowledge for future generations. What followed was my deep engagement with Katuruka-initiated research during which I was a key collaborator and co-producer—a trajectory in my professional career that I did not anticipate at the time.

The Katuruka initiative first acknowledged that the profile of keepers of knowledge had changed significantly. The death of a disproportionate number of elderly males during the HIV/AIDS pandemic had changed how and by whom history was kept and disseminated (Schmidt 2010, 2017a). Instead of dominantly male collaborators/participants, females were openly recognized as the new keepers of historical knowledge. This transformation in heritage values brought to the surface vitally important subaltern accounts held by women (Schmidt 2010, 2014b, 2016). During inquiries led by local elders, female elders emerged as some of the most prominent keepers of oral knowledge, a major break from previous norms of androcentric control over heritage knowledge. By listening closely to elderly women, we together learned of a heretofore unrecognized female ritual authority with significant political and religious power in the region (Schmidt 2017a). Driven underground by dominant male discourses, these subaltern accounts significantly revise our interpretation of one of Africa's most sacred shrines, Kaiija, and the religious and political roles of its ritual officiant (Figures 9.1a and 9.1b).

Female elders of Katuruka revealed during interviews that life surrounding the burial estate of King Rugomora was deeply influenced and governed by a

Figure 9.1. Two descendants of ritual officials of the Balama clan that supervised New Moon ceremonies: (*above*) Ma Eudes Bambanza at age 86 (2009); (*below*) Ma Zuriat Mohamed at age 71 (2009). Photos by author.

female ritual official named Njeru (the White Sheep). Njeru was married in 1900 to King Rugomora (d. 1675), a marriage that transformed the 12-year-old virgin into the bride of King Rugomora as well as the ritual officiant of his burial estate. In this capacity, she was responsible for oversight of the monthly New Moon rituals that renewed the kingdom's prosperity (Schmidt 2014a, 2014b, 2016, 2017a). Moreover, she was called a king, received tribute from those living within the huge burial estate (the former royal holdings), and was a much respected and revered patron and neighbor. Once male participants realized that Njeru was being openly discussed among female peers, they eagerly contributed their memories of her. We listened closely, amazed with the contrast to past testimonies and intent to learn about a powerful community member heretofore treated with silence.

While conducting interviews, my male counterparts were deeply attentive to narratives about Njeru, hanging on each word and wanting to explore details with follow-up interviews. They knew little about her history and its significance, though some who were raised next door to her palace had detailed information about her life. Among the most significant findings was the role of Njeru in New Moon ceremonies. As part of the monthly ritual of renewal, Njeru oversaw ritual processes conducted by Cwezi spirit mediums at Kaiija shrine (Schmidt 2016, 2017a). The Cwezi cult had earlier co-opted ancestral spirit possession of animals such as leopards and snakes (also associated with renewal rites) by social groups with long occupation on the landscape and their own histories of appropriating places associated with nature spirits. The ancestors of ancient social groups, such as the Bayango iron workers, possessed animals associated with key shrines like Kaiija and Kya Rugomora—later appropriated by the Cwezi *kubandwa* cult at the turn of the second millennium AD and then taken over and transformed by the Hinda royals in the seventeenth century. This final appropriation was manifest when the spirit of King Rugomora possessed a snake, which was kept by Njeru and her long line of ancestral predecessors.

Understanding of Njeru and her significance to the heritage of the Haya and, more broadly, the Great Lakes region, developed from interviews that project leader Benjamin Shegesha conducted with Ma Eudes Bambanza, Ma Zuriat Mohamed, Ma Eudes's brother Leveriani Bambanza, and Faustin Kamaleki, once a neighbor and then the CCM (Chama Cha Mapinduzi) regional party secretary (Schmidt 2017a). As we listened to these participants in the Katuruka project, we learned that Njeru was a descendant of the clan of King Rugomora's first wife. As a member of that clan, her marriage to King Rugomora marked an important thread of continuity through the centuries. Considered a *mukama* (king) by her subjects, she could withdraw their estates or levy fines against those who disobeyed her will, even the local king of Maruku: "People received her with great honor; the palace was built, fences were erected and by protocol she was higher than the Mukama of Maruku. If she became angry, heads of cattle had to be paid" (Ma Eudes Bambanza, November 26, 2009, Katuruka; Schmidt 2017a).

During our first interview with Eudes Bambanza, Benjamin asked her about the sacred Kaiija shrine and its associated rituals, a line of questioning that provoked her to share memories of Njeru and her snake—the spirit of Rugomora Mahe:

> As far as I know the *snake . . . used to come to Njeru and coil three times on her thighs.* That snake used to drink milk. It did not stay long; it went back to its house. . . . There was the house of Rugomora the Great [later the palace house of Njeru]. *It was there that he [King Rugomora] came out as the snake which married the woman.* (Ma Eudes Bambanza, November 26, 2009, Katuruka; emphasis added; Schmidt 2017a)

Perhaps the most remarkable occurrence in this interchange is Benjamin's close listening to Eudes's narrative in my presence. In years past, say, 20–30 years ago, he would never have discussed Njeru, let alone pursue the topic during a historical conversation—the usual androcentric treatment of oral history (Schmidt 2017a). Yet, in the throes of vast losses of oral heritage, Benjamin was hyperattentive to any shreds of Katuruka's past that might emerge during the project. Njeru's life, and the proscriptions placed on it, fascinated Benjamin, who as a younger man missed knowing Njeru because of his residence outside the village. He and I learned:

> But she, too, wanted to be happy . . . she . . . could [not] bring a boyfriend into Nyaruju [the palace]. . . . In Nyaruju no beer was kept; people brought beer in their containers, enough to drink while they conversed in the house. (Ma Eudes Bambanza, November 26, 2009, Katuruka; Schmidt 2017a)

Eudes explicitly mentioned the prohibitions placed on Njeru's romantic life and the types of tribute brought to the royal palace. Months later, Eudes's brother Leveriani elaborated on the topic of Njeru's romantic life, ending with a tour of the former farms and homes of her forbidden paramours—a distinctly male perspective that also emphasized the misfortunes of those who forgot to respect taboos about any sexual contact with Njeru.

It is Njeru's role as spiritual coordinator and head of royal rites at Kaiija and the royal burial estate that interests us most. Her marriage to Rugomora's spirit through a snake is a deep-seated metaphor for reproduction. Fertility, already the central symbolic axis of the Kaiija shrine due to its association with reproductive metaphors associated with iron working, is a core focus. Reproduction is renewal, a continuation into the future. The snake trope in this instance is transforming: It was the king again uniting with his virgin wife Njeru—always re-represented as a recent bride. Zuriat, a member of the clan handling ritual protocols at New Moon, shared an enlightening perspective on Njeru's relationship with the snake. "The ancient Mukama was represented by Njeru, who was regarded as his wife. On such occasions she was regarded as a *newlywed bride*. That is what it meant, the appearance of the Mukama" (Ma Zuriat Mohamed, December 1, 2009; Schmidt 2017a). Thus, with the advent of New Moon ceremonies, Njeru became a newly wedded bride to Rugomora: we witness yet another ritual renewal, transforming Njeru's status from his wife to his new bride. New Moon was also a time when trusted advisors took up residence at Njeru's and neighbors, kin, and subjects gathered to celebrate; these minifestivals, often called bacchanals among elders today, included the performance of the royal orchestra beneath the Kaiija tree:

People came from Maruku and it became a great festivity, that appearance of Mukama [Rugomora Mahe] at the occasion of the New Moon. . . . I even witnessed the royal orchestra at Kaiija when it came there at the occasion of the New Moon. On that day one heard the orchestra. I worked there. I am explaining what I witnessed. *I saw Mukama Njoka [snake]*. The day the Mukama appeared, we made a great celebration; we ate and drank. . . . I worked there, following instructions [and giving instructions] to those who came to work under my supervision of six years. (Ma Zuriat Mohamed, December 1, 2009, Katuruka; emphasis added; Schmidt 2017a)

The king's spirit within the snake was empowered to mate with Njeru, his wife and new bride. The son of one ritual official told us:

She would sit, legs stretched out, and the snake would come onto her thighs; that is, her husband slept with her. . . . Those were magic happenings. It knew that she was already clean and it came and got on her thighs. She stretched out her legs, it settled on her thighs for some time and then left. (Ta Leveriani Bambanza, May 1, 2010, Katuruka; emphasis added; Schmidt 2017a)

Lest we begin to think this narrative is influenced by the gender of the story-teller, similar interpretations are found among many women, as when Ma Zuriat made perfectly clear her understanding of Njeru's ritual role in reproduction:

How can you explain a marriage between a snake and a human being? *But at the time when the snake was about to appear, Njeru was smeared with fat.* People like my father would not sleep on their beds. If I am pulling your leg, go and ask another person. On that day, there was plenty of beer for your fathers and grandfathers. *It was a feast. It was the arrival of the king. Njeru was as quiet and collected as a new bride on wedding day. The fat was dripping from her face. Then the snake came and rolled itself and coiled on her naked body.* We children were told to keep away but we understood what was happening. . . . I wish I could take Maria [her daughter] to where such marvels still exist. How lucky those people in the past were! (Ma Zuriat Mohamed, May 10, 2010, Katuruka; emphasis added; Schmidt 2017a)

Even women raised outside the ritual orbit acknowledged the reproductive power of Njeru's ritual coupling with Rugomora:

No, sir! I am glad I didn't see it. Up to now I hear people [only] talk about it. Even when I walk at midday when it is very warm, *I ask myself, "What should I do if I met the snake which lived here and which people said copu-lated with Njeru?"* But I pass and go my way. That thought does not deter me from walking by. (Ernestina John, April 9, 2010, Katuruka; emphasis added; Schmidt 2017a)

Once liberated from values under which they had silenced female voices, men also significantly enriched knowledge about Njeru. A former next-door neighbor vividly remembered seeing Njeru with the snake during New Moon ceremonies:

It [the snake] was spotted. I remember it had a few spots. *Njeru stretched her legs and the snake came; then something mysterious happened. She sat respectfully in there. When the snake came and entered, it crossed Njeru's thighs. He came to marry.* . . . Oh, then bulls were slaughtered, now meat was roasted. All the people worshiped respectively. Before the snake ar-rived, all the people assembled, for it is the day Njeru became wife of King Rugomora. Thereafter Rugomora Mahe, through the form of this snake, disappeared into the plantation. . . . I witnessed that when I was a small child. That was a big celebration. That was the ceremonial marriage of that day. (Faustin Kamaleki, February 2, 2010, Katuruka; emphasis added; Schmidt 2017a)

Through their participation in the Katuruka heritage project, women were instrumental in making the key research contributions in ways not previously imagined. They warmly embraced the need to discuss topics and activities once woven into their daily lives at the Kaiija shrine and King Rugomora's burial estate. As significant knowledge appeared in their narratives, so, too, did women develop an awareness that they had important contributions to make to local history as well as the heritage project within their village (Schmidt 2017a).

These never-before-recorded narratives open new historical vistas and deeply enrich the substance of ritual history and politics in east-central Africa. Elaborate narratives about rites of reproduction that incorporated symbolic copulation with King Rugomora are ethnographic revelations; no similar phenomena are recorded in eastern Africa, though there are bits and pieces, really scraps, of information about a python cult dedicated to fertility rites, suggesting that such rites occurred at Kaiija long before King Rugomora (Roscoe 1909; Schoenbrun 2014; Tantala 1989). The extension of power of Njeru's office to include sanctions against the local king, the exclusion of the king from Njeru's palace or burial estate, and the confiscation of plantations from a wide variety of people, including princes speak to significant political autonomy unknown outside the traditional political structure.

Njeru ruled during a political vacuum caused by colonial machinations with several Haya kingdoms that meant the loss of the Kanyangereko section (chiefdom) of Bukara to her archrival and competitor, King Kahigi II at Kanazi Palace of Kihanja Kingdom. Njeru took advantage of opportunities to exercise her power and authority from her base in Katuruka after traditional patterns of power were interrupted by intrigues and colonial gullibility. In 1900 King Kahigi pulled off a successful ruse—deceiving German authorities by planting guns in the house of the prime minister of his kinsman and neighboring king in Bukara (across Kemondo Bay to the east). Kahigi's hegemony over Kanyangereko (of which Katuruka is a part) unfolded the same time that Kahigi appointed Njeru as the ritual officiant at Kaiija shrine. Thrust into this political breach, Njeru became a new and vital authority, working with her troop of serving girls and drawing on the tribute of those within Kanyangereko to lead a prosperous life filled with ritual festivals that drew widely on her capacity to receive local tribute.[4]

Beyond the informative testimonies, there is little knowledge about the ritual requirements of Njeru's office. Lwamgira (1949a), a local administrator and historian, identifies the office as *muka gashani* (wife of the burial estate, i.e., the king) in Kiziba Kingdom, north of Bukara.[5] Information from the White Fathers' diary at Kashozi Mission relates how Catholic nuns took special notice of young girls who carried out these ritual duties at the burial estates of Kiziba. They had fallen on hard times, forgotten by their patron, the King of Kiziba. Severe internal conflicts for the throne and other difficulties made sustaining the royal house very difficult. Seen as destitute victims, some of these girls were encouraged to settle at Kashozi Mission and take up Christian practices (Larsson 1991). No other mention prepares us for the scale of influence and power that such ritual officiants could rise to. The heritage research initiative in Katuruka was energized by these revelations. The organizing committee and research participants both realized that Kaiija and the *gashani* estate had been enriched with a powerful new dimension to their common heritage. The Katuruka-initiated research makes a major contribution to East African and Tanzanian history.

Because the ritual office of Njeru relates so specifically to the content and structure of the Rugomora Mahe site, it also holds great significance for heritage specialists and archaeologists seeking better interpretation of the spatial orientation of sacred structures and activities. During the Katuruka project, villagers took the initiative to reconstruct the Buchwankwanzi ("Spitting Pearls") house of King Rugomora. Buchwankwanzi was the house in which the king entertained his closest advisors and consulted his Cwezi spirit mediums (Schmidt 2017a; Figure 9.2). After the king's death, it became the depository for his relics: his knives, his shield, his ritual hoes, the ritual paddles of Mugasha (god of waters and storms), his spears, his stool, and other key paraphernalia. Each Buchwankwanzi was an ancient museum for the Haya, a place where the material symbols of kingship were curated, helping to activate and retain memories. It was also the location of the king's jawbone or skull, kept over time as part of the royal memorabilia. Buchwankwanzi was a key ritual structure for Njeru, a place where she continued to consult spirit mediums and advisors and where she used King Rugomora's regalia in the New Moon rituals of renewal. Buchwankwanzi was at the ritual core of the burial estate, a placement verified by archaeological evidence. With an archaeology of listening, a more complete interpretation of Katuruka heritage now compellingly includes Njeru's ritual and political activities.

Figure 9.2. The Buchwankwanzi house constructed by the Katuruka committee in 2010. In the past it hosted the diviners of King Rugomora and then the diviners of Njeru. It also served as the repository of the ritual regalia of King Rugomora, a function related to its service as a museum today. Photo by author.

Listening and Then Forgetting—Then Listening Again

Listening ipso facto places one in an advantageous position to understand how and why Haya changed in their concerns over what is significant heritage in village life. Shortly after the Katuruka community project was launched, we were again called on to listen, this time to a call for action from a local primary school near Katuruka village. The headmaster wanted us to examine some human skulls and long bones gathered by students as part of a biology lesson that led to more than chicken and cattle bones being brought to class. At the time, we were very busy, right in the middle of Katuruka interviews. Benjamin Shegesha was taken by the idea, so we made time to travel to Nyarubale Primary School to look at the bones from a nearby rock shelter. Such a significant and unexplained presence of human remains caused us to return to organize the materials and document the rock shelter (Figures 9.3a and 9.3b). We found high-caliber bullet wounds in several of the skulls, suggesting death by gunshot (Daniels 2013). Not one of the elders in neighboring villages could explain the reason(s) for the presence of ancestors in a rocky ledge, let alone how some came to die from gunshot wounds.

Benjamin and I took the problem to the Katuruka committee, which incorporated an appropriate line of questioning among its experts, finding that not one person could recall loss of life leading to the placing of dead kin at Mazinga Cave. This left us at a dead end. Then I remembered something that I had forgotten for 40 years: my record of several detailed texts from 1969, spelling out the order of battle and command and the ultimate massacre that resulted below Kanazi Palace at the border with Kihanja Kingdom. I did not remember the theme or the core focus of these oral traditions, long ago recorded, archived, and forgotten, until I helped pose a direct question about significant killings near Katuruka.

I remembered that in 1969 I listened to and recorded several oral accounts with highly specific details about a major massacre of local people by the German military government, approximately in 1901. I also remembered that at the time I heard these oral accounts I was struck by the magnitude of the killings, several times asking my collaborations to repeat their testimony. These conversations took place during the same months when other elders were guiding me to Kaiija, when I roamed the villages listening to and learning from elders for months. It was some months before I could excavate my archives back in Florida and identify the oral traditions of great historical importance. I was shocked, again, by their specificity, detail, and credibility. The first text is riveting:

> They met the Germans at their camp in Ngogo. When the German officer Hauptmann [Captain] Lionel [Richter] saw the Bakara and their leaders, he asked for their Mukama. *When he asked who was Mukama, [the Katikiro (prime minister)] said that he was, and within moments he had been shot dead with a pistol by the German officer. Then the German African* askaris *[police/soldiers] present started firing into the seated crowd;* the askaris *had tried to warn the people, but their signs had not been understood. Of the hundreds there, there were only a few survivors. It took the relatives of the dead nine days to retrieve and finish burying their dead at the same place. Some were not buried, and their skulls could be seen for years thereafter.* (Lugimbana Bandio, November 5, 1969, Maruku; emphasis added; Schmidt 2017a, 2017b)

Figure 9.3. Mazinga Cave: (*left*) the waterfalls and (*below*) the rock ledges where multiple human skeletons were placed. Photos by author.

Upon reading these texts, I immediately wondered why some bodies were left on the field of death. Lwamgira (1949a) addressed this issue, observing that those killed in battle cannot be returned to the homestead for burial. They must either be thrown in a hole in the bush or put in a cave. It appears that such ritual proscriptions explain the presence of human bodies killed by heavy guns, both in the place of battle and in nearby rock shelters:

> When [Kishebuka's troops] arrived, a German asked them where Kishe-buka was. Gradually, they were looked over by Korongo as he searched for Kishebuka. As he asked for Kishebuka, the Katikiro spoke up and an-nounced that he was [the *mukama*]. When Korongo asked the people if [he] was Kishebuka, they replied that he was Katikiro of Kishebuka. Dur-ing Korongo's inspection, one *askari* [African soldier] who was a friend of Kishebuka's tried to warn the people that they were in danger and would be shot. *When Korongo learned that Kishebuka was not present, he was very angry and ordered his* askaris *to open fire. The Abendere were the first to die, then the Bakara. Those who escaped the deadly fire were those who happened to be standing in the proximity of Korongo. Those not killed by rifle fire were killed by the Bahamba* (citizens of Kihanja Kingdom ruled by Kahigi II) *and their spears.* Those who escaped to Kiizi (near the whites) were not killed but those who went to Kitembe forest were pursued and killed by the Bahamba (there and two other forests—Rugege and Kyama-konge). After this slaughter, the Germans went to Kahigi's *kikale [palace]* in Kanazi, Kihanja. (Byakela Rusinga, November 29, 1969, Maruku; em-phasis added; Schmidt 2017a, 2017b)

These stories immediately sent me to historical writings about the Haya, including those that discuss the impacts of colonialism (e.g., Austen 1968; Cory 1959; Curtis 1989). What I found was a complete erasure of any mention of this massacre. Even local histories, such as Lwamgira's (1949b) small booklet about Kanyangereko (Bukara), whitewashed this atrocity. This omission is no surprise, for Lwamgira was a major German and British client, known for his deep collaboration with both colonial powers. While other abuses by German administrators appear in the historiography (see Austen 1968), there is only silence for Ngogo.

Stories like that told by Byakela Rusinga were once an active a part of daily storytelling in some families. By the second decade of this millennium, this heritage was no longer passed on from generation to generation. Why? How is it possible that vital second-generation accounts disappeared over the course of five generations? These were questions that I puzzled over. Were the brutal and egregious colonial abuses so traumatic as to be dismissed by later generations as improbable or fantastic? Did local preaching help suppress memories of colonial atrocities? A more accessible explanation had already emerged in the Katuruka research—a marked diminishment of elderly male testimonies. The absence of these important oral narratives was linked to the ravages of HIV/AIDS, leading to a significant elimination of elderly keepers of oral traditions (Schmidt 2010, 2017a). This change occurred in nearby Katuruka and Nkimbo villages, both experiencing deep personal losses as well as loss of knowledge-keepers accompanied by the deep loss of their oral narratives.

Such deep erosion of the intangible heritage, particularly the loss of once vital, multiple oral traditions that animated the tragedy of the 1901 massacre, mobilized the Katuruka committee to launch a follow-up community research project in the vicinity of the primary school (Schmidt 2017a). Local elders contributed their knowledge and registered their strong support for an educational exhibit about Mazinga Cave at Nyarubale Primary School, which was mounted in 2013. While they could not provide any direct knowledge about the events that contributed to the presence of human bodies at Mazinga Cave, they provided keen insights into burial practices associated with spirit mediums—sufficient to eliminate any association of the Mazinga Cave materials with ritual authorities. Their testimonies also underlined the fragility of the oral form when chains of transmission suffer serious rupture.

The texts from my archive bring the story around to how I was "trained" to listen as an anthropological archaeologist. I admit to being a selective listener, but I was sensitized by my training to recognize that foible. Listening was close to my sole purpose during 1969. It remains a constant part of my archaeological practice. As part of my apprenticeship in listening, I was able to proffer a solution to a local mystery: Whose bones are in Mazinga Cave? Without listening closely to elders in 1969, there would have been no way to explain how these human remains came to Mazinga Cave, because it was an appropriate setting for those killed in battle. Most importantly, the historical evidence needed to explain Mazinga Cave would never have been preserved, ensuring forever the subaltern condition of a major colonial atrocity (Pandey 1995; Spivak 1996).

Contemporary heritage knowledge about this genocidal event was entirely erased, a victim of the HIV/AIDS pandemic that broke chains of transmission (Schmidt 2010). Today a small exhibit at the primary school places the remains into historical context and restores pride in the way that heritage was once maintained so meticulously in the region (Schmidt 2017a). The unspoken lesson from these vignettes is that it is impossible to practice an archaeology of listening without residing in communities for extended periods and enlisting local knowledge-keepers as trusted partners. This is precisely the advantage of a community archaeology that affords insights and understandings of the past otherwise inaccessible to many archaeologists.

Notes

1. During my early graduate training in archaeology, Stuart Struever was completing his Ph.D. under the supervision of Lewis Binford. Along with my peers, we were fed positivist pablum in huge helpings. It was not until my stay with the Haya that I came to an awareness that history making could follow alternative pathways.

2. This was not a deeply stratified rock shelter with distinct stratigraphy. The site was situated in a working farm where for generations if not centuries hoe agriculture reached to–40 cm to homogenize deposits, making continuous multiple dating for the multiple occupations impossible. Continuous occupation is affirmed by ceramic evidence, and by deep-time genealogical ties to the land and documentation of successive cult utilization of the site in ritual performance related to fertility, renewal, and iron working.

3. A horizon with burned forest trees on part of the site dated to the late-second millennium BCE had been broken up and had, with disturbances, penetrated into other features near the forge, at first confusing some; it was clearly a distinct phenomenon derived from burned forest evidence (Clist 1987).

4. Girls given as gifts to chiefs and kings were called Bazana. They remained in service until they were married. Their children also became Bazana.

5. Ray (1991) in his study of Buganda ritual offices provides skeletal sketches of minor female officials whose only apparent responsibility was to safe-keep the royal jawbone.

References Cited

Atalay, S.

2012   *Community-Based Archeology: Research with, by, and for Indigenous and Local Communities.* University of California Press, Berkeley.

Austen, R. A.

1968   *Northwest Tanzania under German and British Rule: Colonial Policy and Tribal Politics, 1889–1939.* Yale University Press, New Haven.

Clist, B.

1987   A Critical Appraisal of the Chronological Framework of the Early Urewe Iron Age Industry. *Muntu* 6:35–62.

Colwell-Chanthaphonh, C., and T. J. Ferguson.

2008   Introduction: The Collaborative Continuum. In *Collaboration in Archaeologi-*

cal Practice: Engaging Descendant Communities, edited by C. Colwell-Chanthaphonh and T. J. Ferguson, pp. 1–32. AltaMira, Lanham, MD.

Cory, H.

1959   *History of the Bukoba District.* Lake Printers, Mwanza, Tanganyika.

Curtis, K.

1989   Capitalism, Fettered: State, Merchant, and Peasant in Northwestern Tanzania,
        1917–1968. Unpublished Ph.D. dissertation, Department of History, University
        of Wisconsin, Madison.

Daniels, R.

2013   Report on the Osteology of Human Remains at Mazinga Cave. Manuscript on
        file, Kagera Region Development Office, Bukoba, Tanzania.

Hollowell, J., and G. Nicholas

2009   Using Ethnographic Methods to Articulate Community-Based Conceptions of
        Cultural Heritage Management. *Public Archaeology* 8(2–3):141–160.

Kaindoa, A.

2013   *Rugomora the Great, the Haya Iron King of the 17th Century: An Oral History.* Com-
        piled by P. R. Schmidt. Best Deal Publishers and Booksellers, Bukoba, Tanzania.

Larsson, B.

1991   *Haya Christians Conversion to Greater Freedom? Women, Church and Social
        Change in Northwestern Tanzania under Colonial Rule.* Acta Universitatis Upsa-
        liensis, Uppsala, Sweden.

Lwamgira, F. X.

1949a   *Amakuru G'Abakama ba Kiziba.* Rumuli Press, Kashozi, Tanganyika.

1949b   *Amakuru G'Abakama ba Kanyangereko.* Rumuli Press, Kashozi, Tanganyika.

Lwihula, G., L. Dahlgren, J. Killewo, and A. Sandstrom

1993   AIDS Epidemic in Kagera Region, Tanzania—The Experiences of Local People.
        AIDS CARE 5(3):347–357.

Mason, R. J.

2000   Archaeology and Native North American Oral Traditions. *American Antiquity*
        65(2):239–266.

Mutembei, A. K.

2001   *Poetry and AIDS in Tanzania: Changing Metaphors and Metonymies in Haya Oral
        Traditions.* Research School of Asian, African, and Amerindian Studies, Leiden
        University, Leiden, the Netherlands.

Ndamugoba, D., M. Mboya, K. Amani, and K. J. Katabaro

2000   *The Impact of HIV/AIDS on Primary Education in Bukoba Rural and Kinondoni
        Districts of Tanzania.* UNICEF, Dar es Salaam, Tanzania.

Oliver, R.

1979   The Earliest Iron Age? Review of P. R. Schmidt, *Historical Archaeology: A Struc-
        tural Approach in Africa. Journal of African History* 20:289–290.

Pandey, G.

1995   Voices from the Edge: The Struggle to Write Subaltern Histories. *Ethnos* 60(3–
        4):223–242.

Pikirayi, I., and P. R. Schmidt

2016   Introduction: Community Archaeology and Heritage in Africa: Decolonizing

Practice. In *Community Archaeology and Heritage in Africa: Decolonizing Practice,* edited by P. R. Schmidt and I. Pikirayi, pp. 1–20. Routledge, New York.

Pyburn, A.

2003   Archaeology for a New Millennium: The Rules of Engagement. In *Archaeologists and Local Communities,* edited by L. Derry and M. Malloy, pp. 167–184. Society for American Archaeology, Washington, DC.

Ray, B.

1991   *Myth, Ritual, and Kingship in Buganda.* Oxford University Press, Oxford.

Rehse, H.

1910   *Kiziba: Land und Leute.* Verlag van Strecker und Schröder, Stuttgart, Germany.

Roscoe, J.

1909   Python Worship in Uganda. *Man* 9:88–90.

Rugalema, G.

1999   It Is Not Only the Loss of Labour: HIV/AIDS, Loss of Household Assets and Household Livelihood in Bukoba District, Tanzania. In *AIDS and African Smallholder Agriculture,* edited by G. Mutangadura, H. Jackson, and D. Mukurazita, pp. 41–52. Southern African AIDS Information Dissemination Service, Harare, Zimbabwe.

Schmidt, P. R.

1978   *Historical Archaeology: A Structural Approach in an African Culture.* Greenwood Press, Westport, CT.

1997   *Iron Technology in East Africa: Symbolism, Science, and Archaeology.* Indiana University Press, Bloomington.

2006   *Historical Archaeology in Africa: Representation, Social Memory, and Oral Traditions.* AltaMira, Lanham, MD.

2010   Trauma and Social Memory in Northwestern Tanzania: Organic, Spontaneous Community Collaboration. *Journal of Social Archaeology* 10:255–279.

2013   Oral History, Oral Traditions and Archaeology: Application of Structural Analysis. In *Oxford Handbook of African Archaeology,* edited by P. Mitchell and P. Lane, pp. 37–47. Oxford University Press, Oxford.

2014a   Rediscovering Community Archaeology in Africa and Reframing Its Practice. *Journal of Community Archaeology and Heritage* 1:38–56.

2014b   Hardcore Ethnography: Interrogating the Intersection of Disease, Human Rights, and Heritage. *Heritage and Society* 7(2):170–188.

2016   Historical Archaeology in East Africa: Past Practice and Future Directions. *Journal of African History* 57(2):183–194.

2017a   *Community-Based Heritage in Africa: Unveiling Local Research and Development Initiatives.* Routledge, New York.

2017b   Contests between Heritage and History in Tanganyika/Tanzania: Insights Arising from Community-Based Heritage Research. *Journal of Community Archaeology and Heritage* 4(2):86–100.

Schmidt, P. R., and S. T. Childs

1985   Innovation and Industry during the Early Iron Age in East Africa: KM2 and KM3 Sites in Northwest Tanzania. *African Archaeological Review* 3:53–96.

Schmidt, P. R., and I. Pikirayi (editors)

2016   *Community Archaeology and Heritage in Africa: Decolonizing Practice.* Routledge, London.

Schoenbrun, D.

2014   Python Worked: Constellating Communities of Practice with Conceptual Meta-
phors in Northern Lake Victoria, ca. A.D. 800 to 1200. In *Knowledge in Motion:
Constellations of Learning Across Time and Place,* edited by A. Roddick and A.
Stahl, pp. 216–246. University of Arizona Press, Tucson, AZ.

Smith, C., and G. Jackson

2008   The Ethics of Collaboration: Whose Culture? Whose Intellectual Property? Who
Benefits? In *Collaboration in Archaeological Practice: Engaging Descendant Com-
munities,* edited by C. Colwell-Chanthaphonh and T. J. Ferguson, pp. 171–199.
AltaMira, Lanham, MD.

Smith, L., and E. Waterton

2012   *Heritage, Communities and Archaeology.* Bristol Classic Press, Bristol.

Spivak, C. G.

1996   Subaltern Talk: Interview with the Editors. In *The Spivak Reader,* edited by D.
Landry and G. Maclean, pp. 287–308. Routledge, New York.

Tantala, R. L.

1989   The Early History of Kitara in Western Uganda: Process Models of Political and
Religious Change. Unpublished Ph.D. dissertation, Department of History, University of Wisconsin–Madison.

Tully, G.

2007   Community Archaeology: General Methods and Standards of Practice. *Public
Archaeology* 6:155–187.

10

Listening, Hearing, Choosing?

The Challenge of Engaging Archaeology
in Conflict Transformation

AUDREY HORNING

Archaeologies of listening should foster ethical, inclusive practice. But that is not always easy, especially when we may not like what we hear. How we negotiate the politics of the present while staying true to the evidence of the past is the central challenge of responsible, ethically engaged archaeological practice. Drawing from efforts to engage archaeology as an integral part of peacebuilding in post-Troubles Northern Ireland, I want to address the risks and the rewards of collaborative cross-community practice. Positioning archaeology as a means of bridging the divisions in postconflict settings toward the creation of a stable, shared society requires an ability not only to listen but also to hear and respect the strength of personal and community narratives, even when those narratives may be founded on fundamental misrepresentations of the past.

In Northern Ireland, society remains divided into two communities, broadly drawn as Catholic/Nationalist/Republican and Protestant/Unionist/Loyalist. Today's divided identities are understood to be rooted in the seventeenth-century expansion of British power over Ireland, expressed in part through the importation of loyal British settlers as part of the Ulster Plantation scheme, launched in 1609—plantation in this instance meaning the planting of people. Engaging people in the present with the archaeological evidence relating to this contested period, seen as the origin of what has been termed an ethnic conflict between the Catholic descendants of the Gaels and the Protestant descendants of the planters by some analysts (e.g., McGarry and O'Leary 2000), carries considerable risk. The deconstruction of long-held narratives can render community collaborators anxious and sometimes angry. Fundamentally, the mobilization of this past for the benefit of the future involves choices over the exploration and interpretation of archaeological evidence and in so doing destabilizes oppositional community identities, making cross-community collaborative practice essential.

The need to balance issues of evidence, ethics, and respect for individual and community narratives is the subject of constant negotiation but is core to the development of an empirically informed, ethically engaged archaeological practice. Echoing Wylie's (2015) endorsement of collaborative practice as the locus for "some of the most creative archaeological learning," perspectives gained from cross-community collaborators not only have improved archaeological practice and methodologies but have opened up new interpretative possibilities. Furthermore, working alongside trained facilitators has emerged as a productive approach to embedding an empirically honest archaeology within conflict transformation (Horning and Breen 2017; Horning, Breen, and Brannon 2015). Listening is core to successful peace negotiation and is core to an archaeology that is actively engaged in the process of building shared, nonviolent futures.

Background

In 1998 the Good Friday Agreement ushered in a welcome, if still unstable, end to the 30 years of violence known as the Troubles. Since 2006 and the signing of the St. Andrews Agreement, a power-sharing executive has been in place, initially dependent on an unlikely alliance between the Republican Sinn Féin leader Martin McGuinness, once an Irish Republican Army (IRA) commander, and the Presbyterian firebrand Reverend Ian Paisley, leader of the Democratic Unionist Party (DUP) at the time of the agreement. The political structure is wholly reliant on and defined by a consociational model employing a principle of parity of esteem between the two traditions (Coakley 2009), politically represented by the two main parties, Sinn Féin and the DUP. While there are other political parties, the population overwhelmingly continues to vote according to community identity; only one mainstream party, Alliance, attempts to court the interests of people across the divide. Any major decision-making requires cross-party, cross-community support, and, crucially, leadership is shared between the two largest parties—the Office of the First Minister and Deputy First Minister (OFMDFM). Inability to agree means the Assembly is prone to collapse. The Assembly was dissolved in January 2017.

Notwithstanding this latest political crisis, the Troubles probably seem like distant history to anyone outside of Northern Ireland. Visitors to Belfast no longer routinely encounter police barriers, empty blockaded streets, and the ruins of bombed-out buildings. British Army bases have been decommissioned, central Belfast streets have reopened to automobile traffic, and there has even been a softening of the hard-line sectarian imagery on Belfast's legendary painted gables. Economic policy encourages development and seeks foreign investment. Tourist numbers are up, but not just because of Belfast's trendy urban scene or the undeniable beauty of the Ulster countryside. The Troubles themselves now serve as an attraction, with several firms offering voyeuristic black taxi and bus tours of Troubles hotspots along the back streets of North and West Belfast, where over 1,000 lost their lives in sectarian violence (Sutton 2001). The extent to which tourism can contribute positively to peace-building in post-conflict societies is a matter of considerable debate (Farmaki 2017). Economic gains can be more than overshadowed by insensitivity and the negative impacts of constant reminders of conflict. In Northern Ireland, the touristic desire to observe the physicality of the sectarian conflict may bring much-needed revenue to tour operators (often ex-prisoners); at the same time, it provides a considerable economic imperative for the retention of hard-line murals and other overt symbols of violence and division (Cochrane 2015).

In cruising past the many "peace walls" and separation fences that continue to divide Belfast neighbourhoods, few visitors are likely to guess that the majority of those living in close proximity to the walls strongly advocate their retention and cannot envision a time when they would not be necessary (Byrne, Heenan, and Robinson 2012). Furthermore, for those who grow up in peacetime but in the shadow of these physical barriers, negotiating their own personal safety is fundamentally linked to the perpetuation of sectarian division (Browne and Dwyer 2014). Most of these barriers are also located in neighborhoods that experience high levels of economic deprivation and low educational attainment, both key risk factors for paramilitary recruitment (Hargie, O'Donnell, and Mc-Mullan 2011) (see Figure 10.1). The tourist gaze in this respect is inconsequential to the daily realities of those who dwell nearby.

In short, contemporary Northern Ireland remains a deeply divided society. Geographical segregation is the norm; only 6.9 percent of schoolchildren are educated in an integrated (Catholic and Protestant) environment (Hayes, McAllister, and Dowds 2006; Hughes et al. 2016:1092; McCully and Barton 2009). The majority of the 88 peace lines (walls dividing neighborhoods in conflict) in Belfast were constructed after the Good Friday Agreement (McDonald 2009). While the high levels of violence have decreased and society has become

Figure 10.1. Peace wall, North Belfast. Photo with permission of Rachel Tracey.

"normalized," security alerts still occur on a daily basis and the risk of a return to violence is ever present. For example, in 2013, the bomb disposal unit was called out on average once every day of the year (Kilpatrick 2013); in 2016 security alerts occurred daily and MI5 raised the alert level for a terrorist attack by Northern Ireland dissidents on Great Britain from moderate to substantial (Kearney 2016). Security alerts routinely precipitate road closures that impact on that most mundane of activities (the daily commute), affecting even the most privileged members of society.

The psychological impact of conflict is manifested in high levels of post-traumatic stress disorder and elevated suicide rates that have been directly attributed to the legacy of conflict (Ferry et al. 2011; Tomlinson 2012), particularly affecting those who grew up during the height of the conflict in the 1970s. Furthermore, clinical evidence suggests that the negative impacts of trauma, if left unacknowledged and untreated, can be passed down to the next generation (Downes et al. 2012). Given the small size of Northern Ireland, it is rare to encounter someone whose life was not impacted in some way by the violence. However, perceptions of victimhood are widely variable not just among those individuals who personally suffered or directly witnessed violence (Brewer and Hayes 2013; Cairns et al. 2003). More pertinently for peace-building, there is political disagreement over whether all those who died in the conflict (including perpetrators) should be considered victims (Little 2012:89). To create "moral equivalency" between perpetrators and their victims is anathema when some of the root causes of the divide—the historical narratives addressed below—have not been meaningfully tackled. The political failure to establish a widely acceptable means of addressing Troubles-related violence, crime, and alleged collusion between security forces and paramilitaries exacerbates the psychological trauma.

The June 2016 Brexit vote, in which the United Kingdom as a whole narrowly voted in favor of leaving the European Union (EU), has further increased levels of anxiety and uncertainty in the province. The majority of people in Northern Ireland voted to remain in the European Union and now face uncertainties over the financial and political impact: strengthened border controls, loss of EU Peace and Reconciliation funding that has supported a multitude of cross-community initiatives (including those aimed at former paramilitaries and at-risk youth as well as our heritage-related programs), and loss of market access as well as agricultural subsidies for Northern Ireland's farms (Hayward 2017). When the United Kingdom leaves the single market and customs union, border controls will have to be implemented—most likely reinstating borders either between Northern Ireland and the Republic of Ireland in some form or, less likely, surrounding the whole island of Ireland, notwithstanding the Republic's continued membership in the EU. Neither is conducive to building and maintaining a peaceful society with strong links to both the Irish Republic and Great Britain. Brexit has rendered an already challenging future even more precarious.

The archaeology students at Queen's University Belfast whom I have taught are overwhelmingly from Northern Ireland and are drawn from both traditions. Although most grew up during peacetime and all certainly profess mutual respect and tolerance, it is clear from talking to them that differences, division, distrust, and even despair remain common. After reading Hamilakis (2009) and others on archaeology and the Iraq War, and Blakey (2008) and others on the New York African Burial Ground, the conversation about archaeological ethics, stakeholders, and responsibilities often turns to the local. Students commonly volunteered their opinion that they thought it was much better that archaeologists from outside Northern Ireland came into the province to deal with the contested period that lies at the heart of the Troubles and at the center of my own research, "because we can't get past our own bias." Insofar as I was not born in Northern Ireland, these comments may have been meant for me specifically. But my family ties to the region are strong and deeply rooted, and I have worked in Northern Ireland longer than some of them have been alive. Put simply, like anyone else in Northern Ireland, I have my own perspective and biases.

So why are 18–21-year-olds so despondent about their own future? The answer lies in the paradoxical reality that the structure of the peace process itself impedes full integration because it is founded on a principle of ensuring parity between the two communities. In all aspects of government funding, for example, equivalent amounts must go to initiatives from each tradition, while the dominant political parties break down along sectarian lines, as noted above. Parity and mutual respect were and are critical aspects of peace-building but inevitably reify difference, rendering efforts to explore and encourage commonalties over difference extremely challenging yet all the more critical to building a truly peaceful society.

Archaeological Interventions

What role can archaeological sites play in conflict transformation? Conflict is a deeply complex phenomenon with multiple and interlinked root causes. Among the central facets of many conflicts across the globe are historical power relations where particular groups advocate for cultural or political supremacy over other groups (Jeong 2000:32). Directly implicated in contemporary difference in Northern Ireland are the still contested and unresolved histories of the sixteenth and seventeenth centuries, when the English Crown extended control through the mechanism of plantation, a colonial effort to supplant the Gaelic Irish population that, despite its intent, did not succeed. The archaeological record of this period overtly complicates the accepted dichotomous narratives through highlighting complexity and particularly extensive evidence for the emergence of shared, syncretic practices drawing on Irish, Scottish, and English traditions; the reliance of plantation settlements on the demographically dominant Irish population (Breen 2012a and 2012b; Donnelly 2005; Horning 2001, 2013a); and continuity in preplantation settlement patterns and landscape use (Breen 2012b; Donnelly 2007; Donnelly and Horning 2002; O'Keeffe 2008). In the present, such tangible evidence possesses a profound capacity to challenge understandings of the perceived divide between Irish and British identities and contribute to the emergence of a shared Northern Irish identity.

That the evidence from the seventeenth century so strongly contradicts accepted narratives about the primordial divide between the two traditions raises legitimate questions about the construction of ethnonationalism in Northern Ireland. Some analysts (e.g., McGratton 2010:183) outright reject the notion of the Troubles as an ethnic conflict at all, instead arguing for an approach in which "an emphasis is placed on how historical processes, power disparities, and the perception of shifting threats and opportunities may influence political transitions and create the context for nationalist mobilization." McGratton's perspective of identity as fluid rather than fixed is welcome and in step with contemporary archaeological understandings, particularly in relation to colonial encounters. That said, rejecting the importance of identity as a cause of the Northern Irish conflict and barrier to peace-building is fine as an academic exercise, but it does not play out very well as part of public discourse in which the Troubles are understood to have been fundamentally about identity. People's sense of self and identity remains grounded in essentialist narratives; as such, the strength of those narratives must be appreciated and addressed if they are to be effectively challenged as part of building a more peaceful society. More succinctly, the Troubles undoubtedly resulted from a complex admixture of political, economic, and geographical factors. But most who lived through it understand it to have been principally the result of (as yet unresolved) ethnic rivalry and antagonism, so it is from that standpoint that any effort to effect positive change must begin. The tangibility of archaeological evidence can provide a refutation of mythic narratives in ways that are much more viscerally powerful than words on a page.

Over the last decade, archaeological projects focusing on the late sixteenth and early seventeenth centuries have begun to tap into that power by incorporating community groups and schools in excavations, with an emphasis on field experience and the potential for shared discovery (Horning, Breen, and Brannon 2015). Such immersive practice gives individuals the opportunity to physically engage with process of discovery and, importantly, the space to individually decide what the evidence actually means. As such, engagement and conflict transformation become embedded in the practices of archaeological fieldwork and material interpretation (Horning 2013c; Horning, Breen, and Brannon 2015). Being complicit in the discovery process makes individuals responsible for seeking an interpretation and an understanding of what is found. The excavation process thus can become transformative through this encounter with evidence and negotiation over meaning, provided that all participants understand that they are working together in a safe space, which has to be created through consensus. Participants acknowledge feeling empowered. One local community group involved in a project directed by my colleague Colin Breen of Ulster University acknowledged not only that they had learned about the complexity of the plantation period but that their members were also more "willing to reconsider their own identities in light of what they have learnt through engaging with professional archaeologists" (Ballintoy and District Local Archaeological and Historical Society 2013).

The process of community archaeology itself often matters more to our collaborators than does the outcome in the form of the data that get carted back from the field and analyzed in the lab. As such, a critical distinction must be drawn between inclusive archaeological projects that aim to enhance community cohesion and coproduction of narratives from the more traditional versions of community archaeology that employ volunteer labor to perform otherwise traditional archaeological projects (see the extended discussion in Horning 2013c as well as the discussion in Martindale and Nicholas 2014). How we move from one model to the other is not straightforward, as shifting from traditional top-down models of public archaeology into collaborative practice effectively requires philosophical reskilling.

Advocacy and inclusivity necessitate a lessening of control and a conscious (not tacit) acknowledgment that one is making a choice in how to interpret and approach the past. Doing so without compromising or abandoning our concomitant ethical responsibilities to the dead and the actualities of their experiences is extraordinarily difficult. The real risk here is that in relinquishing control and in prioritizing the present over the past we simply construct usable pasts that may not be empirically honest. Usable pasts have long been at the heart of nation building and empire building and in those contexts inevitably privilege the elite and, in a capitalist world, justify inequality. Focusing intentionally on the marginalized other is a common riposte to concerns over elite bias and can be very effective in situations where there are clear structural inequalities and an imbalance of power. This is most aptly demonstrated in the increasing number of projects that aim not only to engage indigenous communities but to actively collaborate and incorporate different forms of knowledge-making (see, e.g., discussions in Atalay 2012; Colwell-Chanthaphonh and Ferguson 2008; Martindale and Nicholas 2014; Nicholas 2010; Silliman 2008).

The particularities of the Northern Ireland situation preclude any such easy choice over which histories should be rediscovered, prioritized, or mobilized. A focus on a marginalized other does not work in Northern Ireland, where both communities self-identify as marginalized others. Choosing one voice to prioritize over another would hardly aid the cause of peace and would implicate the researcher in fostering continued division and unrest. Such a choice would de facto be understood as a political stance.

The two communities are roughly equivalent in population, so neither has the upper hand. On the island of Ireland, the Catholic, Nationalist community is numerically dominant. Despite the assumptions of many in the broader global Irish diaspora, however, there is actually little public or political appetite in the Republic for reunification of the island. Many in the Republic have never traveled north of the border and view Catholics in the north more with suspicion than with any kindred connection. In the context of the United Kingdom, the Protestant Unionist community has a demographic majority. Within the United Kingdom, it is often Ulster Protestants who argue the loudest for the Union and for a British identity. Yet that identity is always understood as contingent on a contractual agreement—that Great Britain will continue to protect the Ulster British. Significant numbers in Scotland and Wales seek independence, while, as cogently argued by Colley (1992) two decades ago, being British more often than not really has meant being English. The notion of a UK identity has been, if not wholly shattered, certainly fragmented by the Brexit vote of 2016. The English, like the Irish of the Republic, are also ambivalent about Northern Ireland, viewed as a financial drain on the Exchequer and a source of anxiety, as represented by the "substantial" status of the terror alert. Whatever the future holds for society in the north of Ireland, arguably it will have to come from within. When no one else wants you, you have to forge your own identity and your own future.

What role can presentations about the past play in peace-building? Since the Good Friday Agreement, the museums sector has endeavored to strike the difficult balance between critically engaging the past and trying not to alienate its audience. Since 1998 the Ulster Museum has mounted a series of temporary exhibits aimed to address a range of contested histories. The most challenging of these exhibits, interestingly, date to the first few years of peace. The *Icons of Identity* exhibit (October 2000–April 2001) juxtaposed symbolic objects relating to iconic figures sacred to one tradition or the other tradition (e.g., St. Patrick and William III), and aimed to challenge the Two Traditions model of understanding these figures through historical context. However, there is a fine line between challenging the divide and reifying the divide. Displays that overtly juxtapose perspectives from either side run a risk of essentializing those differences. Reactions are often extremely strongly worded, as was the case with the recent *Remembering 1916: Your Stories* exhibit at the Ulster Museum (Blair

2016), which used community-sourced objects to tell the connected stories of the 1916 Rising in Dublin and the 1916 Battle of the Somme, respectively core parts of Republican and Loyalist narratives.

Perhaps the most provocative museum display mounted in the early years of peace was the *Conflict: The Irish at War* exhibit (December 2003–August 2006), which explored the role of conflict on the island of Ireland from the Mesolithic to the present. Critics charged the museum with "giving the impression Ireland is a place of interminable violence." Furthermore, the museum was accused of harboring a Unionist bias by implying that "the Irish are a race apart, genetically predisposed to conflict . . . [which] provided ideological cover for the British state and its claim that it is somehow a neutral arbiter in the conflict" (Mclaughlin and Baker 2010, 46).

My take on the exhibition was more positive for two reasons. First, the displays relating to twentieth-century conflict explicitly acknowledged the active role played by material culture. The gallery was packed full of weapons, flags, uniforms, bullets, and the ordinary possessions of people who found themselves caught up in violence. Second, the museum acknowledged its own role in relation to social memory and the ongoing negotiation of narratives by inviting visitors to pen and post their comments not only on the display but on their own experiences of violence. This approach made the museum space active in healing and the process of conflict transformation. Others were less impressed with the open-ended nature of the display: "the plurality of voices might just as easily be considered a way of avoiding any genuine effort to interpret and explain the past where it is so vociferously disputed and open to sectarian interpretation" (McLaughlin and Baker 2010:47). Perhaps to the relief of its staff, the museum then closed its doors for major refurbishment. When it reopened in 2009, all the color had been drained from the displays on the recent past. The very small Troubles gallery featured no material culture and relied solely on stark black-and-white photographs, perhaps in an effort to distance the experience from the present.

In November 2014 a new permanent modern history gallery opened, focusing on Ulster from 1500 to 1968 (the Troubles were still relegated to the black-and-white annex). Curatorial staff worked closely with academics (including myself) to select objects that would convey the complexities of the period and invite contemplation over its lasting significance. My top choice was the enigmatic "Dungiven Costume," the name given to a set of threadbare clothes found in a bog that incorporates elements of sixteenth-century Irish fashion (woolen mantle), English fashion (jacket), and Scottish fashion (tartan trews), along with leather shoes constructed in a traditional English manner (stitching) but repaired with Irish lacing technique (Horning 2014). The hybridity and ambiguity of the clothing inevitably provoke questions about the identity and experiences of the last person to wear these clothes. The small space of the gallery and the limited text (in keeping with current museological practice) lessen some of the potential power of the objects on display. Visitors must engage with a touch table to receive contextual information about objects in the exhibit. This is perhaps a strategic approach: only those prepared to be challenged will take the time to watch the short video clips. Reviews have mainly been positive, with one critic commending the museum for "producing an exhibition that carefully walks the tightrope of Irish history" (Crooke 2015:45).

If public institutions like museums that are charged with curating the past and giving it meaning in the present struggle to balance on the tightrope of sectarian legacies, what hope is there for archaeology, a discipline that has not always paid attention to the contemporary significance and impacts of archaeological stories? I would argue that it is actually easier for archaeology to make a difference than it is for museums, because we have the ability to involve community members in the discovery process, as discussed earlier. Rather than being confronted with the end product of research in a carefully crafted museum exhibit, where the choices made and the depth of research are left implicit and thus impossible to assess easily, we can involve others in the co-production of knowledge. The acknowledged subtext for the Modern History gallery is that Irish history is a shared history, like it or not. That, too, is the message coming from the archaeological record. But arguably the messages are all the more powerful and are rendered more palatable when based on shared practice.

Archaeological sites, places, or excavations therefore can serve as shared spaces where dialogue is encouraged through informed and participatory investigation, functioning as a joint recovery of narratives. Challenging people's understanding of the past means challenging their identity in the present, so it does carry risk. Archaeologists are not generally trained to handle such risks: to understand when you might inadvertently do someone psychological harm and to know the best ways to carefully manage the destabilization that can occur. To date, the immersive projects, incorporating community partners into archaeological projects, have concentrated more on those groups who traditionally would be open to explorations of the past—local history groups and schools. The success of these engagements efforts thus far has led to a more challenging series of projects in conjunction with the Corrymeela Community, a shared governance civil society formed in 1965 with the aim of bringing people together from across the sectarian divide in safe and neutral surroundings. The members of the steering group for the project (see the acknowledgments), made up of trained Corrymeela facilitators, archaeologists, and museum professionals, generally agree about the importance of engaging more difficult to reach groups (including ex-paramilitaries, survivors of Troubles-related violence, at-risk youth, etc.) with the tangibility of plantation-period archaeology in an effort to impact on the present and future. But agreement on precisely how to do this and, indeed, what the evidence might actually have to contribute to peace-building is less straightforward but has led to some very productive discussions.

Most important has been the evolution of the program itself, which is focused not on fully formed collaborative practice but on creating the conditions that may lead to such working in the future (Pettis 2015). The aim is simply to begin a conversation over the meaning of the past in the present and to facilitate engagement with the tangible evidence of the plantation period. Together, the members of the steering group drafted and signed a code of practice to be accepted by participants at the start of any program. In addition to being up-front about our aim to connect an exploration of the past with peace-building in the present, the contract is based on a series of five principles: (1) facilitators should work to create a safe environment where people feel valued, accepted, and respected; (2) those who hold expertise should use knowledge in a manner that acknowledges this power dynamic and empowers participants; (3) participants should have an opportunity to explore their values and beliefs in freedom and without expectation that they should change; (4) when exploring history, care should be taken to honor and respect the stories of those in the past; and (5) participants should be given opportunities to own their learning process and shape the direction of programs. A key outcome from the Corrymeela perspective lies in just bringing people together and creating a space in which participants can feel free to express themselves and listen to others with respect. For my part, what I have hoped for in addition is for individuals to develop awareness that people in the past—the Irish and English and Scots who for better or worse were compelled to engage with one another—had no foreknowledge of the present. The Troubles may seem an inevitable outcome of the plantation period from the perspective of the twenty-first century, but from the vantage point of 1609 or 1611 or 1630 the events of the late twentieth century were far from inevitable. Of far greater concern to the majority, of whatever identity, was negotiating the needs and realities of the day, from the quotidian to the creative.

Our programs involve a full weekend residential where participants stay at the Corrymeela residential center situated on the scenic north coast of County Antrim. Costs for participants in the first stage of our project were covered by our grant funding from the Heritage Lottery fund, while we experts donated our time. Friday evenings focus on ice-breaking activities and a bit of a discussion about the Ulster Plantation, then on Saturday we visit a series of plantation-period sites with complicated histories and also have an artifact handling session (see Figure 10.2). In the evening the groups produce posters (what my museum colleagues call memory maps), then on Sunday we discuss what has been learned. I have found it much easier to undertake this kind of work in cooperation with the Corrymeela partners. I have listened and learned from them, just as they have become vested in the notion that understanding the past—and the past that is further back than the Troubles—has merit in the present and the future. Indicative of that commitment and recognition was the way that Corrymeela showcased the project during the 2015 visit of Prince Charles, which was explicitly about forgiveness (McCleary 2015).

Figure 10.2. Audrey Horning and a community group exploring the complicated history of Dunluce Castle. Photo with permission of Sean Pettis.

But Does It Work?

As part of the overall process, feedback is solicited to understand if people find the experience to be positive or negative. One respondent expressed a common sentiment: "Bit of both—unsettling as there's a lot of things need clarified. It will help me look at things differently—question them more and look for the real meaning." In the discussion that follows, I have chosen to generalize rather than relate the specifics of each group to protect the identities of the participants. Each group was profoundly different, depending on its expectations, background, and composition. Listening to the participants and participating in their discovery processes significantly enhanced my own understanding of the complexities of contemporary Northern Irish society as well pointing me in new directions in terms of research questions about the past.

Going into the first series of programs I harbored my own concerns not just about the efficacy of what we were trying to do but about the likely responses from the participants. I expected some to be more open to new understandings than others, which turned out to be the case. However, I was wrong about which groups were more likely to find the program challenging and threatening, forcing me to confront my own misconceptions. I was dubious about the likely engagement of participants from working-class Loyalist communities, not just because of their experience of Troubles-related violence and ongoing social and economic deprivation but because of the dominant Loyalist and Unionist perspective that the Belfast Agreement that ushered in peace was "little more than a surrender process" to the forces of Republicanism (McAuley 2008:19). Given the importance of the Protestant narrative of the plantation period being one in which hard-working Protestants transformed a savage land in the face of continued opposition, I expected that my archaeological stories about the haphazard and incomplete nature of plantation might be unwelcome, as would my tales about Protestant incomers drinking with the numerically dominant Irish, living in Irish houses, and consuming their meals from Irish-made pottery.

I could not have been more wrong. My tales of intercultural drinking sparked recognition, while descriptions of Irish building techniques employed in English plantation villages resonated with those in the building trades. A fragment of Chinese porcelain that made its way around the globe to early seventeenth-century Ulster proved an unexpected item of fascination to people who have long been taught that they live in a backward, marginalized land. A visit to Dunluce Castle, where a Catholic Highland Scot built a plantation village and funded a Protestant church while facilitating the activities of Scottish Franciscan missionaries (Breen 2012a), evoked knowing laughs about the advantages of "playing both sides." Evocative sites like Dungiven priory, once the center of the Gaelic O'Cahan lordship but later transformed into a plantation manor (Brannon and Blades 1980), inspired awe and reflection. Our visits include entering the chancel, not usually open to visitors, to see the rare survival of a fifteenth-century effigy tomb. The special viewing opportunity to "touch" the past inevitably provokes discussion of why the resident English planters, Sir Edward Doddington and his wife, Anne, who held the site for decades after her husband's death, chose not to destroy the O'Cahan tomb, clearly a Catholic Irish symbol. Whatever the explanation, the survival of the tomb forces a rethinking of sectarianism and religious violence in the implementation of plantation, and participants of all backgrounds seek plausible explanations rooted in their own social understandings.

Groups split up to create their memory maps in the evening, which were then shared and discussed in the morning in discussions that were often strikingly honest and reflective. Many struggled with how much responsibility they personally should bear for present-day division: "I had no say in the matter," said one man, in relation to his ancestors' decision to settle in Ulster, while another asked, "How long do you have to be in a place before you belong?" One gentleman (again echoing my own students) asked, "Is it better that outsiders deal with this period? Will we ever get over ourselves?" Several freely admitted that they had their doubts about why we were doing these programs and what we might be trying to "feed" them. One man confessed to having Googled some of the historical terms used on the first night, to make sure that they were not loaded with bias. Trust has to be developed, and the process can only just begin in a short weekend program.

In all of our programs, regardless of the community affiliation of the participants, what emerges is that no one knows about the history of the north of Ireland because it has traditionally not been taught in school. Prior to the introduction of a shared history curriculum, if you attended a predominantly Protestant school, you learned more English history. If you attended a Catholic school, you more often read histories from the Republic. Even with the shared history curriculum, teachers are often too nervous or simply lack the confidence to teach it, valuing classroom cohesion over historical knowledge (Kitson 2007; McCully 2012). There remains a vacuum that gets filled with sectarian narratives without any evidentiary basis. And people know that and recognize it, and they want and deserve something better. But this does not mean that the process of learning should be unidirectional, with experts like myself imparting knowledge to those who seek it. The questions asked by participants, often drawn straight from their own experiences, have given me multiple fruitful new directions for my own research and challenge my own construction of the nature of society in the plantation period. By way of one small example, one man who works with youth offenders was very interested in systems of justice in the seventeenth century and the ways in which they were implemented and understood in Ulster. This has led me to think seriously about the cultural implications of the intersections and disjunctures between two very different systems of law, Gaelic Brehon law and English civil law, and how they were implemented in plantation settlements.

Surprisingly, the biggest challenge to the aim of the program came from cross-community groups, forcing me to ask a fundamental question: What is actually more important: peace-building or correcting understandings about the past? Cross-community groups derive their strength from resolutely looking forward, not backward. Cohesion and friendship are often based on not going there—not going into the reasons and rationales for division, not talking about politics or violence, but instead working together toward a better future. In a follow-up meeting with one such group, it was clear that there were problems. Sean Pettis (2016:9), our Corrymeela facilitator and partner, described it this way: "The content of the programme had made them somewhat 'wobbly' with regards to who they are as a group." I recalled one participant saying that she wanted to believe that the Ulster Plantation was all about Protestants coming and taking away what she smilingly described as Seamus and Roisin's wee whitewashed cottage. When faced with the reality that Seamus and Roisin in the seventeenth century probably did not live in a whitewashed cottage and that incoming planters did not necessarily evict them from whatever they were living in, it was difficult for her to accommodate that perspective. Nationalist identity is strongly rooted in narratives of dispossession, just as Unionist narratives are founded on a belief in a savage land transformed through hard work and dedication. Stories about the mutual entanglements of planter and Gael are therefore challenging for everyone at a very basic level. Neither narrative was the reality in the past. But what is more important in the present?

Ethically, I don't feel that I should force the members of such groups, who have become friends often against all odds, to acknowledge the complexities of the past if it means that the peace and goodwill they have developed will be undermined and possibly damaged forever. Yes, I would like for everyone in the present to know and understand the experiences of those in the past, especially as they are routinely mobilized in the present. However, engaging in an archaeology of listening does not mean only listening—it means actually hearing, and acting accordingly. An archaeological version of the Hippocratic oath may be what is actually required: An archaeology of listening means an archaeology that overtly seeks not to cause harm. Harm in this instance refers to people in the present, but it should equally apply to people in the past. While I will not force any individual or group in the present to accept new historical narratives, I do not wish to do harm to people in the past by shading or over-looking the evidence of their lived experiences. So I will continue to share the evidence from the past, but I will do so in a manner that respects the needs of the present. Deciding on a specific course of action—when to push and when to step back—requires active listening and active hearing.

Conclusion

I want to conclude with a consideration of positionality and pragmatism. Re-turning to the comments made both by students and participants about the perceived objectivity of outsiders, there is a pragmatic advantage to being per-ceived as something of a neutral authority, even if as a self-reflexive archaeolo-gist I can't afford to believe in objectivity (also discussed in Horning 2013a). Fol-lowing one early program, one anonymous respondent commented about "how by involving archaeologists they can exert such influence" (Causeway Museum Service 2009). In peace negotiations, it is the neutral position of the interlocutor who brokers discourse. I have to think carefully when to employ my identity as a neutral authority and when to be wholly honest about my own positionality. I tend to make that choice based on the most likely outcome, when I want that outcome to be a greater appreciation that people in the past could not predict the future. Here I would take particular inspiration from Mrozowski's (2014:343) argument for a pragmatic approach that specifically requires practitioners to "explicitly identify the practical outcomes of their research" and recognize that "social science needs to be politically engaged." Of course, the aim of situating archaeology as political engagement is neither necessarily complementary with nor conducive to true inclusivity in archaeological practice. Yet I believe the two are not incompatible and that the combination, with all its inherent tensions and contradictions, may in fact lead to more meaningful, deeper understand-ings and potentially new praxis.

Questions of moral obligation and the imperative to respect multiple perspectives are of particular resonance when dealing with contested histories in conflict-ridden and postconflict societies. Archaeology in these contexts carries risks but also the potential for transformative social benefit. Precisely what the future holds for Northern Ireland is not clear, but I have made my own choice, as a citizen, to participate in the forging of that future through the tools I have at hand. Those tools include an empirically grounded understanding of the experiences of people in the past, whose lives have been too often mobilized in the service of violence and conflict in the present. I, too, am mobilizing their lives—but I hope that my training as a professional archaeologist, coupled with my constant questioning of my own motivations and ethical positioning, allows that mobilization to have at least some honest grounding in the lived actualities of their existence. I keep my ear to the ground as well as attuned to the voices around me.

Acknowledgments

I am extremely grateful to my colleagues and friends in the steering group for the Culture, Contact and Conflict around the Causeway project: Shona Bell, Colin Breen, Colin Craig, Robert Heslip, Susan McEwan, Helen Perry, Sean Pettis, and Gemma Reid, as well as the rest of the staff at Corrymeela and especially all the participants. I would like to thank and acknowledge the Heritage Lottery Fund for supporting the first phase of the project. I am grateful to the Ulster Museum, particularly William Blair, Sinéad McCartan, and Fiona Byrne for their support, interest, and willingness to take risks. In addition, my insights have been shaped by many other friends and colleagues in Northern Ireland, particularly Nick Brannon, Colm Donnelly, Paul Logue, Ruairí Ó Baoill, Siobhán McDermott, and Rachel Tracey, but I hold none of them responsible for my opinions. I am also extremely grateful to my listening colleagues for all that I have learned from them, and to Peter Schmidt and Alice Kehoe not only for bringing us all together but for serving as exemplary models.

References Cited

Atalay, S.
2012   *Community-Based Archaeology: Research with, by and for Indigenous and Local Communities.* University of California Press, Berkeley.
Ballintoy and District Local Archaeological and Historical Society
2013   Letter to Queen's University Belfast, August 26, 2013.

Blair, W.

2016   Remembering 1916: Legacy and Commemoration. Keynote address at *Remembering 1916: The Easter Rising, the Battle of the Somme, and the Impact on Lowell: a Public Engagement Conference.* University of Massachusetts Lowell and Queen's University Belfast, Lowell, MA, September 7, 2016.

Blakey, M.

2008   An Ethical Epistemology of Publicly Engaged Biocultural Research. In *Evaluating Multiple Narratives: Beyond Nationalist, Colonialist, Imperialist Archaeologies*, edited by J. Habu, C. Fawcett, and J. Matsunaga, pp. 17–24. Springer, New York.

Brannon, N. F. and B. Blades

1980   Dungiven Bawn Re-edified. *Ulster Journal of Archaeology* 43:91–96.

Breen, C.

2012a   *Dunluce Castle, History and Archaeology*. Four Courts Press, Dublin.

2012b   Randal MacDonnell and Early Seventeenth-Century Settlement in Northeast Ulster, 1603–30. In *The Plantation of Ulster: Ideology and Practice*, edited by M. Ó Siochru and E. Ó Ciardha, pp. 143–157. Manchester University Press, Manchester, UK.

Brewer, J., and G. Hayes

2013   Victimhood Status and Public Attitudes towards Post-conflict Agreements: Northern Ireland as a Case Study. *Political Studies* 61:442–461.

Browne, B., and C. Dwyer

2014   Navigating Risk: Understanding the Impact of the Conflict on Children and Young People in Northern Ireland. *Studies in Conflict and Terrorism* 37:792–805.

Byrne, J., C. G. Heenan, and G. Robinson

2012   *Attitudes to Peace Walls*. Research report to the Office of First Minister and Deputy First Minister, Belfast.

Cairns, E., J. Mallett, C. Lewis, and R. Wilson

2003   *Who Are the Victims? Self-Assessed Victimhood and the Northern Irish Conflict.* Northern Ireland Statistics and Research Agency, Belfast.

Causeway Museum Service

2009   1613–2013: Exploration of the Causeway Comment Sheet Evaluation, on file, Causeway Museum Service Office, Coleraine Borough Council, Coleraine.

Coakley, J.

2009   Implementing Consociation in Northern Ireland. In *Consociational Theory: McGarry and O'Leary and the Northern Ireland Conflict*, edited by R. Taylor, pp. 122–145. Routledge, London.

Cochrane, F.

2015   The Paradox of Conflict Tourism: The Commodification of War or Conflict Transformation in Action? *Brown Journal of World Affairs* 22:51–69.

Colley, L.

1992   *Britons: Forging the Nation, 1707–1837*. Yale University Press, New Haven, CT.

Colwell-Chanthaphonh, and T. J. Ferguson (editors)

2008   *Collaboration in Archaeological Practice: Engaging Descendant Communities*. AltaMira Press, Lanham, MD.

Crooke, E.

2015   Review: Modern History Gallery, Ulster Museum, Belfast. *Museums Journal* (February):43–45.

Donnelly, C.

2005   The I.H.S. Monogram as a Symbol of Catholic Resistance in 17th-Century Ireland. *International Journal of Historical Archaeology* 9:37–42.

2007   The Archaeology of the Ulster Plantation. In *The Archaeology of Post-medieval Ireland, 1550–1850*, edited by A. Horning, R. O'Baoill, C. Donnelly, and P. Logue, pp. 37–50. Wordwell, Dublin.

Donnelly, C., and A. Horning

2002   Post-medieval and Industrial Archaeology in Ireland. *Antiquity* 76:557–561.

Downes, C., E. Harrison, D. Curran, and M. Kavanagh

2012   The Trauma Still Goes On: The Multigenerational Legacy of Northern Ireland's Conflict. *Clinical Child Psychology and Psychiatry* 18(4):583–603.

Farmaki, A.

2017   The Tourism and Peace Nexus. *Tourism Management* 59:528–540.

Ferry, F., Bolton, D., Bunting, B., O'Neill, S., Murphy, S. and B. Devine

2011   *The Economic Impact of Post-Traumatic Stress Disorder in Northern Ireland*. onlinelibrary.wiley.com/doi/10.1002/jts.22008/pdf. Northern Ireland Centre for Trauma and Transformation (Belfast); accessed August 15, 2018.

Hamilakis, Y.

2009   The "War on Terror" and the Military-Archaeology Complex: Iraq, Ethics, and Neo-Colonialism. *Archaeologies* 5:39–65.

Hargie, O., A. O'Donnell, and C. McMullan

2011   Constructions of Social Exclusion among Young People from Interface Areas of Northern Ireland. *Youth & Society* 43:873–899.

Hayes, B. C., I. McAllister, and L. Dowds

2006   In Search of the Middle Ground: Integrated Education and Northern Ireland Politics. *Ark Research Update* 42: (unpaginated).

Hayward, K.

2017   A Frictionless Border Is an Oxymoron, an Invisible One Is Undesirable. *Irish Times*, July 15, 2017. https://www.irishtimes.com/opinion/a-frictionless-border-is-impossible-an-invisible-one-undesirable-1.3155222; accessed December 16, 2017.

Horning, A.

2001   "Dwelling Houses in the Old Irish Barbarous Manner": Archaeological Evidence for Gaelic Architecture in an Ulster Plantation Village. In *Gaelic Ireland 1300–1650: Land, Lordship, and Settlement*, edited by P. Duffy, D. Edwards, and E. Fitzpatrick, pp. 375–396. Four Courts Press, Dublin.

2013a   *Ireland in the Virginian Sea: Colonialism in the British Atlantic*. Omohundro Institute for Early American History and Culture and the University of North Carolina Press, Chapel Hill.

2013b   Exerting Influence? Responsibility and the Public Role of Archaeology in Divided Societies. *Archaeological Dialogues* 20:19–29.

2013c   Politics, Publics, and Professional Pragmatics: Re-envisioning Archaeological

Practice in Northern Ireland. In *Engaging the Recent Past*, edited by C. Dalglish, pp. 95–110. Boydell and Brewer, Woodbridge, Suffolk, UK.

2014   Clothing and Colonialism: The Dungiven Costume and the Fashioning of Early Modern Identities. *Journal of Social Archaeology* 14 (3):296–318.

Horning, A., and C. Breen

2017   In the Aftermath of Violence: Heritage and Conflict Transformation in Northern Ireland. In *Post-Conflict Archaeology and Cultural Heritage: Rebuilding Knowledge, Memory and Community from War-Damaged Material Culture*, edited by P. Newson and R. Young, pp. 177–194. Routledge, London.

Horning, A., C. Breen, and N. Brannon

2015   From the Past to the Future: Integrating Archaeology and Conflict Resolution in Northern Ireland. *Conservation and Management of Archaeological Sites* 17:4–20.

Hughes, J., C. Donnelly, R. Leitch, and S. Burns

2016   Caught in the Conundrum: Neoliberalism and Education in Post-Conflict Northern Ireland-Exploring Shared Education. *Policy Futures in Education* 14(8):1091–1100.

Jeong, H.-W.

2000   *Peace and Conflict Studies, an Introduction*. Ashgate, Surrey, UK.

Kearney, V.

2016   Dissident Republican Threat Reaches New Level. BBC News, May 11. http://www.bbc.co.uk/news/uk-northern-ireland-36269175; accessed December 16, 2017.

Kilpatrick, C.

2013   One Security Alert in Northern Ireland for Every Day of the Year. *Belfast Telegraph*, December 28. http://www.belfasttelegraph.co.uk/news/northern-ireland/one-security-alert-in-northern-ireland-for-every-day-of-the-year-29871264.html; accessed March 27, 2014.

Kitson, A.

2007   History Education and Reconciliation in Northern Ireland. In *Teaching the Violent Past: History Education and Reconciliation*, edited by E. A. Cole, pp. 123–154. Rowman and Littlefield, Lanham, MD.

Little, A.

2012   Disjunctured Narratives: Rethinking Reconciliation and Conflict Transformation. *International Political Science Review* 33:82–98.

Martindale, A., and G. Nicholas

2014   Archaeology as Federated Knowledge. *Canadian Journal of Archaeology* 38:434–465.

McAuley, J.

2008   Constructing Unionist and Loyalist Identities. In *Transforming the Peace Process in Northern Ireland*, edited by A. Edwards and S. Bloomer, pp. 15–27. Irish Academic Press, Dublin.

McCleary, M.

2015   A Royal Visit. *Corrymeela Magazine* 15:6–9.

McCully, A.

2012   History Teaching, Conflict and the Legacy of the Past. *Education, Citizenship and Social Justice* 7(2):145–159.

McCully, A., and K. Barton

2009　When History Teaching Really Matters: Understanding the Intervention of School History on Students' Neighbourhood Learning in Northern Ireland. *International Journal of Historical Learning and Teaching Research* 8:28–46.

McDonald, H.

2009　Bridge over Troubles Water. *Guardian*, July 29.

McGarry, J., and B. O'Leary

2000　*Explaining Northern Ireland: Broken Images.* Blackwell, Oxford.

McGratton, C.

2010　Explaining Northern Ireland? The Limitations of the Ethnic Conflict Model. *National Identities* 12:181–197.

McLaughlin, G., and S. Baker

2010　*The Propaganda of Peace: The Role of Media and Culture in the Northern Ireland Peace Process.* Intellect, Bristol, UK.

Mrozowski, S. A.

2014　Imagining an Archaeology of the Future: Capitalism and Colonialism Past and Present. *International Journal of Historical Archaeology* 18:340–360.

Nicholas, G.

2010　*Being and Becoming Indigenous Archaeologists.* Left Coast Press, Walnut Creek, CA.

O'Keeffe, J.

2008　*The Archaeology of the Later Historical Cultural Landscape in Northern Ireland: Developing Historic Landscape Investigation for the Management of the Archaeological Resource: A Case Study of the Ards, County Down.* Unpublished Ph.D. thesis, University of Ulster, Faculty of Life and Health Sciences.

Pettis, S.

2015　Contact, Culture and Conflict around the Causeway. *Corrymeela Magazine* 15:12–13.

2016　Evaluation: Contact, Culture and Conflict around the Causeway. Report submitted to the Heritage Lottery Fund, Belfast.

Silliman, S.

2008　*Collaborating at the Trowel's Edge: Teaching and Learning in Indigenous Archaeology.* University of Arizona Press, Tucson.

Sutton, M.

2001　An Index of Deaths from the Conflict in Ireland. http://cain.ulst.ac.uk/sutton/; accessed March 27, 2014.

Tomlinson, M. W.

2012　War, Peace, and Suicide: The Case of Northern Ireland. *International Sociology* 27(4):464–482.

Wylie, A.

2015　A Plurality of Pluralisms: Collaborative Practice in Archaeology. In *Objectivity in Science*, edited by J. Y. Tsou, A. Richardson, and F. Padovani, pp. 189–210. Springer Verlag, Berlin.

11

Sigiriya Rock

Global Heritage Commodified, Local
Heritage Forgotten, and Who Is Listening?

JAGATH WEERASINGHE AND PETER R. SCHMIDT

Sigiriya is one of the most important archaeological sites in Sri Lanka, hugely popular and widely visited both by local and by international visitors. This fifth-century palace and its magnificent gardens entered the annals of archaeology in the late nineteenth century. Preservation and management have been in the forefront of Sri Lanka's archaeological agenda ever since.

Sigiriya is also one of the most majestic and complex World Heritage Sites in Asia. Located in central Sri Lanka, the primary, late fifth-century development (in a site dating back to 300 BC) is an extraordinary example of town planning, garden design, architecture, hydraulic engineering, and wall painting traditions. The apex of the site is a royal palace located on the summit of a granitic monolith rising about 165 m above the surrounding plain (Figure 11.1). The royal complex consists of the palace, water gardens, and ritual and administrative buildings that are buttressed by a series of massive earth ramparts, wide moats, and entrance gateways—all constructed during the 18-year reign of King Kassapa I. The Royal Pleasure Gardens with their water fountains, ponds, and miniature water gardens are the earliest surviving landscaped gardens of Asia. They are serviced by an ingenious system of hydraulic engineering that is connected to a larger system of moats, canals, and reservoirs. Wall paintings on the western façade of the rock are the finest ancient murals of Sri Lanka.

Sigiriya was designated as a World Heritage Site under United Nations Educational, Scientific and Cultural Organization guidelines (UNESCO 1982). Very prominent and senior archaeologists, such as Roland Silva (president of International Committee on Monuments and Sites [ICOMOS] for many years) and

Figure 11.1. Sigiriya Rock from the southern rampart overlooking the water gardens, looking north. Photo by Peter Schmidt.

Senake Bandaranayake, pushed forward the initiative to protect and develop sites in the Cultural Triangle (e.g., Bandaranayake 1992, 2005; Guruge et al. 1994; Silva, Bandaranayake, and de Silva 1993). Sigiriya's nomination and designation as a World Heritage Site was a process controlled by and restricted to these professional archaeologists and heritage experts. Since their successes, the Central Cultural Fund (CCF) of Sri Lanka has been carrying out archaeological inquiries and heritage management at Sigiriya. It is a powerful example of the Authorized Heritage Discourse in action, with experts holding all the power over its management, its development, and its interpretation. Surrounding communities have no substantive role in its management of interpretation, though many individuals seek and find employment in a wide range of employment as groundskeepers, excavation laborers, guards, and daily-paid workers.

Sigiriya's inscription came at a time when there was a global rush to designate sites and when management plans required by UNESCO were poorly implemented or not implemented at all. This haste has carried with it a variety of advantages and increasingly clear disabilities over the years. The economic advantages of designation are enormous—high numbers of foreign visitors over the years along with high admission fees for foreign visitors have been a bonanza for the CCF.

Despite significant income from Sigiriya and other world heritage sites in the Cultural Triangle, little infrastructural investment has resulted in the areas surrounding the archaeological site. Revenue earned from sales of tourist tickets are largely spent on conservation and restoration of archaeological remains, museum construction, site maintenance, staff training, and administration of 11 heritage projects across the country. This translates to little being done to enhance visitors' experience and little effort to monitor and to enforce the originally demarked buffer zones in early but ephemeral, unimplemented management plans.

More serious is the failure to implement a mandated management plan after an ICOMOS monitoring review in 1994, the report for which was delayed until 1998. At that time, UNESCO required that Sri Lanka present a full management plan along with details of the buffer zones around Sigiriya Rock—16 years after inscription. The ICOMOS findings presented to UNESCO were pointed and specific, citing Sri Lanka's failure to follow UNESCO guidelines plus the uncontrolled growth of development activities around the site, both of which have led to commercial intrusions into the site and commercial development in surrounding villages, a crisis that local citizens find alarming and want to see changed:

> Amongst the comprehensive information and various recommendations presented in the report, ICOMOS experts noted that the area surrounding the rock of the outer moat at the Ancient City of Sigiriya site, which clearly was intended to be included in the original 1984 nomination dossier, is not indicated on the map of the nomination file. ICOMOS recommended that this be officially included in the protected area and that the World Heritage Committee be officially notified of the boundaries of the Ancient City of Sigiriya site. (UNESCO 1998:65)

Sri Lanka responded to this critical report four years later, in 2002, presenting coordinates for key bench marks and setting out a 12,600-acre buffer zone inside of which development would be restricted, including a 365 m buffer imposed by the director general of archaeology under the provisions of Section 24(1) of the Antiquities Ordinance of Sri Lanka, 1956 revisions that are applicable to all development (Legislative Enactments of Ceylon [1956] 1960). Twenty years after inscription, the CCF finally submitted its buffer zone map. The CCF report also admitted the urgent need to protect ancient sites endangered within this zone, including five remote ancient village settlements dating to the period of Anuradhapura, third century BC to tenth century AD, as well as a need to arrest uncontrolled development on this heritage landscape, including:

ancient irrigation system centered on the "Sigiriya Mahawewa," a man-made reservoir with a tank [reservoir] bund [dam] extending 7 miles and a catchment of 1000 acres. This cultural landscape still exists in unique biodiversity value. *Recent settlement growth due to socio-economic developments within the Sigiriya region has resulted in a demand for land, causing encroachments into the archaeological landscape and, therefore, currently presents a serious threat to the values of conservation.* Hence, there is a need to extend the borders of the World Heritage Property to include its archaeological landscape of the sites. (UNESCO 2002:10; emphasis added)

Moreover, the report openly admits that "Unauthorized and haphazard development activities in the buffer zone are on the increase. The State Party should pay more attention in the enhanced implementation of regulations" (UNESCO 2002:20). "The State Party," of course, is Sri Lanka, but the authors are representatives of that state authority. Ironically, the report also maintains that no changes in the "authenticity" of the site are anticipated (UNESCO 2002:11) while these rapid changes in the allegedly protected landscape are occurring. This document was written *with the hope* to implement long-delayed management policies yet omits the required management plan in its concluding responses without comment. This anomaly elicited no response from UNESCO, perhaps because the document repeatedly references the Sigiriya Heritage Foundation Act No. 62 (1998), which sets out explicit principles for the management of Sigiriya. Passed by Parliament in 1998, *this act has not been implemented,* leaving managers with ephemeral and unenforceable guidelines. Yet, in a direct answer to the UNESCO critique, the 2002 CCF document claims that there is a management plan, with the following observations:

Conservation strategies for this zone have been outlined in the plan accepting the reality that although *the Sigiriya region is still relatively under developed, the politics of socio-economic improvements in the area will eventually conflict with Heritage Management. The plan therefore attempts to forestall this inevitable conflict by suggesting policies that will harness economic development to achieve the final objectives of conserving and protecting the heritage values of the site. The plan is pending implementation subjective to funding.* (UNESCO 2002:13; emphasis added)

Notably, the CCF report of 2002 does not include the text of the Sigiriya Heritage Foundation Act of 1998. Rather, it presents a weak lament: "The State is duly required to implement 'Sigiriya Heritage Foundation Act'" (UNESCO 2002:22), suggesting that those in the heritage hierarchy of Sri Lanka were aware that a management plan was by then a hopeless cause without parliamentary action.

The development trends acknowledged in the 2002 report are contrary to the objectives of the original development plan that highlighted the importance of both archaeology and contemporary living culture and heritage values of other Sigiriya stakeholders in both urban and rural environments (Urban Development Authority 1998:5). Specific plans to link surrounding communities and their economic aspirations as well as their heritage traditions with the Sigiriya World Heritage Site have long been forgotten, at significant cost. There are many reasons for this oversight, but it mainly derives from the way that some think about heritage management—managing heritage as the prerogative of the heritage experts, with the associated communities and other stakeholders acting as passive recipients of the "scientific" decisions and procedures of the experts (see Smith 2006). Yet the experts themselves have avoided scrutiny, a smoke and mirrors approach that evidently has hoodwinked UNESCO but not residents, who, as the stewards of Sigiriya heritage, now see management issues reaching crisis proportions.

Digging Deeper Than Inside Moats: Local Views of Heritage

During March 2016 we embarked on a suite of interviews designed to listen to what local heritage practitioners in communities around Sigiriya think about heritage and how it is performed in their daily lives, a perspective that bears affinities to participatory community gaining popularity and pertinence in other parts of the world (e.g., Atalay 2012; Colwell-Chanthaphonh and Ferguson 2008; Schmidt 2017). We also believed that if we listened closely and seriously, we might learn how local experience and ideas might point to a new way to management and interpretative perspectives that might be used to interdict negative impacts on the site and its immediate communities. By listening to local people who are respected by village residents for their expertise in traditional medicinal and craft practices, we also hoped to gain understanding of how new management principles and ideas might be derived from local insights (Moccasin, this volume). Later in this chapter we propose several components of a management plan influenced by local heritage experts. Its premise is an integrated and inclusive approach involving villagers, local leaders, village youth, heritage practitioners, craft-specialists, hoteliers, guest-house owners, vendors, guides, tourist helpers, monks of village temples, and government officials.

Since Sigiriya was inscribed, stakeholders have been mostly ignored. Inclusiveness later became a mandate of UNESCO guidelines for world heritage sites—requiring that cultural, social, economic, and demographic components be engaged, not just the inscribed site. The UN General Assembly has since passed the Declaration on the Rights of Indigenous Peoples, with Article 27 pertaining:

> States shall establish and implement, in conjunction with indigenous peoples concerned, a fair, independent, impartial, open and transparent process, giving due recognition to indigenous peoples' laws, traditions, customs and land tenure systems, to recognize and adjudicate the rights of indigenous peoples pertaining to their lands, territories and resources, including those which were traditionally owned or otherwise occupied or used. Indigenous peoples shall have the right to participate in this process. (United Nations 2008:10)

Like the directive to implement a management plan for Sigiriya, these mandates were not applied to the site, leaving it in jeopardy today.

We began our interviews among villagers living on the margins of Sigiriya. Local heritage values, currently overwhelmed by the physical and cultural presence of Sigiriya Rock, were a key focus. Of significant interest, too, were the workings of a central bureaucracy and its laissez-faire approach to enhancing the presentation of heritage by using yet more excavations and restoration. While many local people derive their livelihoods from tourism and from employment at the site, they nonetheless remain seriously marginalized in terms of its management and the interpretation of Sigiriya values. Local people poignantly express this alienation, viewing the site as "a rock" that has little relevance to their heritage. One elder observed, "Sigiriya is much more than the rock. It is the rock and everything around it." As we listened to villagers talk about their lives, their visions, and their heritage, we more profoundly came to comprehend the potential heritage contributions of those living in greater Sigiriya.

By listening to healers, snakebite healers, healers of eye injuries, basket weavers, and carvers, we learned of their alienation from the central administrative and interpretative apparatus but also of their strong optimism about helping solve some of their contemporary heritage problems. Snakebite healers serve one of the most important community functions, given the very high incidence of snakebites. Still highly valued, though compensated meagerly, they see their offspring attracted to other lives and thus seriously worry about their abilities to pass on their heritage knowledge. A wise healer of eye injuries and former postman mused that the real heritage of Sigiriya was the very land on which they lived and carried out their daily lives—the village settlement, paddies, and forests with their extraordinary array of reservoirs and irrigation systems developed some 1,500 years ago. Remarkably, they continue to manage this complex system of dams, reservoirs, sluices, canals, and water allocation and, moreover, express deep concern about the knowledge systems being adequately passed to future generations. Collectively, they see informed heritage tours with specific foci on their distinctive heritage and technology as a real ecotourism with deep historical depth.

Other discussions centered on the improvement of policy-making and administration, with strong feelings about a local council charged with advising and participating in the Sigiriya Board of Management—currently restricted to heritage professionals. As we listened to these local heritage discourses, we also learned that many see a decay of their cultural heritage and historic landscapes, as shown in: (1) inappropriate new developments disrespecting the cultural heritage; (2) destruction of historic forest areas and heritage landscapes, due to unregulated economic ventures; (3) invasion of mass tourism, displacing local inhabitants; (4) congestion and visual contamination of historic areas by inappropriate structures inside villages, particularly those lodging visitors but also harboring prostitution. These were deep-seated, spontaneously expressed sentiments, often expressed as desires for change.

People wanted accelerated participation and adoption of a more comprehensive heritage umbrella for Sigiriya. Healing knowledge, in particular, is seen as a possible vehicle for public education of students and visitors, a way of integrating the formal (and mostly unvisited) botanical gardens at Sigiriya with performances/practice by local knowledge-keepers. Our interlocutors convincingly argued that regular performances as part of the Sigiriya experience would be a means to train a younger generation in their healing heritage. These diverse heritage perspectives—some with significant economic and cultural implications—are now central principles in future management plans for the greater Sigiriya Heritage Site. Thus, listening to local wisdom about heritage enriches us and simultaneously changes our heritage management philosophy; it grows knowledge from diversity, accepting the guidance of indigenous knowledge, leaving behind practices that marginalized and alienated local life.

The Knowledge-Keepers

We start with a short review of the different ways of life and knowledge discussed here, our insights into local heritage meanings, and possible heritage management approaches. Our focus included both craftspeople and healers, who have always played key social roles in Sri Lanka communities. The concerns that all express—about how they see their culture changing and their heritage threatened—are real and vivid. They are deeply troubled about their knowledge being forgotten, left behind by children attracted to more lucrative jobs.

They see their neighborhood changing—illegal chalets going up in forest settings, heavy traffic on their rural roads, prostitution, drugs, and congestion, all threatening their rural lifeways. Beyond these concerns lies a strong determination to do something to change the status quo, to make local lives less stressful, to change how Sigiriya operates, and to contribute to and enhance the way Sigiriya is managed in the future for the well-being of all communities and interest groups. One of the primary concerns that residents of Greater Sigiriya express is their anxiety over the impending loss of their heritage. While we in the scholarly world call this knowledge of medicinal practices intangible heritage, they make no such qualification, seeing it as *their heritage*, under threat.

The Snakebite Healers

Envenoming and death due to bites is a common morbidity and mortality problem in Sri Lanka (de Silva 1980; Ediriweera et al. 2016). The dry zone of Sri Lanka is inhabited by five of the six highly venomous snakes found in the country. More than 80,000 bites, 30,000 envenomings, and 400 deaths due to snakebites occurred in a 12-month period in Sri Lanka. The North Central Province, the southern border of which is only a few kilometers from Sigiriya, has the highest frequency: 623 snake bites per 100,000. The medicinal and cultural role of the snakebite healers in Sigiriya is significant. They play a crucial role in healing snakebites and in managing their possible aftereffects, both physical and psychological. Many villagers bitten by snakes visit a traditional medicinal healer after their treatment in government hospitals. Snakebite healers create

Figure 11.2. A. G. Ranbanda (*right*), a snakebite healer, talks with Jagath Weerasinghe (*left*) and Jane Schmidt (*far left*). Photo by Peter Schmidt.

their treatment concoctions with medicinal oils and pastes made from plants, roots, and leaves foraged in the Sigiriya forest. Villagers believe that traditional medicines prevent the long-term effects of envenoming.

A. G. Ranbanda is a snakebite healer. He sits on a bench in a lean-to, wrapped in a sarong and talking about his life as a snakebite healer in a region where snakebites are endemic (Figure 11.2). When asked if others followed his example and learned this knowledge system (*shastraya*) after he was instructed, Ranbanda said, "Nobody. That's very sad. There are children, but none are interested. Once I am gone, this medicinal practice will disappear" (Ranbanda, personal communication, March 8, 2016). The fragility of this knowledge system, so central to the health and well-being of residents, is illustrated in Ranbanda's commentary on the erosion of knowledge over his lifetime through the death of colleagues: "There were plenty in this area. Now dead. I am the only one left. They were in Sigiriya, Pidurangala, Talkote, Kimbissa [villages around Sigiriya]. But . . . when all of them failed, the patient came to me" (Ranbanda, personal communication, March 8, 2016). In this poignant acknowledgment of the disappearance of knowledge that led to his rise to prominence in the community, Ranbanda did not hesitate to point out his own value as a healer.

Ranbanda went on to frame his concerns in more explicit terms of heritage loss: "The medicinal practices that have come down from [our] ancestors are our heritage. It [that heritage] came all the way to me, but *it is over after me*" (Ranbanda, personal communication, March 8, 2016). His comment about loss of heritage knowledge also peppers the discourse of other participants in our research. Though such concerns arise out of diverse personal, familiar, and community experiences, they have culture change in common, particularly the impact of growing education and economic opportunities. Among those opportunities was the archaeological development of Sigiriya, where many people in the early 1980s found employment as laborers who helped uncover the ramparts, walls, and moats. Even Ranbanda was attracted to such work while he continued his healing: "We built [restored] the stone-wall of the *seethala maligawa* [Summer Palace]. We broke [apart] the ones that were there and rebuilt all anew. When we were *breaking* the old one we saw another wall underneath built in a different way. That's why I said that not only King Kassapa had reigned here" (Ranbanda, personal communication, March 8, 2016; emphasis added). While such employment was episodic and temporary, it marked a suite of new jobs in a wide range of occupations at this World Heritage Site, but none with any effort to listen to the intelligent workers.

Competition came from other sectors, too. While residents continue to value local snakebite healers, even when receiving hospital treatments, healers receive meager payments from their patients, who assume that such knowledge comes cheaply:

> Medicinal goods are so expensive. Our people don't get it. When you go to the doctor, the fee is specified and you pay it and come. When you go to the *wedamahattaya* [traditional medicinal person], you just give Rs. 200 or 100 with a handful of betel leaves. I am not complaining, but recently a patient was brought here having been bitten by a *mapila*—treated him till 11 p.m. and cured him. The patient came with his folks—about seven or eight of them. So we welcomed them with tea and betel leaves. But then they paid for my treatments only Rs. 200. Then, you see, I can't say that you must pay this much. I spent about Rs. 500 [for treatment and treats for the patient's folks]. (Ranbanda, personal communication, March 8, 2016)

Thus, a central problem is that such traditional healing also carries with it unchanged client expectations that traditional payments are adequate, when in fact they are insufficient to sustain the practitioner, let alone cover basic expenses. Hospital costs escalate and are absolute, yet the traditional healer is expected to take a token payment, even when it far less than fair recompense. Yet Ranbanda and others cannot turn away needy patients. His children, however, see that this is not a viable future, avoid learning such knowledge, and invest their time in paddy farming or work associated with Sigiriya.

The dilemma for Ranbanda and others is young people's lack of interest in learning snakebite healing. Ranbanda wishes that he could reverse the trend by instructing youth: "I'd give this knowledge even to an outsider, if interested. I have rescued more snakebitten people than the number of hairs on my head. No one died. . . . I have rescued [patients] who were proclaimed to be dead in half an hour" (Ranbanda, personal communication, March 8, 2016). A deep-seated desire to keep this knowledge alive is seen in the pride of accomplishment and respect that such a position commands, even in the era of hospital treatments.

G. G. Seelawathi is a female snakebite healer, having learned through apprenticeship to her father in both physical and ritual expressions of healing. She took up healing full-time after her father was killed by an elephant. She takes pride in her skills, yet worries about the future of snakebite healing. She sees the problem of continuing important heritage practices in the future much like her male counterpart, Ranbanda:

> No one is interested. Grandchildren are still school-going age. My eldest son is in Kayanwala. He does it somewhat. It is difficult for them do this. I also find it difficult to do this. With current economics it's difficult, sir. To make medicine and to make oils you need various kinds of oils. Stuff like mee oil and tala oil, etc., are needed. These are very expensive. It's the nature of snakebite medicinal practice that one has to have the medicines ready at home when a snakebitten patient comes. You don't have time to make the oil when a patient comes. You need the medicines right away. (Seelawathi, personal communication, March 10, 2016)

Seelawathi openly shares the outline of ritual technology, evoking deep ritual meanings not easily mastered, and bemoans the absence of apprentices. Yet her personal mission is to provide services despite the increasingly rare plants, now so expensive to collect and process:

Now there are *few* medicinal stuffs in the forest. I had a few grown. Now dead. Then animals also eat and break them. Snakebite medicinal practice is not easy. First you have to chant the *mantaras* to lower the venom. It is after that you do treatments. Treatments must be given soon after *mantaras* to protect the liver and the brain. It's not good that venom goes to these two things. If these two things are protected, then treatments can follow. (Seelawathi, personal communication, March 10, 2016)

When asked if she was willing to train others in snakebite healing, Seelawathi quickly replied that she would welcome such an opportunity but that she could not train someone from the same village for fear of conflict of interest in drawing patients—a principle taught by her father. This is certainly not holding back the training of others in the surrounding villages. Rather it is the expense that already modest families incur by acting out these heritage performances: they are honor-bound to share their knowledge through healing, even though it is a burden, "Let's say a poor person comes for medicine. You can't have the idea that there is no return by treating this poor guy because you won't be able to get any money from the person" (Seelawathi, personal communication, March 10, 2016). With such principles governing heritage performances, there is little mystery as to why younger people fail to take it up as a profession. We learned from our discussions that development of another mechanism to ensure viable performance is a subject of significant concern.

Weavers and Other Crafts Workers

G. G. Anulawathi is a weaver of reeds, a maker of mats, baskets, and other objects; she is also known as a storyteller. Her husband worked for several decades as an archaeological laborer in the Sigiriya excavations, as does a son today. They carefully maintain a special traditional visitors' (pillow) bench outside their main entrance, an addition made when she was featured in a TV special. Like her healer counterparts' concerns over vanishing heritage, she also worries that no one will continue weaving practices: "My daughters did it as long as they were with me. After marriage, [they had] no interest in this. They are at many different places. Also, now you have any object in plastic!" (Anulawathi, personal communication, March 16, 2016). When asked if the younger generation has an interest in continuing mat weaving, she forthrightly admits:

Those days [when we were children] wet-rice cultivation was what we did, but not so now. Because of education, time is spent day and night on that [by the younger generation] and have no interest for other work. . . . "Studying" [doing schoolwork] is more important than paddy cultivation work. If you don't study today, you can't live tomorrow. Today youngsters don't work as hard as we did. [They] do not step into a paddy field. (Anulawathi, personal communication, March 16, 2016)

As we listened to this incisive commentary about modern life and education, a more profound pattern began to emerge. The idea that paddy work is anathema to current youth signals a crisis in Sigiriya heritage—an absence of engagement with an ancient heritage of management principles for reservoirs, canals, and paddy field allocations. Without such engagement, the core of Sigiriya heritage is at risk.

While earning a modest income from reed weaving, Anulawathi has virtually no contact with the buyers, the tourists who frequent Sigiriya, yet another commentary on the distance between residents and visitors: "Most [of the woven products] go to hotels. There is a hotel in Habarana. What they have are all my goods. They either order [what they want] or take what I have woven" (Anulawathi, personal communication, March 16, 2016). Commercial brokers create a cultural and financial barrier between heritage practitioners and visitors—something that some participants felt could be avoided by having village heritage tours that would expose visitors to a wide range of heritage performances, allow them to interact with local people, and learn about heritage from those who practice it daily. To reinforce this point, Anulawathi noted:

The day before yesterday a foreign couple visited me—saw me weaving. But that doesn't happen every day. Now see, white tourists are brought, the rock is shown, then taken to hotels, which get the commission [that's all]. But there is no interest to show things like this to them. (Anulawathi, personal communication, March 16, 2016)

The goal to address poverty alleviation, as stated in the CCF report to UNESCO in 2002, is another unenacted management principle, yet it has the potential for rapid enactment by integrating craftspeople and their heritage knowledge into heritage tourism around greater Sigiriya. The alienation resulting from the restrictive and limiting range of heritage experiences coordinated by hotels, tour leaders, and guides emerges from most of our interviews.

This poignant disenchantment can be also traced back to the beginnings of Sigiriya as a World Heritage Site, when people were displaced from their traditional villages and resettled in zones outside of a 12,600-acre general buffer zone, the Phase I relocation (with Phases II and III not yet implemented). This displacement, deeply disorientating in terms of ages-old responsibilities to the landscape and its multitude of hydraulic engineering developments requiring informed management, was not accepted passively. Instead, many families moved back to traditional plots, especially to the north of Sigiriya, where they rebuilt houses and today practice paddy agriculture with impunity.

Resettlement after initial replacement has been assisted by the failure to implement a comprehensive management plan for Sigiriya. On the southern side of Sigiriya Rock, some residents were never permanently resettled in the new homes constructed in New Town, west of Sigiriya; they remained in original structures that were not destroyed because people refused to abandon them (Figures 11.3a and 11.3b). Some of these are situated within the 400-yd buffer zone mandated by Sri Lanka Antiquities Law and have organically grown over the decades to include expansive restaurants and accommodations along the main road—a kind of ticky-tacky tourism that clashes with an otherwise notable heritage landscape. Residents are fed up with inconsistencies in enforcement, with special favors given out to people who are building hotels and other commercial enterprises within the general buffer zone, not to mention jobs at Sigiriya that are handed out as political favors: "There is yet another thing. The minister in charge of the Triangle—he sends people from his area as workers to Sigiriya. That deprives the people of the area of opportunities" (U. G. Punchibanda, personal communication, March 9, 2016). This strongly stated grievance, factually accurate in its recognition of favoritism that works against local interests, marks a clear awareness that local heritage keepers are keenly aware of political manipulations that work against their interests.

R. G. Wijerathna is a former healer and a carver. He commands a charismatic presence and performs for an array of tourists who are brought to his home to hear his ideas about wood carving, another lost art at Sigiriya. Local tourist shops are filled with carvings, but most are done by artists from outside the district. Indigenous carving is almost dead, with Wijerathna being the last wood-carver. His many awards for his carving are prominently displayed. While he is proud of his accomplishments, he is also keenly aware that his heritage is threatened. He is willing, like others, to teach young people: "I welcome youths to come here to learn how to celebrate our heritage, but I do not see them coming" (Wijerathna, personal communication, March 8, 2016).

A

B

Figure 11.3. Remaining occupied houses after relocation of the Sigiriya community, within the mandated antiquities buffer zone: (*a*) a house that has expanded over more than three decades, with Sigiriya in the background; (*b*) another remaining home, contiguous to the main road but within the buffer zone. Photos by Peter Schmidt.

Traditional Doctors

M.G.K. Amma is a local medical doctor licensed to dispense various traditional medical concoctions. She was trained by a monk and cannot share knowledge given to her privately. She is a very popular doctor, with a large clientele and a well-stocked pharmacy. Her heritage, though, is much more than being a licensed traditional doctor. She traces her lineage of complex engagements with healing: "I have been] doing this since '72/'74. The medicinal practitioners of our lineage did snakebite treatment, *sarvaanga* [full body] treatments, and sorcery/incantations" (Amma, personal communication, March 9, 2016). She failed to obtain training in the lineage arts from her great grandfather, so she turned to a reverend (monk), known as Wedahamuduruwo.

Amma faces the same dilemma as the other Sigiriya heritage practitioners: There is no one to pass knowledge to. "This practice, then, must be learned by a grandchild. No one is interested to learn this. . . . Nobody learns. According to our lineage, and also according to Reverend Sumangala, if there is no one to learn this practice, then the medicinal-books [*wedapoth*] will have to be given to the temple" (Amma, personal communication, March 9, 2016). Listening to her, we learn how urgent local initiatives are in the face of a dominant discourse that ignores and exploits local heritage. All are last-generation keepers of heritage knowledge. Heritage knowledge stops with them or will be deposited in a local temple, perhaps to be referenced incidentally in future studies about what went wrong at Sigiriya. Amma has no illusions:

> The current generation (*now children*) sees no value in these [heritage values] . . . as long as I am alive, these things will be done. After me, I've no idea. I also find it difficult to continue to do these things. If helped to buy a machine to make oils, that would be a great help. (Amma, personal communication, March 9, 2016; emphasis added)

Her focus is economic, in the present, knowing that her children will not learn this heritage knowledge. Listening to Amma and her compatriots compels reflection and questions, some of which we explored to see what directions might be taken to overcome what appears to be a crash-dump for heritage values around Sigiriya.

Underwriting all experiences is the frustration that failure to perpetuate heritage practices lies at home—the interruption of heritage performance by the lack of interest and time for youth to learn skills and knowledge that do not provide a living under contemporary economic conditions. Among all collaborators, U. G. Punchibanda (Figure 11.4), the postman/eye healer, was most explicit about this failure to continue key heritage practices: "They [his sons] have no interest whatsoever" (Punchibanda, personal communication, March 14, 2016). Some answers began to emerge spontaneously in our discussions with Punchibanda. As observed earlier, he shared a vision about the heritage landscape of great antiquity and its deeply embedded knowledge being the foremost heritage value around Sigiriya Rock. Stewards of this knowledge understandably are concerned, even agitated, by the threats that impinge on a way of life that goes back two millennia, yet they also have clear and pointed ideas—if

Figure 11.4. U. G. Punchibanda, the retired postman and eye healer, during a moment of reflection while he advocated an approach to heritage that incorporates the inclusion and active engagement of local communities in maintaining the vitality of living heritage and managing greater Sigiriya. Photo by Peter Schmidt

we listen closely—about what might be done to make positive changes in how Sigiriya heritage is treated and represented by central authorities:

> Things like herbal gardens can be made. Currently medicinal plants are disappearing. Those days the herbal garden [at Sigiriya] was maintained beautifully. Today it is neglected. If such a thing is developed, how useful would that be today? In past days, it was beautiful. I have been there several times. . . . Many people from here took use of the herbal garden those days. (Punchibanda, personal communication, March 14, 2016)

Punchibanda identifies a resource at Sigiriya that has been used by local healers for generations—the Botanical Gardens. Long neglected and marginalized as peripheral to the primary Sigiriya heritage message (most visitors stand alongside or walk past the gardens while waiting for the admissions line to move forward—completely unaware that one of Sigiriya's best-kept heritage secrets is only meters away), the Botanical Gardens are a key point of articulation between the local communities and the CCF. While Punchibanda sees development of the Botanical Gardens with local healers acting as docents, teachers, and managers as an attractive way to recognize, integrate, and preserve local heritage at Sigiriya, he has taken up his own medicinal gardening. Despite this, he is willing to train youth, like others, "If an outsider is willing to learn this, I am ready to give." He hastens to note, however, that this is a collective responsibility: "It can't only be me who gets [involved there]; there are many medicinal practitioners around here" (Punchibanda, personal communication, March 14, 2016).

A Template for Change Emerges

The wisdom manifest in Punchibanda's commentary is striking in its vision and insight, compelling us to listen even more closely to his observations. He quickly identifies the shortcomings of tourism:

> Now look at this—guides bring the tourists to Sigiriya and put them in hotels. Then make them climb the rock. Do not look around [the countryside]. Go back to hotels. Sir, Sigiriya is not only this rock. How much more is there to see? These paddy fields, the tanks, this village. (Punchibanda, personal communication, March 14, 2016)

Indeed, the very environment of Sigiriya Rock is a living heritage that goes back millennia. Yet all of this is missed in the programmed mass tourism experience that Sigiriya has become. Punchibanda suggests that an integrated, inclusive treatment of heritage at Sigiriya helps everyone—residents, visitors, and the nation.

Specific grievances are real and must be addressed in a comprehensive management plan that includes community participation, including community interests in cultural tourism:

> How much do these *suddo* [European tourists] spend to come to our country? Is it correct to show them this rock only? If they are shown the beauty of these villages that would bring money to the government and to the villages as well. The *suddo* come here only for one day. If they could be retained here for a couple of days, that would good for us. These [people] like to buy our traditional things. These guides take the tourists only to those places that they have associations with, because they get a commission. . . . Because such things are made in villages . . . then a program to bring them to the villages, that will be good for our incomes. (Punchibanda, personal communication, March 14, 2016)

The preservation of heritage practices in this manner arises out of a concern to keep such knowledge vital into the future. Yet some kinds of change threaten family values and neighborhood integrity when moral values are eroded through tourism development that has invaded the buffer zone with impunity:

> These hotels are the biggest threat to this area. Various types of illicit activities happen in these hotels. These activities have political support. Women are brought from outside to the hotels and things happen. Now people in these villages with land sell their lands to make hotels [through others]. The coming of hotels can bring good or bad to the villages. Youth in the villages have jobs. (Punchibanda, personal communication, March 14, 2016)

Punchibanda is ambivalent, seeing the positive economic benefits but overwhelmed by the intrusion of unwelcome unsavory life, through corrupt means, into the midst of their neighborhoods. Moreover, it is also an intrusion into forests where healers for generations have obtained important medicinal plants. But, perhaps most alarmingly, his analysis announces the interest of outside, unknown investors served by local agents. Punchibanda sees beyond these daily concerns to refocus attention on the real, lived heritage of Sigiriya:

> What we have as our heritage is tanks [dams and reservoirs], stupas, lakes, brooks, etc. Then such things as medicinal practices are also there. We need to educate others about these things. There are *parani-minissu* [old-people or ancient-people] in our villages. These people know a lot. I think that what should be done is to gather these senior people to a place and discuss about these things. (Punchibanda, personal communication, March 14, 2016)

Again, Punchibanda brings us back to the realization that heritage is embedded in the lived landscape—one that stretches over several millennia into deep time. He views the need to educate as a collective responsibility, one that could possibly be satisfied by a locally developed and managed eco-cultural tourism that features the deep heritage of hydraulic engineering and management around Sigiriya. He went on to elaborate how he would organize a Council of Elders with all villages of greater Sigiriya represented. This council could then advise the CCF and participate in CCF decision-making in the future.

What Now? Future Strategies at Sigiriya

There is no way to avoid the conclusion that failure to implement a management plan for Sigiriya has led to clear and unambiguous results: an overused, quickly eroding, poorly interpreted cultural property; a remote bureaucracy that provides only routine employment; a history of alienation from the local community dating back to relocations; a severely diminished cultural and natural environment due to poor buffer-zone enforcement; and exclusion of local heritage as it is lived today. Iconic of past Sinhalese glories, Sigiriya shrinks in value as the sustaining values and heritage of land use and ingenuity are lost around the rock.

By listening to those with local heritage knowledge, we learn that awareness about and fear of loss of heritage knowledge are key concerns among a last generation of knowledge keepers. Given their diverse heritage interests, they have no way to gather together to express their concerns, save for the Council of Elders proposed by the Punchibanda, the postman/eye healer—a positive direction that should be an integral part of the future management plan. Younger Sri Lankan archaeologists are asking for a program they might follow that departs from presentation of archaeologically defined structures to include a wider spectrum of heritage around Sigiriya. We suggest one here. What we have mentioned early in this chapter about management approaches at Sigiriya captures a broader Sri Lankan attitude toward heritage management: It is expert-centered and carried out with a bureaucratic outlook that sees the communities traditionally associated with the heritage sites as hindrances and problems not as potential and necessary participants in heritage preservation and interpretation.

Local desires for development and control over heritage tourism in the villages also emerged from a perception that those asking about local heritage were listening seriously to learn how change in the way heritage is treated at Sigiriya could be affected. The idea of a Heritage Cooperative also arose—a micro-loan fund disbursement facility made up of village elders (Council of Elders) with expertise in traditional medicinal and craft practices—to provide assistance *and advice* to those seeking to develop more direct control over local heritage performances and tourism. This institutional innovation was suggested by local heritage leaders with the aim of creating a climate of collaboration among Sigiriya project managers and local citizenry to encourage new entrepreneurial ventures, enhance heritage knowledge preservation, and govern economic development to benefit all parties.

Creating a heritage experience that includes and goes beyond archaeology alone is seen as critical to keep living heritage practices vital, with longevity over generations to come, thus meeting an express need of local knowledge-keepers. As local heritage practitioners came to understand that they were being listened to carefully, they also shared their hope to develop a new generation of local heritage experts through training programs that revitalize and preserve heritage values in the communities surround the World Heritage Site, keeping heritage values alive over the coming generations. A fresh generation of heritage experts trained by willing elders in mat weaving and basketry, snakebite medicine, general traditional medicine, indigenous woodcarving, metal-working, and storytelling, among others, draws on a holistic approach in a proposed partnership that sees value in local practices and their cultural and economic vitality.

The heritage values of Sigiriya lie in equal measure in its surrounding traditional-cultural landscape, consisting of the vast forest cover, village tanks (reservoirs), and villages as well as the ancient knowledge systems that make up complex archaeological landscapes that host protohistoric cemeteries, ancient iron-producing centers, and a number of Buddhist monastic sites. Taking this inimitable combination of the archaeological, the natural, and the traditional into consideration, a management plan for Sigiriya and its hinterland demands a heritage practice that sees the communities traditionally associated with the heritage traditions of the sites as necessary participants in heritage preservation and interpretation. Most fundamental here is a change in the governance protocols to incorporate local participation in decision-making, moving toward an inclusive process, not one dominated by central authorities alone (see Abungu 2012, 2016; Pikirayi and Schmidt 2016; Schmidt and McIntosh 1996). Such a management approach promises to give rise to the most-needed next generation of local heritage experts and instill a notion of belonging in the discourse of heritage preservation among the local population in Sigiriya.

References Cited

Abungu, P.
2012   *World Heritage and Local Communities: The Case of the "Rabai Kaya Conservation Community Project," Kenya.* National Museums of Kenya, Nairobi.
2016   Heritage, Memories, and Community Development: The Case of Shimoni Slave Caves Heritage Site, Kenya. In *Community Archaeology and Heritage in Africa: Decolonizing Practice*, edited by P. R. Schmidt and I. Pikirayi, pp. 91–111. Routledge, New York.

Atalay, S.

2012   *Community-Based Archaeology: Research with, by, and for Indigenous and Local Communities.* University of California Press, Berkeley.

Bandaranayake, S.

1992   *Sigiriya Project.* Vol. 1. Central Cultural Fund, Colombo.

2005   *Sigiriya: City, Palace, Gardens, Monasteries, Paintings.* Central Cultural Fund, Colombo.

Colwell-Chanthaphonh, C., and T. J. Ferguson (editors)

2008   *Collaboration in Archaeological Practice: Engaging Descendant Communities.* AltaMira, Lanham, MD.

de Silva, P.H.D.H.

1980   *Snake Fauna of Sri Lanka—with Special Reference to Skull, Dentition and Venom in Snakes.* National Museums of Sri Lanka, Colombo.

Ediriweera, D. S., A. Kasturiratne, A. Pathmeswaran, N. K. Gunawardena, B. A. Wijayawickrama, S. F. Jayamanne, G. K. Isbister, A. Dawson, E. Giorgi, P. J. Diggle, D. J. Lalloo, and H. J. de Silva

2016   Mapping the Risk of Snakebite in Sri Lanka—A National Survey with Geospatial Analysis. *PLoS Neglected Tropical Diseases* 10(7):e0004813. doi:10.1371/journal.pntd.0004813.

Guruge, A.W.P., T. G. Kulatunga, A. Amarasedera, H. Ratnayake, T. W. Sirisena, P. L. Prematilleke, L. K. Karunaratne, S. Bandaranayake, L. Alwis, N. de Silva, R. Silva, and C. Ellepola

1994   *The Cultural Triangle of Sri Lanka: International Campaign.* Central Cultural Fund, Colombo.

Legislative Enactments of Ceylon (1956)

1960   *Antiquities Ordinance.* Government Publications Bureau, Colombo.

Pikirayi, I., and P. R. Schmidt

2016   Introduction: Community Archaeology and Heritage in Africa: Decolonizing Practice. In *Community Archaeology and Heritage in Africa: Decolonizing Practice,* edited by P. R. Schmidt and I. Pikirayi, pp. 1–20. Routledge, New York.

Schmidt, P. R.

2017   *Community-Based Heritage in Africa: Unveiling Local Research and Development Initiatives.* Routledge, New York.

Schmidt, P. R., and R. J. McIntosh

1996   The African Past Endangered. In *Plundering Africa's Past,* edited by P. R. Schmidt and R. J. McIntosh, pp. 1–17. Indiana University Press, Bloomington.

Silva, R., S. Bandaranayake, and N. de Silva

1993   *The Cultural Triangle of Sri Lanka.* Central Cultural Fund, Colombo.

Smith, L.

2006   *Uses of Heritage.* Routledge, New York.

United Nations

2008   *Declaration on the Rights of Indigenous Peoples.* United Nations, New York.

United Nations Educational, Scientific and Cultural Organization (UNESCO)

1982   World Heritage Committee, Sixth Session, Paris, December 13–17. UNESCO, Paris.

1998   World Heritage Committee, Twenty-Second Session, Kyoto, Japan, November 30–December 5. UNESCO, Paris.

2002   World Heritage Committee, Sri Lanka. Periodic Reporting Exercise on the Application of the World Heritage Convention. Section II, State of Conservation of Specific World Heritage Properties. State Party: Democratic Socialist Republic of Sri Lanka. Property Name: Ancient City of Sigiriya. UNESCO, Paris. http://whc.unesco.org/en/statesparties/LK/documents/SriLanka; accessed March 15, 2015, but since removed. On deposit at the Postgraduate Institute of Archaeology, Colombo, Sri Lanka.

Urban Development Authority

1998   *Development Plan for Sigiriya Heritage City*. Vol. 1. Central Cultural Fund, Colombo.

PART III

Biographies of Archaeologies of Listening

12

A Lineage of Listening

ALICE B. KEHOE

I arrived on the Montana Blackfeet Reservation with a fresh B.A. from Barnard College as an anthropology major, a ticket for graduate work at Harvard, and three summers of archaeological fieldwork behind me. I was to be assistant curator, for three and a half months, at the Museum of the Plains Indian in Browning, the reservation agency town. The museum had been a Works Progress Administration (WPA) project, with a regular staff of two, the director and the maintenance man, who would be Blackfeet. What I found was an acting director, a young man named Tom Kehoe, and the maintenance man, Joe Schildt. The director, Claude E. Schaeffer, was on medical leave.

Tom had been hired by Schaeffer two years earlier to conduct an archaeological survey of the reservation. He had just completed course work for a master's degree in anthropology at the University of Washington (Seattle), following an anthropology B.A. from Beloit College, and had worked on River Basin Surveys crews along the Missouri River, excavating Indian villages that would be flooded by dams. Like me, he had been admitted to Harvard for doctoral work, in his case pending the completion of his M.A. His M.A. thesis drew on his survey of the reservation, focusing on the question of the function of rings of stones commonly termed tipi rings (Figure 12.1). Dr. Schaeffer had suggested the topic and informally directed Tom's research. The thesis was completed and submitted a few months after I had decided to remain on the reservation to marry Tom and participate in his research.

Tom's thesis featured interviews with older Indian people on the reservation. They told him where there had been camps and explained that, before the extinction of the bison herds in the 1880s, stones had been used to hold down the bottoms of their tipis. When the tipi was lifted, the stones rolled off a little and formed a ring.[1] Hearths were only sometimes built inside tipis, as people preferred to cook outside if weather permitted. All the older Indians, whose grandparents

Figure 12.1. Thomas F. Kehoe pointing out a tipi ring, in a field of tipi rings, Blackfeet Reservation, Montana. Photo by Alice B. Kehoe.

had been the generation forced to settle on the reservation, concurred that, except for a few unusually large rings, the stone rings had secured tipis. The common designation "tipi rings" was correct. Thanks to Mary Ground, a Blackfoot born in 1883, we even ground-truthed this claim, when she pulled up her tipi after the reservation's 1956 powwow and revealed the tipi ring it had left (Figure 12.2).

This might seem like a routine, straightforward archaeological interpretation for the millions of such rings once found all over the prairies, if not for professors who scorned Indians' histories. William Mulloy (1952) had argued that "tipi ring" is a folk term, to be rejected in favor of the noncommittal phrase "manifestation of unknown relationship." In support of his skepticism, he cited Lewis (1889), a report on Lewis's explorations and recording of stone constructions on the plains. Lewis, too, had urged scientists to be wary of common labels for precontact phenomena. A member of the audience who heard his report politely told him that tipi rings are indeed tipi rings, stones that once weighted down hide tipis and were left as rings when the tipis were pulled up. Dr. Washington Matthews had served as a surgeon in Dakota Territory/the Great Sioux Reservation and per-

Figure 12.2. Mary Ground, Blackfoot, explaining how she made her tipi very traditional by using rocks to hold down its curtain-like liner. When she lifted the liner, a tipi ring was left. Photographed at the conclusion of North American Indian Days, 1956, Browning, Montana, Blackfeet Reservation. Photo by Thomas F. Kehoe.

sonally observed this many times (Lewis 1889:164–165). Lewis apologized and accepted Dr. Matthews's empirical knowledge of tipis and camps. Mulloy apparently had not read the smaller-print "Discussion" following Lewis's paper.

Thus, at the beginning of my professional research, I saw the gap between empirically based inductive scientific work and its opposite, academic arrogance privileging formal Western training over any other means of interpreting archaeological data (Figure 12.3).

Over the years, I have seen and pondered the contrast. Spending some weeks each summer in Blackfoot territory, visiting with friends and collaborators there, I comprehend something of Blackfoot reality, the world in which these people live. It is as if I take off the formal tailored jacket I wear in the city; I experience the prairie wind and sun and cold rain and what distances are on that landscape, how the mountains are alive and other species of people speak— ground squirrels and birds and horses and deer and plants. Archaeological data lie in this world. They are not lab specimens to be measured and tagged with academic labels.

Figure 12.3. Elder Theodore Last Star, with clipboard, and interpreter informing archaeologist Ruth Gruhn about Blackfoot bison drives, at the Boarding School Bison Drive
site, Browning, Montana, on the Blackfeet Reservation. Photo by Alice B. Kehoe.

Frank Speck and Bedside Ethnology

The history of archaeology (and of anthropology, which to me encompasses
archaeology) reveals a persisting tension between rational theories and discom-
forting data. Private interests and ambitions, often masked, are considerations
not easily remarked. Social class was once a criterion for recognizing a scientist

(Shapin 1994) and remains, along with "race," a condition affecting opportunities for doing science. All these factors come into play in considering the work and teaching of Frank G. Speck, Claude Schaeffer's professor (Figure 12.4).

Speck (1881–1950) was an outsider, literally and professionally. From boyhood he roamed the woods and marshes of New England and New York, learning from local people, Indians, and books the habits of fauna and flora. Speck was also a sociable person who made friends easily and enjoyed eating and traveling with companions. At the same time, he meticulously and faithfully documented every specimen he acquired, whether animal, plant, or handicraft, and contributed substantial collections to a number of museums, large and small (Medoff 1991). He earned his living as a professor of anthropology at the University of Pennsylvania, taking students with him on field trips; among his students were William Fenton, A. I. Hallowell, Anthony F. C. Wallace, Edmund Carpenter, and John Witthoft (Blankenship 1991; Darnell 2006). All of these anthropologists developed close relationships with Indian people, listening and expanding their universes with other-than-human beings (Figure 12.5).

The Speck family descended from Dutch settlers in the Hudson Valley, including, they said, some Mahican ancestry. At 18, Frank finished high school in Hackensack, New Jersey, and enrolled in Columbia University. Spending a few days at Fort Shantock, Connecticut, during his holidays, Speck fell in with three Mohegan youths who took him to their community, introducing him to older relatives who spoke Pequot/Mohegan (Bruchac 2018:140–175). During his junior year at Columbia, Speck took a course in comparative philology. His professor was interested in Algonkian. When Speck revealed that there was at least one community where Pequot/Mohegan was the daily language, the professor teamed with him in collating and analyzing it. Their work was nearly ready for publication when the professor's home, with the study materials in his office, burned. All the manuscripts, including extensive journals in Pequot/Mohegan lent by matriarch Fidelia Fielding, were lost. The professor also introduced Speck to Franz Boas, with whom Speck began graduate work in anthropology, writing a dissertation on the Yuchi, whom he visited in their exile home in Oklahoma. Speck was awarded the Ph.D. by Pennsylvania, with Boas as his dissertation director. He then commenced his lifelong employment at Penn.

Speck's devotion to the tiny marginalized remnant Indian communities east of or within the Appalachians made him an anomaly in American anthropology. His position on the faculty at Penn, and Boas's approval, kept him respectable. His indefatigable and superbly documented collecting made him welcome

Figure 12.4. Frank G. Speck (*right*) and Chief Jasper Blowsnake at Winnebago Camp, Elk River Reservation, Minnesota, 1936. Photo: University of Pennsylvania Museum UPM Neg. #148615. Jasper Blowsnake was the elder brother of Sam Blowsnake, narrator of *Crashing Thunder: The Autobiography of an American Indian* (1926).

in museums, and his encyclopedic knowledge and rich fieldwork won him first-rank students, without fully negating the unease with which most anthropologists viewed his recognition of apparent "Negroes" and people who looked white as authentically of Indian descent and tradition. Speck ignored the color and class lines of American society. He recorded and published observational

Figure 12.5. Adam White Man showing Tom Kehoe a medicine rock near White Man's home, Blackfeet Reservation, Montana, 1955. He explained that he knows it is a medicine rock, because he observed that it had moved on its own. Photo by Thomas F. Kehoe.

data that supported Indian affiliations. That, like his natural history papers on amphibians drawn from field data, was solid science.

Fogelson (2016) quotes Anthony Wallace on Speck's method, expounded to his students:

There are three kinds of ethnologists; the doorstep ethnologists, the kitchen table ethnologists, and the bedside ethnologists.

The doorstep ethnologist takes a room in town at a good hotel; he comes out to the reservation and interviews people on their doorstep. [Here he fixed an imaginary monocle in his eye and scowled] "Would you marry your sister?" Then he goes back and writes a book telling all about the Indians. Then there is the kitchen table ethnologist. He comes in the morning and stays all day. He sits at the kitchen table and takes notes and asks people questions. But he wouldn't stay the night there! [Here Speck straightened up haughtily] It might be dirty upstairs! The bedside ethnologist is the only one who really gets to know the people and their culture. He stays all day; he eats with the family; he learns the language; and he sleeps in the same house. He never learns everything; but he learns a lot more than the doorstep ethnologist or the kitchen table ethnologist.

I want all of you to be bedside ethnologists.

The present book's "archaeologies of listening" approximates Speck's bedside ethnology. Niceties of terms aside, we who advocate listening are in the Frank Speck mode, never learning everything but learning a lot more than the archaeologist who only talks to community representatives or does not talk to anyone.

Whom Should We Listen To?

Frank Speck was notorious for fraternizing with communities marginalized by the United States and Canadian governments—neither recognized as Indian nor accepted as white. Their ways of speaking were judged to be uneducated dialects, their subsistence from woods, waters, and marshes to be primitive.[2] Speck heard words and phrases that he recognized as Algonkian or another American Indian language stock and saw technologies and field knowledge that he could link to early historic descriptions of Indians. East of the Appalachians, Indian nations had been forced to adapt to European colonizations for three centuries before Speck's fieldwork: Frank knew that some of Fidelia Fielding's fellow Mohegans "looked Indian" as she did, while others, equally kin, appeared phenotypically white or black. A single family can exhibit the range, as parents' genetics sort out.[3] In the heyday of White Anglo-Saxon Protestant eugenicists for whom Franz Boas was the nemesis (Spiro 2009:317–319), Speck's deep history for unrecognized tribes cast him as a radical.

With his broad range of friendships built up since youth, Speck apparently listened to hundreds of Algonkians, Iroquoians, Cherokee, and craftspeople who, by implication although not always stated, were of Indian descent. See, for example, his masterly study of *Eastern Algonkian Block-Stamp Decoration* (1947), in which he quotes a number of basketmakers and their immediate descendants, including the wonderfully named Miss Pocahontas Pharaoh, a Montauk descended from their hereditary chief Wyandank (Speck 1947:11). Using the scientific method, Speck recorded a range of variation rather than demanding the "true" or *ur*-text sought by most of his contemporaries; one of these, Clark Wissler, instructed his interpreter to find the "most common arrangement of incidents" in recording Blackfoot myths, until "a venerable old man pulled up a common ragweed, saying 'The parts of this weed all branch off from the stem. They go different ways, but all come from the same root. So it is with the different versions of a myth'" (Wissler and Duvall 1908:5).

The communities where we work may be municipalities, tribes, or bands— units in bureaucratic structures of modern nation-states, whatever the legal form. Governments require the units to elect or appoint (or accept) officers who will pass down decrees and speak for the community to the government agents; these may be selected by the actual most influential persons in the community to fulfill the government's position. When I lived in an Aymara village in Bolivia, to learn how a project to restore Tiwanaku-period raised fields met villagers' needs, I was told that the official *alcalde* (mayor) had no power. I observed that the real headman of the community was the appropriately named Don Plácido, who would speak only Aymara. It is normal for principal investigators or their field directors in an archaeological project to go to the local community, ask to speak with its officers, likely men whose names have been provided by the district governor, and formally inform them about the project. Casting a project in this colonial structure may be necessary. It is after this step, if required, that an archaeologist can hang out in the community, sit in kitchens listening to women, walk along when food or medicines are collected: brush past the ragweed, as it were, picking up its sticking seeds. One never gets the full range of variation; on the other hand, one can begin to develop a feel for the landscape, social relations, weather, and other-than-human beings including animals. Archaeological data begin to have dimensions outside conventional experience.

Boas, with his historical particularism (every society has its particular history), and Speck, with his naturalist orientation, opposed the fundamental Western Enlightenment supposition that science can discover universal regularities, "laws" to all intents and purposes. At its worst, the Western premise of universal laws led to twentieth-century fascism, not only in Adolf Hitler's Germany but also in the Rockefeller Foundation's bankrolling of projects in "[t]he social sciences, [that] like all science, are primarily concerned for analysis, prediction, and *control of behavior and values*" (Barber 1952:259; emphasis added). Less ambitious but still pernicious was, and is, conventional Western science including archaeology that "has nomothetic, generalizing, interests . . . [a] responsibility to" render non-Western peoples' experience and ideas "into the language of modern scientific and historiographic discourse" (Mason 2006:241). Such hegemony attempted by an invasive, conquering power over American Indians was consistently resisted by Fidelia Fielding. Her foster son carried on the struggle, teaching a cohort of outstanding scholars to eschew reductionism and racist hierarchies. Not incidentally, Speck recruited young American Indians to assist him in the field and to come to Penn for a university degree. They had little success there, given the impediments set before them at that time: only Gladys Tantaquidgeon, a Mohegan, is generally known today as an Indian historian trained by Speck.

Claude Schaeffer was reserved and scholarly where Speck was extroverted and an outdoorsman. Schaeffer taught Tom Kehoe how to proceed systematically through a research agenda, checking sources against sources—both oral and published—as one moves along. The published thesis (Kehoe 1960) is organized according to a Western rational schema: Historical Evidence, excerpting nineteenth-century explorers; Ethnological Considerations (Kehoe was advised to say "considerations" rather than "evidence") from Blackfoot informants and informants of other tribes; Archaeological Considerations, including environmental factors, ethnological background, and archaeological fieldwork; and, finally, "Discussion, Conclusions, and Appendix: A Modern Blackfoot Camp" (the 1956 North American Indian Days powwow in Browning, Montana, where Mary Ground put up her tipi with its ring of stones). Schaeffer liked to talk with Indians in his office in the Museum of the Plains Indian in Browning, a place filled with their families' beautiful craftwork, where they felt welcome. He worked with older Blackfoot men and middle-aged interpreters to create what he hoped would be definitive lists of Blackfoot (or at least Amskapi Pikuni, the Montana Blackfeet) bands, their leaders, and households. To do this, he laid large sheets of paper on the desk and drew up lists and genealogical connections with the men's help. All this was significant knowledge to the Pikuni men, the bones of their recent history and with real-world utility in land claims (Figure 12.6).

Figure 12.6. Chewing Black Bone, Blackfoot, a valued teacher concerning the Blackfoot world. Photo courtesy of the U.S. Department of the Interior, Indian Arts and Crafts Board, Museum of the Plains Indian. Original by D. J. Schmidt, Browning, MT, 1947.

Schaeffer advised Tom Kehoe to go out in the museum van to the homes of many respected elders, listening to them tell where there were tipi rings, why (in many instances) the camp had been there, and perhaps what family had camped there and then eventually asking whether all the rings called tipi rings were indeed rocks that had held down tipis. This was, in Speck's terms, kitchen table ethnology. The second phase of the research was Listening Part 2, taking the Blackfoot to sites that they had told him about and talking about the observed phenomena on site. After months of listening and tying verbal information to actual places and observed data, Tom hit the libraries to search explorers' journals and classic ethnographies for mentions of rocks and tipis.

Working for the People of Saskatchewan

I lived with Tom on the Montana Blackfeet Reservation for three years. He then successfully applied for the new position of provincial archaeologist for the Canadian province of Saskatchewan, and we moved to its capital, Regina. At that time (the 1960s), middle-aged residents of the province included a high proportion of people who had grown up during the Dirty Thirties, the droughts and erosion in the 1930s when few farms got any crops. There was no money. Almost no one could afford college. They stayed on the land, walking the dry, blowing fields. These were perfect conditions for noticing sites, with intelligent literate people having time to collect, read what they could find, and document their artifacts. The Saskatchewan Museum of Natural History, where Tom was based, had homegrown self-taught naturalists (especially the incomparable Fred Lahrman) and a geologist, Bruce McCorquodale, who worked at a professional level in the province. They knew hundreds of farmers, knew the landscapes, and knew the local collections. Tom drove the grid roads to the farms that his museum colleagues recommended, sat at the kitchen tables with hundreds of artifacts laid out before him, walked out with the farm people to their sites, and recorded what they told and what he saw. Many of the blowouts of the Dirty Thirties were by then blown over; the local collectors provided evidence of occupations since the Terminal Pleistocene.

There had been a little professional archaeology before Tom, mostly relatively recent salvage work by a Saskatchewan man who had archaeological training but not at the doctoral level. With so many data available and the eager cooperation of museum staff and residents of the province, Tom could construct a plan for excavating a few key sites that promised critical material for radiocarbon and stratigraphic chronologies and artifact diagnostics. We and several leading nonprofessional archaeologists who lived in the Regina area organized the Saskatchewan Archaeological Society in 1963 to link all those collectors into a democratic science for the province—as a century earlier, Joseph Henry and Spencer Baird had worked to make the Smithsonian a central node for the widely scattered self-taught naturalists of the young United States (Hinsley 1981:34).

We decided that two projects would be crucial to the program to map and manage Saskatchewan archaeological sites. A site with deep and clear stratigraphy was needed to discover a chronology of artifact types and occupations, and a site from the first European traders in the province was needed to establish both indigenous and imported artifact types at that time of historic contact. Avocational archaeologists John and Jean Hodges told us that the Gull Lake bison drive, in the southwest of the province, had indicated deep, clear stratigraphy when the avocationalists had tested it. Fur trade histories described a 1768 independent traders' post on the Saskatchewan River as the first successful post in the province. Tom decided to undertake Gull Lake, which more than fulfilled its promise, yielding a sequence of bison pounds from 200 CE to 1876, near the extinction of wild bison herds (Kehoe 1973). I took the fur trade post, called François' House after the French-Canadian voyageur who was a partner in it with the Scots immigrant merchant James Finlay (Kehoe 1978).

Neither Gull Lake nor Nipawin, where François' House was located, had First Nations communities in their areas. Gull Lake may have been used by the Blackfoot before they retreated in the early nineteenth century and may have been used by Cree during the nineteenth century, and possibly by Assiniboine. Nipawin was Cree territory historically. For the two seasons of excavation at François' House, I hired a crew of local laborers, middle-aged men who had worked on farms when they were younger, before machines made day labor redundant. Nipawin was homesteaded at the turn of the twentieth century, and some of these men had grown up in cabins not much different from the François and Finlay post cabins. They knew the history of the river running beside the terrace on which the post was built, the timber and carpentry, the soils, and how to deal with the bear and her cubs eating chokecherries for three days on the edge of our clearing. One day Reinhardt Lehne looked up from troweling and said to me, "I remember this floor. It has the fine black dust that my mother's floor had from her sweeping the cabin every day with her twig broom." Prompted, I realized that the floor of what was probably Finlay's cabin was a finer texture than the floor of another cabin likely to have been the room for the men of their brigade. Checking texts later on eighteenth-century vernacular construction methods, sedimentology, Nipawin ecology, and so on showed me how much the crew's knowledge from experience had facilitated recognition of the site's data.

Lehne's explanation of the quality of the floor of Finlay's cabin made me think about the trader's companion, mentioned in fur-trade histories as "a Saulteau woman" (Kehoe 2000:174). She bore Finlay a son, Jacques Raphael Finlay, called Jaco, conceived during the time they lived at Nipawin. Finlay had a legal, white wife back home in Montreal, whose son, James Jr., was a fur trader like his father and half-brother. The Saulteau woman was a "country wife," an

Indian woman married à la façon du pays (country custom, as the traders and historians term it). François LeBlanc, the other partner in the post, had married a young woman, perhaps the daughter of a country wife, in a Catholic ceremony at Michilimackinac, the principal depot for the inland fur trade. She and their young son accompanied François. Rival Hudson's Bay Company traders reported that François and Finlay casually permitted Indians to enter the post and kept no night guard, "even when the Natives are lying on their plantation" (Matthew Cocking quoted in Morton 1939:286).

I noted that indigenous artifacts—some small pots, stone knife and scraper blades, bone harpoon, awls, and thong softener, antler flaker, bone and shell beads—lay immediately outside the walls of the post, testimony to the "Natives lying on the plantation," particularly women, to judge by the number associated primarily with women's activities. A few sherds found close to the wall seemed impressed with traders' stroud cloth, in place of the usual twined bag fabric on Woodland sherds. I was not doing "feminist archaeology," a standpoint just breaking through into the discipline when I analyzed Francois' House. I was doing straightforward inductive inference to reach the best explanation for the range of artifacts and their positionings in the site (Kehoe 2000). Underlying my interpretations were my ethnographic experiences with Blackfoot, Cree, and Dakota women, watching and occasionally helping with their tasks, and listening to their reasons for allocations of activities to women and to men.

Wearing the Ethnographer's Cap to See Conventional Archaeology

Political upheaval, precipitated when Saskatchewan's agrarian socialist government instituted provincial health care that drew wrath and a million dollars from the American Medical Association to call for an election, cut out the province's heritage programs and my expectation to teach anthropology in the University of Regina. We moved to Lincoln, Nebraska, where Tom became director of the Nebraska Historical Society Museum and I started teaching in the university's Anthropology Department. There, in the state capital, we both experienced, head-on, life in hierarchies. My department chair, Preston Holder, actively discouraged the five faculty members from talking with one another; he apparently feared that we would plot his ouster. Tom discovered that he was to operate a program given to him by his superior in the Historical Society, a patriotic Nebraskan who wanted monuments to Pony Express stations installed with ceremony, rather than research into the state's history, postcontact or precontact. We were saved by an opening for a curator of archaeology in Tom's home state's premier museum, the Milwaukee Public Museum. Tom got the appointment, and I was hired to teach at Marquette University, a Jesuit institution that realized it needed some anthropology to look fully credited. We were both free in summer to continue fieldwork, mostly projects in Saskatchewan. We could build on collegial relationships with archaeologists there and in Alberta, professional and nonprofessional, and with Indian people I knew from my dissertation research in the province. Once again, we could drive the grid roads to sites and reserves and listen to knowledgeable people.

Now we became tenured and published members of committees in our regional and national disciplinary organizations. These brought us into association with denizens of ivory-tower major research universities. It was the heyday of Lewis Binford. The only worthwhile archaeology would be "scientific" archaeology, which exclusively used hypothetico-deductive methodology and relied on statistics. "Culture history" was damned. Neither local people nor Indian people lived in that universe. Tom, employed in a civic museum with the excellent ethnographer Nancy O. Lurie, became more active in museology matters, stubbornly ignoring Binford as more and more midwestern archaeologists became his followers. I read seriously in history/philosophy of science, discovered the sociology of science, tried to publish papers showing how inappropriate Binford's method was, and accumulated a pile of rejected papers. Only by clapping on my ethnographer's cap could I make sense of the national meetings. I observed a phenomenon that resonated with my experience in high school: my suburban school had one (officially not permitted) boys' fraternity and one girls' sorority. Most of the girls who were excluded by the sorority sisters sat around sad. We certainly could have created our own sorority, but no one did. The excluded girls were disdained and that was that. The same thing happened, I saw, with so many marginalized by announced "theorists" in anthropology and by Binford and other self-appointed "scientists" in American archaeology. Out on the margins, we talked to one another without mounting any concerted challenge to the dominant claques. Only a sociology of science can explain such failure of rational behavior.

Frank Speck had that experience of being marginalized, alongside his "Negro-looking" or Indian or "river people" research communities. Overt racism had a lot to do with that marginalization, yet there was more: dominance and marginalization are the means supporting ideologies. Those in power are the elect; those marginalized bear irredeemable defects. I found it curious that very few of the purportedly very rational scientific practitioners would read history, philosophy, or sociology of science, although they routinely cited Binford's consultant Merrilee Salmon and her husband, Wesley, whose field was philosophy of physics (see Turner 2007 for crucial differences not noted by the Salmons). Two exceptions were my friends out on the margins, Jane Kelley and Guy Gibbon.

Kelley from childhood accompanied her father, William Curry Holden, on his naturalist excursions in southern New Mexico and Arizona and adjacent Mexico. They listened to several generations of Yaqui, in Mexico and in Arizona, coming to know the land through Yaqui eyes. Jane recorded harrowing histories of Yaqui women during the Mexican war against the nation, when thousands of Yaqui were sent as slaves to plantations far away to the east (Kelley 1978). Disturbed by the "New Archaeology" subverting work like hers, Kelley teamed with Marsha Hanen, whose doctorate was in philosophy of science, to publish *Archaeology and the Methodology of Science* (Kelley and Hanen 1988). Guy Gibbon, a University of Minnesota faculty member specializing in northern Midwest archaeology, used a sabbatical to spend a year studying at the London School of Economics, at that time the center of philosophy of science debates. He then published *Explanation in Archaeology* (Gibbon 1989). No matter how sound their foundations and demonstrations of scientific reasoning appropriate to American archaeology were, Kelley and Gibbon did not inspire followers.[4]

Something much greater than reason organizes mainstream and marginal archaeology in North America (Mirowski 2005). We are all immersed in American culture. From early childhood, we listened to, saw, and moved in a society where white Christian men rule. Our school textbooks and school holiday celebrations steadily reinforced Anglo-Christian white male dominant status as the natural order of the world. *Natural Order* is the book that cracked open that ideological hegemony for me in 1981 (Barnes and Shapin 1979). It anthropologizes science, describing the cultural contexts of scientific researches. World War II shattered the centers-and-colonies structure of the "long century" from the early nineteenth to mid-twentieth century. The story of America, its frontiersmen with their axes and rifles creating civilization out of the wilderness, was being undermined as the disenfranchised struggled for rights. In reaction came a resurrection of nineteenth-century unilinear cultural evolution, constructed to scientifically prove the natural superiority of white men (Kehoe 1998:172–187). Archaeologists were welcomed to demonstrate the "law" (in quotation marks, to be sure) or regularities of cultural evolution, posed as working hypotheses to be validated by deductively sought data analyzed by means of statistical formulae. Was it just coincidence that the leader of the New Archaeology professing this science was a big blond man from the heartland of Christian Fundamentalism?

Now I was in the level of *verstehen*, a deeper, empathetic understanding. I was also engaged in anthropological efforts to contest creationism, doing ethnography with local fundamentalist churches and creationist groups and publishing on creationist culture and its contexts in American society. Parallels between evangelical fundamentalists and mainstream American archaeology, from the dominance of white men to the tautologies of proving hypotheses by deductively selecting supportive data, were all too apparent. The ethnographer's cap filtered out superficial differences. From the 1493 papal bull Doctrine of Discovery, through Supreme Court Justice John Marshall's trilogy of court decisions (1823–1832, 1840s), Manifest Destiny propaganda, Frederick Turner's 1893 frontier hypothesis, and the entrenched paternalism of the Bureau of Indian Affairs, Anglo dispossessions of American First Nations are legitimated. Challenges evoke uneasy emotions of insecurity. Acknowledging that racism continues to bedevil descendants of slaves and of "primitive" tribes is easy charity; acknowledging five centuries of deliberate deceits perpetuated by ironically revered men such as Thomas Jefferson subverts our whole edifice of common knowledge.[5]

Listening as Radical Critique

A "Fact" printed in 1776, to be read by "the candid world" concerned over 13 American colonies' Act of Rebellion, is that King George "has excited domestic insurrections amongst us, and has endeavoured to bring on the inhabitants of our frontiers, the merciless Indian Savages whose known rule of warfare, is an undistinguished destruction of all ages, sexes and conditions."[6]

Who were the "Indian Savages" on the colonies' frontiers? Primarily the Five Civilized Tribes—Cherokee, Choctaw, Chickasaw, Creek, and Seminole—whose successful plantations competed with those of the English settlers. Jefferson himself, in "Logan's Lament," which he published in 1782, acknowledged that the most mercilessly savage attacks were those of the white vigilantes upon Indian families such as Logan's (Wallace 1999). Is there any more succinct example of social charter myth than the Declaration's final "Fact" that every American schoolchild is expected to read?

Jefferson's chicanery, continued during his presidency (Miller 2008:96; Onuf 1997), laid a pragmatic foundation for the United States' inexorable expansion across the continent. Indians were to be a vanishing people, physically surviving only as assimilated persons of color in the lowest stratum of society. Frank Speck's uncovering of communities that against all odds had persisted through three centuries of persecution was a radical challenge to American hegemony. Furthermore, his bedside ethnology deliberately transgressed bedrock societal norms: *sleeping in the beds of the uncivilized*. Listening at the kitchen table is only somewhat less radical, for do we not often sip coffee from *their* cups? Our "archaeologies of listening" follow in this unfashionable practice that subverts the dominant role of "civilized scientists" in academic research.

Archaeology's own philosopher of science, Alison Wylie (2015:208), explicates what Frank Speck knew well: "those who are socially marginal may be epistemically advantaged" not only to bring into view data overlooked or misidentified by mainstream archaeologists but also "may catalyze counter-narratives and counter-norms that have the conceptual resources to capture forms of experience, dimensions of the world (social and natural) and ways of navigating it that are lacking in dominant culture."

Wylie chooses her words with care. "Dominant culture" dominates: refusal to accept its decreed boundaries is a radical move. Both Wylie and her frequent interlocutor, Sandra Harding (2016), assert the value of recognizing standpoint (Wylie 2012), and both locate their work in postcolonial critique (Harding 2016; Wylie 2015). Speck antedates postcolonialism, yet his life and work take its standpoint.

Neither Tom nor I perceived an archaeology derived from listening to Indian people to be a radical move. As Claude Schaeffer laid it out, it was an obviously efficient method to get to the sites most likely to be significant in regional precontact history and gain information about them that would not be discovered by excavation. The method worked in Saskatchewan, too, although with a settler rather than indigenous populations. After we moved into academia, we put a name to the method: the direct ethnographic approach in archaeology (Kehoe and Kehoe 1985). In the heyday of hypothetico-deductive scientistic archaeology (e.g., Watson, LeBlanc, and Redman 1971) our opposing method was ignored by mainstream academic archaeologists, even as the profession was shifting to a majority of practitioners working through cultural resource management contracts.

The Native American Graves Protection and Repatriation Act (NAGPRA) and the subsequent authorization of THPOs (tribal historic management officers) overturned the power hierarchy (Colwell 2017). With lawyers hovering in the background, museum officials and archaeologists opened doors to listen to Indian people examining collections and designating areas where archaeology might be permitted or would be out of bounds. Now listening may take place in tribal government offices more often than at kitchen tables. Archaeology has taken a historical turn (Sassaman 2010; Sassaman and Holly 2011). Even as academic subfields are broadened to include studies of the unenfranchised, the Doctrine of Discovery and Manifest Destiny still structure the way American history is taught. Seismic shifts take time.

In this chapter I have endeavored to highlight an anthropologist whose unusual naturalist bent provided him with an "epistemic advantage," enabling him to conduct ethnographies of listening among socially marginalized communities. Frank Speck created a lineage of anthropologists who were comfortable listening at kitchen tables. It was my good fortune to take a summer job that led into this lineage.

Notes

1. We interviewed Mrs. Duck Chief, an aged Siksika Blackfoot who had lived in a bison-hide tipi as a child. She told us that hide stretches under rocks, while canvas tipis don't stretch and rocks roll off. She said that people had to give up using rocks to anchor tipis when hides were no longer available. Canvas tipis are secured by pegs driven through loops on the tipis into the ground, like modern tents.

2. See, for example, John Wesley Powell's description of American Indians in his report as director of the Bureau of Ethnology (Powell 1881:xxvii–xxx). He states unequivocally that before European invasions America was occupied only by "semi-nomadic . . . savage tribes" (Powell 1881:xxvii).

3. When we lived on the Blackfeet Reservation, we were befriended by Mae Aubrey Williamson (1892–1985), a leading citizen whose father was a white trader and whose mother was from a prominent Blackfeet family. Mrs. Williamson told me that her brother was blond and blue-eyed like their father; she and one sister looked "mixed-blood"; and the third sister looked Indian. All spoke fluent Blackfoot and knew the protocols of religion and custom.

4. Fogelin (2007) is a gentle, clearly written effort to defuse New Archaeology's claim to scientific method. He explains how inference to the best explanation is generally followed by archaeologists, even those claiming to be more rigorously scientific, and emphasizes "empirical breadth" (encompassing "a wide variety of observations or evidence") as a criterion of adequate explanation (Fogelin 2007:618). Fogelin specializes in the archaeology of South Asia Buddhism, outside American archaeology's principal arena.

5. This position is expounded in Kehoe (1998, 2014) and in Wallace (1999). There is a growing scholarly literature on the Doctrine of Discovery and settler colonialism (see, e.g., Areal 1996; Ford 2010; Kennedy 1994; Robertson 2005). Miller et al. (2010) document in legal detail the continuing force of the Doctrine of Discovery in the four Anglo-founded colonial nations.

6. Declaration of Independence, "The unanimous Declaration of the thirteen united States of America," signed July 4, 1776. The quotation is the last of "27 Facts" (the document's phrase) presented to justify the colonies' rebellion.

References Cited

Areal, B.
1996   *John Locke and America: The Defense of English Colonialism.* Clarendon Press, Oxford.

Barber, B.
1952   *Science and the Social Order.* Free Press, Glencoe, IL.

Barnes, S. B., and S. Shapin (editors)
1979   *Natural Order: Historical Studies of Scientific Culture.* Sage, London.

Blankenship, R. (editor)
1991   *The Life and Times of Frank G. Speck, 1881–1950.* University Publications in Anthropology, No. 4. University of Pennsylvania, Philadelphia.

Blowsnake, Sam
1926   *Crashing Thunder: The Autobiography of an American Indian.* Prepared for publication by Paul Radin. New York: Appleton.

Bruchac, M. M.
2018   *Savage Kin: Indigenous Informants and American Anthropologists.* University of Arizona Press, Tucson.

Colwell, C.
2017   *Plundered Skulls and Stolen Spirits: Inside the Fight to Reclaim Native America's Culture.* University of Chicago Press, Chicago.

Darnell, R.
2006   Keeping the Faith. In *New Perspectives on Native North America,* edited by S. A. Kan and P. T. Strong, pp. 1–16. University of Nebraska Press, Lincoln.

Fogelin, L.
2007   Inference to the Best Explanation: A Common and Effective Form of Archaeological Reasoning. *American Antiquity* 72(4):603–625.

Fogelson, R. D.
2016   Frank G. Speck (1881–1950) and A. Irving Hallowell (1892–1974): The Generational Divide. Paper presented at American Society of Ethnohistory annual meeting, Las Vegas, NV, November 9.

Ford, L.
2010   *Settler Sovereignty: Jurisdiction and Indigenous People in America and Australia, 1788–1836.* Harvard University Press, Cambridge, MA.

Gibbon, G.
1989   *Explanation in Archaeology.* Blackwell, Oxford.

Harding, S.

2016   Latin American Decolonial Social Studies of Scientific Knowledge: Alliances and Tensions. *Science, Technology & Human Values* 41(6):1063–1087.

Hinsley, C. M., Jr.

1981   *Savages and Scientists: The Smithsonian Institution and the Development of American Anthropology 1846–1910.* Smithsonian Institution Press, Washington, DC.

Kehoe, A. B.

1978   *François' House, an Early Fur Trade Post on the Saskatchewan.* Saskatchewan Ministry of Culture and Youth, Regina.

1998   *The Land of Prehistory: A Critical History of American Archaeology.* Routledge, New York.

2000   François' House, a Significant Pedlars' Post on the Saskatchewan. In *Material Contributions to Ethnohistory: Interpretations of Native North American Life,* edited by M. S. Nassaney and Eric S. Johnson, pp. 173–187. Society for Historical Archaeology and University Press of Florida, Gainesville.

2014   Manifest Destiny and the Order of Nature. In *Nature and Antiquities: The Making of Archaeology in the Americas,* edited by P. L. Kohl, I. Podgorny, and S. Gänger, pp. 186–201. University of Arizona Press, Tucson.

Kehoe, T. F.

1960   Stone Tipi Rings in North-Central Montana and the Adjacent Portions of Alberta, Canada: Their Historical, Ethnological, and Archeological Aspects. Anthropological Papers, No. 62. *Smithsonian Institution Bureau of American Ethnology, Bulletin* 173: 417–473, Plates 48–61. Government Printing Office, Washington, DC.

1973   The Gull Lake Site: A Prehistoric Bison Drive in Southwestern Saskatchewan. Publication in Anthropology and History No. 1. Milwaukee Public Museum, Milwaukee.

Kehoe, T. F., and A. B. Kehoe

1985   The Direct Ethnographic Approach to Archaeology on the Northern Plains. In *Reprints in Anthropology,* vol. 30, pp. 1–10. J & L Reprints Co., Lincoln, NE.

Kelley, J. H.

1978   *Yaqui Women: Contemporary Life Histories.* University of Nebraska Press, Lincoln.

Kelley, J. H., and M. P. Hanen

1988   *Archaeology and the Methodology of Science.* University of New Mexico Press, Albuquerque.

Kennedy, R. G.

1994   *Hidden Cities: The Discovery and Loss of Ancient North American Civilization.* Free Press, New York.

Lewis, T. H.

1889   Stone Monuments in Southern Dakota (with reports of discussion by members of the Anthropological Society). *American Anthropologist* 2:162–165.

Mason, R. J.

2006   *Inconstant Companions: Archaeology and the North American Indian Oral Traditions.* University of Alabama Press, Tuscaloosa.

Medoff, C.

1991   The Frank Speck Collections and the Documentation of the Material He Collected. In *The Life and Times of Frank G. Speck, 1881–1950*, edited by R. Blankenship, pp. 102–127. University Publications in Anthropology, No. 4. University of Pennsylvania, Philadelphia.

Miller, R. J.

2008   *Native America, Discovered and Conquered: Thomas Jefferson, Lewis and Clark, and Manifest Destiny*. University of Nebraska Press, Lincoln.

Miller, R. J., J. Ruru, L. Behrendt, and T. Lindberg

2010   *Discovering Indigenous Lands: The Doctrine of Discovery in the English Colonies*. Oxford University Press, New York.

Mirowski, P.

2005   Economics/Philosophy of Science: How Positivism Made a Pact with the Postwar Social Sciences in the United States. In *The Politics of Method in the Human Sciences*, edited by G. Steinmetz, pp. 142–172. Duke University Press, Durham.

Morton, A. S.

1939   *A History of the Canadian West to 1870-71*. Thomas Nelson and Sons, London.

Mulloy, W. T.

1952   The Northern Plains. In *Archeology of Eastern United States*, edited by J. B. Griffin, pp. 124–138. University of Chicago Press, Chicago.

Onuf, P. S.

1997   Thomas Jefferson, Missouri, and the "Empire for Liberty." In *Thomas Jefferson and the Changing West: From Conquest to Conservation*, edited by J. P. Ronda, pp. 111–153. Missouri Historical Society Press, St. Louis.

Powell, J. W.

1881   *First Annual Report of the Bureau of Ethnology*. Government Printing Office, Washington, DC.

Robertson, L. G.

2005   *Conquest by Law: How the Discovery of America Dispossessed Indigenous Peoples of Their Lands*. Oxford University Press, New York.

Sassaman, K. E.

2010   *The Eastern Archaic, Historicized*. AltaMira, Lanham, MD.

Sassaman, K. E., and D. H. Holly Jr. (editors)

2011   *Hunter–Gatherer Archaeology as Historical Process*. University of Arizona Press, Tucson.

Shapin, S.

1994   *A Social History of Truth*. University of Chicago Press, Chicago.

Speck, Frank G.

1947   *Eastern Algonkian Block-Stamp Decoration*. Archeological Society of New Jersey, Trenton.

Spiro, J. P.

2009   *Defending the Master Race: Conservation, Eugenics, and the Legacy of Madison Grant*. University of Vermont Press, Burlington.

Turner, D.

2007   *Making Prehistory: Historical Science and the Scientific Realism Debate*. Cambridge University Press, Cambridge.

Wallace, A.F.C.

1999   *Jefferson and the Indians*. University of Michigan Press, Ann Arbor.

Watson, P. J., S. A. LeBlanc, and C. L. Redman

1971   *Explanation in Archeology: An Explicitly Scientific Approach*. Columbia University Press, New York. (2nd ed. by Watson and LeBlanc, *Archeological Explanation: The Scientific Method in Archeology*. Columbia University Press, New York, 1984.)

Wissler, C., and D. C. Duvall

1908   *Mythology of the Blackfoot Indians*, Anthropological Papers, Vol. 2, Pt. 1, pp. 1–163. American Museum of Natural History, New York.

Wylie, A.

2012   Feminist Philosophy of Science: Standpoint Matters. *Proceedings and Addresses of the APA [American Philosophical Association]* 86(2):46–76.

2015   A Plurality of Pluralisms: Collaborative Practice In Archaeology. In *Objectivity in Science*, edited by F. Padovani, A. Richardson, and J. Y. Tsou, pp. 189–210. Boston Studies in the Philosophy and History of Science 310. Springer, New York.

13

Colonial Encounters of First Peoples and First Anthropologists in British Columbia, Canada

Listening to the Late Nineteenth-Century Voices of the Jesup North Pacific Expedition

CATHERINE C. CARLSON

COMMENTARY BY ALICE B. KEHOE

In this chapter we discuss the earliest professional anthropological fieldwork undertaken within the Canadian province of British Columbia, led by anthropologist Franz Boas of the Jesup North Pacific Expedition, focusing on the young archaeologist he hired. Boas's pioneering expedition of 1897–1899, under the auspices of the American Museum of Natural History, centered on two culture areas in British Columbia, the Northwest Coast and the Interior Plateau. The expedition involved ethnographic, linguistic, biological, and archaeological data collection on the indigenous peoples of the Pacific Northwest. Boas employed Harlan I. Smith (1872–1940) on the expedition to direct the first archaeological fieldwork in the region.

Smith undertook three years of archaeological fieldwork in British Columbia in 1897, 1898, and 1899. He directed his fieldwork in the Interior Plateau to the Thompson River Valley between Kamloops and Lytton, but he also worked along the Lillooet River and on the lower Fraser River at the coast. His Interior Plateau work took him into the villages of the Secwepemc (Shuswap), Nlaka'pamux (Thompson), St'at'imc (Lillooet), and Halkomelem-speaking (Coast Salish) peoples.

This chapter reexamines Smith's Jesup Expedition publications, along with his unpublished field letters and postcards, with the goal of listening to the unedited informal voices of people, both indigenous and not, who contributed to documenting indigenous cultures during the late nineteenth century. There is reluctance within the indigenous communities of British Columbia today to embrace archaeology as a worthwhile endeavor, and I suggest that this has its roots in the Jesup Expedition. Smith's field letters reflect the beginnings of important issues for archaeologists that persist to this day, including concern with cultural appropriation, ethical practice, community involvement, and patronizing colonial attitudes (Carlson 2005; Thom 2000, 2001).

Smith published several well-illustrated Jesup memoirs. He also wrote several letters and postcards from the field to Franz Boas, although only eight pages of field notes are archived. Smith was an accomplished photographer, producing several scrapbooks of photographs with notes and annotation. Many artifacts, skeletal collections, plaster "life masks," and ethnographic objects were also collected and are still housed at the American Museum of Natural History in New York.

The letters that Smith wrote to Boas provide a firsthand, unedited, informal account of archaeology's beginnings in the Pacific Northwest. Along with the photographs, they are a body of unedited material that provides insight into the early practice of scientific archaeology in North America and also into the early working relations with the indigenous communities. Building on my own archeological work in the region, I researched these documents with the goal of listening to the perspective of the communities on what archaeology might have meant to them.

An important aspect of the letters and photographs is how they portray the dominating influence of Franz Boas on Smith's work. The letters reveal how the majority of Smith's field time and funding went into either excavating human burials, photographing portraits of the Native peoples as specimens or physical types, or making and shipping plaster casts or life masks of peoples' heads, all at the request of Boas. Physical anthropology, not archaeology, was what Boas was focused on. Consequently, the majority of archaeological artifacts recovered were grave goods.

Smith (1900:402–403) describes his 1897 excavations at Spences Bridge on the Thompson River: "At Spences Bridge a single grave was the most interesting site explored. . . . There are numerous old graves near by, which the Indians did not wish us to explore, while they assisted in exploring the first grave, which had been unknown to them."

After Spences Bridge, Smith moved upriver to Kamloops, where he met with both the chief of the band, Chief Louie, and the local missionary, Father Le Jeune. In a postcard to Boas, Smith writes (June 18, 1897, AMNH accession no. 1897–27):[1]

Dr. Boas, Indians here object to my taking bones away—They are friendly & will allow me to dig graves & take all but the bones. I have seen [the Indian] agent, and Indians are on the fence. We hope they will change their minds & allow bones to go to N.Y. for study not for joke as they fear.

The next letter in the files is from the town of Lytton. Smith describes how the issue of removing bones was resolved there with the help of the priest (July 14, 1897, AMNH no. 1897–27):

Both here [Lytton] and at Kamloops the site of work is on Indian re-serves—at both places I was welcome to take stone, shell etc. but refused human bones. At Kamloops they, after holding a big council where my side was presented by the Priest [Le Jeune], telling them I came to get things to use to teach the people in N.Y. decided to let me have a few bones to teach with but I must cover up all I did not take so no bad white men would take them to make fun of the Indians.

What finally swayed the community was the promise that the bones would be used for teaching purposes. The community was shown photographs of the displays at the American Museum to convince them of this. Smith (1899:102) wrote:

Finally the confidence of the people was gained by the help of a number of photographs of the museum, in which it was shown how the people visited the halls in order to see the wonderful works of the Indians, and how they were instructed, by means of lectures, in regard to the meaning of all these objects, and from that time on they rather helped than resisted any endeavor to obtain collections.

In his second year of fieldwork in 1898, Smith brought his new wife, Helena, along. She was interested in the work of women in the communities, publish-ing a newspaper article for the *New York Daily Tribune* entitled "Mrs. Harlan I. Smith Makes a Study of the Indians." Smith (1898) wrote that she was "much interested in the life of the Indian women of this dry interior region. . . . While the Siwashes [men] here . . . engage in irrigating and tilling their ranches, fish-ing for salmon, etc., the Klutchmans [women] are industrious in digging edible roots, making baskets, tanning deerskins and making them into moccasins."

Bruchac (2014) has recently written about how Boas's ethnographic work on the Northwest Coast largely marginalized the role of women in the First

Nations cultures on the coast of British Columbia, which is also true for the communities in the Plateau. Still, the Smiths did record women's work. Harlan wrote to Boas on April 21, 1898:

> While at the village I saw a little girl scraping a skin with a stone hafted in a handle about 3 ft. long similar to the one [James] Teit collected. Closer inspection showed 3 of these hafted scrapers & the skin stretched on a frame. I contemplate photographing her at work tomorrow and then buying the whole outfit for you as I think you will want it for a group [exhibit].

In the 1899 fieldwork at Lillooet on the Fraser River, Smith wrote to Boas about obtaining 16 skeletons, informing him of the secretive nature of his collecting (August 19, 1899, AMNH no. 1899–3): "By taking skeletons out on backs we got them out without Indians realizing the bulk & so free from objections but when the Indians return from fishing it would not be pleasant to be here." Later in the season, Smith wrote again to Boas on various matters, including revisiting the problem of recovering the skeletons in the Lillooet Valley (September 16, 1899, AMNH no. 1899–3):

> I consider that no trouble will arise from my work up the Lillooet, and yet as the work was done while only a few Indians were there, those who were absent and have since returned, might object. Those that were present did not comfort me much, and I feel that I would rather let the matter be digested by them before taking up more extensive archaeological studies which must of necessity to careful work and preservation of specimens be done more openly. The skeletons I collected there and at other places are evidence that I am not trying to get out of running some risks on small insurance.

In 1899 Smith traveled to the Nicola Valley, bringing copies of his complete monograph "Archaeology of Lytton" with him to show drawings of the artifact to the elders from several communities, for interpretation. He wrote to Boas: "I have shown the Lytton Memoir to Indians and have gotten nearly all doubtful points explained" (September 30, 1899, AMNH no. 1899–3). These interpretations were then published in Smith (1900) as appendix II. Smith (1900:440) wrote that the information on interpretation was obtained from "Baptiste[,] an old Indian shaman living in the valley; Michel, an intelligent old Indian of Lytton; Salicte, chief at Nicola Lake; and the brothers of the last named." For example, he showed them a particular artifact: "This Baptiste considered to represent an unfinished pipe. The theory seems plausible, although the pipe would have been very small. Michel of Lytton thought it represented a small hammer, to be hafted in a little handle and used by a slave or servant to crush food for a rich and toothless old person" (440). Another example was an artifact that "Baptiste and Mr. Teit agree was undoubtedly used for such purposes as chipping arrow-points, carving wood, and cutting out steatite pipes. They were not impressed with the opinion of Michel of Lytton, that it was used for cutting nephrite" (440–441).

Listening to sometimes differing or conflicting interpretations about material culture by individual community members creates a layer of complexity to the listening process that Smith felt compelled to present as an appendix to an unrelated volume.

Discussion

Despite the focus in the field on recovering human skeletons, Smith's years at the American Museum following fieldwork, 1900–1911, were spent cataloguing, installing exhibits, and writing publications that focused on material culture. There is only a single paragraph in the Thompson memoir (Smith 1900) about the collection of burials. Smith was not a physical anthropologist, and Boas did not entrust the Jesup skeletal materials to Bruno Oetteking until 1913. None of the burials from the Interior Plateau were analyzed.

It is apparent from both the letters and the published memoirs that Smith, lacking strong research questions of his own, was led entirely by Boas's agenda. In his subordinate position to both Boas and Jesup (who was funding the expedition), combined with his unfamiliarity with the indigenous people in whose villages he was trying to collect, dig, photograph, and cast, Smith sometimes found himself in conflicting and tenuous circumstances. Collecting burdened him with many logistical and ethical challenges. The correspondence only provides hints of the degree of complex cultural negotiations that Smith found himself engaged in. He felt that he needed to collect large numbers of specimens to ensure his job security, produce substantive written materials, and provide adequate specimens for museum displays.[2]

Smith realized that disturbance of Indian graves was probably controversial in every community where he worked. Sneaking out skeletons at considerable risk in Lillooet was ethically problematic for him. Constantly in negotiations with the Native people, Smith was most successful in Kamloops and Lytton/

Spences Bridge and the Nicola Valley, where he was able to rely on the priest Father Le Jeune and Boas's ethnographer James Teit (who was married to an indigenous woman) to function as cultural intermediaries. Long after the publication of the Jesup results, Smith (1913:4) wrote of these sensitive issues:

> In the same way that we desire to cling to the property of our ancestors, so the Indians revere and guard the land of their forefathers. It was sometimes difficult to persuade the Indians who owned the land where most of the explorations were conducted to allow the work to be carried on. But when the purpose of the investigation was explained to them, some of the Indians highly appreciated the work; in fact they favoured it more than many of our own people do.

It is apparent that Smith labored under difficult circumstances to accomplish the goals of the Jesup Expedition. He proceeded with limited funding, minimal and untrained field helpers, and occasional bouts of ill health. He must have been frustrated that he did not entirely share Boas's interest in physical anthropology and coastal archaeology and that the coastal people strongly objected to having their heads cast. He clearly distinguished skull collection from doing archaeology, as noted in a letter about Lillooet (August 25, 1899, AMNH no. 1899–3): "If it had not been that skulls were wanted from there could I have gone for archaeology?"

Smith was aware that he was taking much away from the traditional territories and that he lived in danger of being seen as a "grave robber" like George Dorsey, his competition from the Chicago Field Museum of Natural History. He was cognizant that he not only was removing artifacts from these ancestral villages but was also removing them from the Dominion of Canada. These concerns may explain why he wanted to get assurance from Boas that the people of Spences Bridge, for example, got their own copies of the photographs. Although Smith's letters indicate that he valued the interpretations of material culture from the elders, his published material is largely descriptive and lacking interpretation. It is not known if Smith sent copies of the published memoirs to the chiefs of the villages; his 1913 monograph notes only: "Over one hundred copies [of the memoirs] were given to leading libraries and learned societies in all the great countries of the world" (Smith 1913:4).

The standards of field practice set by Boas greatly influenced the development of the discipline of anthropology in the late nineteenth century and well into the twentieth century. The legacy of the "Boasian tradition" has had an enormous influence on the creation of scientific knowledge of indigenous cultures. In the final analysis, Smith's "series of explorations" *introduced* archaeology to British Columbia's First Nations peoples. Given the strength and continuity of oral history in the First Nations communities today, combined with a reverence for their ancestors, it is not surprising that their nineteenth-century view about what archaeologists do (they steal from graves) persists today.

One of the characteristics of scientific practice is to dismiss old or pioneering studies as obsolete. For archaeology, this practice of dismissal has resulted in obfuscating the political impact of the Jesup legacy on current indigenous views of contemporary archaeology. The early methods of collecting have created a lasting and generally negative view among the First Nations about the practice of archaeology in British Columbia today.

The nineteenth century witnessed the development of an array of new sciences and the beginning of professionalized practitioners of these new fields of study, including anthropology, then in its infancy. Morris Jesup had the goal of making "a museum organized for science" (Freed 2012:60) and turned to vertebrate paleontology and anthropology as two sciences worthy of development in a museum setting. I think that it is important to recognize that the formation of anthropology as a scientific department at the American Museum followed the same path as vertebrate paleontology, with its similar research and collections goals. Both of these sciences were well suited to the amassing of specimens for exhibit.

The publications derived from the first anthropological field projects are in a genre of dispassionate empirical scientific discourse that was intended for an academic audience. The scientific discourse of that time had its own particular powerful genre, a style of writing that persuasively classified and described the natural world with greater accuracy, formality, and authority. Due to that formal and authoritarian style of nineteenth-century scientific writing, one that privileges the scientific approach, the "informal" voices of both the indigenous peoples and their anthropological practitioners are not generally embedded within the published scientific discourse—and, if they are, then only as a brief footnote.

The Jesup publications, along with other anthropological texts, became the privileged authority on how knowledge of indigenous culture was presented to nonindigenous settlers and their governments and are the ethnographic roots of the histories of First Nation culture into the contemporary world. While formal authority was a major goal of the emerging scientific practice, the result was that the indigenous peoples themselves were not listened to and eventually came to feel as if they were treated as mere specimens. As a consequence, archaeology is still viewed with suspicion and misunderstanding in the First Nations communities today.

Commentary on Harlan Smith, Franz Boas, and Their Struggles with Science

Alice Kehoe

Carlson's characterization of the academic style of pioneering professional archaeology opens up a major issue still festering in archaeology: whether writing as a scientist requires a dispassionate, abnegating style. Part of postcolonial positioning calls for recognizing the cultural bias carried by imperial powers' designated scientists. Writing in the objective third-person style of scientific discourse not only precluded reflexivity by authors regarding their reactions and emotions but conveyed a positivist impression of unassailable reporting.

Harlan Smith's grave robbing poisoned relations between British Columbia First Nations and later archaeologists, yet his letters make it clear that he keenly felt himself to be a young recent hire, obliged to follow his employer's orders if he wished to continue in his chosen profession and support a family. He left the American Museum in 1911 to join the Dominion of Canada as an archaeologist, managing data from all over Canada until his retirement in 1937. In an obituary, a colleague wrote that "'recording the facts' was another of his great enthusiasms, and he made the most detailed record of all specimens, all photographs" (Leechman 1942:114). During his tenure supervising archaeology in Canada, he admitted to W. B. Nickerson, funded to work in Manitoba, that "I have enough other things to do that interest me more, so that I would not miss it if I never gave any attention to Manitoba or for that matter to archaeology" (Dyck 2016:204); nevertheless, he performed the duties of his office as he had carried out Boas's directives, with energy and effort.

So, if Harlan Smith had little choice but to follow Boas's directives, what was Boas up to? No ghoul, Franz Boas led liberal attacks on the racism ruling the United States, most famously in his measurements of immigrant children's heads that demonstrated that residents in the United States correspondingly developed broader heads than their parents. Anthropometry, particularly of the skull, was a basic technique of scientific anthropology in the nineteenth century, making skulls the most important data to be collected (Little 2010; see Boas letters in Stocking 1974:202–218). Boas began his employment with the American Museum in 1896, after nearly two years without a job; he, like Smith, had a young wife to support. As Smith had to fulfill Boas's expectations, Boas had to fulfill those of his boss, Morris K. Jesup, president of the American Museum, banker, and philanthropist, who was actively interested in Arctic exploration. Jesup funded the North Pole expeditions of Robert Peary, along with the North Pacific anthropological expeditions bearing his name, which were organized and participated in by Boas. Jesup's patronage was a prize that enabled Franz Boas to establish himself as more than merely a scientist, as a power figure during anthropology's development as a credentialed discipline (Freed 2012:70–72).

Anthropology is somewhat of an anomaly among the sciences. Because it is involved with human beings, it cannot manipulate its research objects. These have the same length of life and needs for space and freedom to move as the anthropologists who study them, in contrast to scientists whose fruit flies or mice or even chimpanzees produce generations during the span of the observers' studies and can be caged. How should anthropologists demonstrate that they are scientists, that their work should be counted in this prestigious profession? Boas and his successor at the American Museum, Clark Wissler, knew quite well that they and their colleagues must adhere to writing in the style of the genre science.

In a frequently cited paper, rhetorician Carolyn R. Miller (1984) argued for "Genre as Social Action." Form and rules in a genre of discourse identify a community; those who wish to participate in that community, in this case the community of recognized scientists, must adhere to the genre's standards. Miller emphasizes that genres are historically and culturally situated, changing over time (Miller 1984:158). From the mid-nineteenth to the mid-twentieth century, scientific discourse was required to look objective by omitting information on the personal experiences and emotions of the science author. Science writing was descriptive, displaying only factual data that, in principle, any other scientist could examine directly. Abundant illustrations, accurate drawings, or photographs did, in fact, allow readers' virtual witnessing of data.

The Anthropological Papers of the American Museum during Boas's and Wissler's tenures carefully present factual descriptions in standard educated English (Wissler [1913] wrote a paragraph in Latin in his monograph on Blackfoot ceremonies, when Horn Society initiation entailed coitus to transfer power). To include experiences and feelings such as Harlan Smith did in his letters, even to include his detailed accounts of negotiations with First Nations communities, would have jeopardized recognition of his work and reports as science. Morris Jesup supported many humanitarian agencies, but the American Museum was a scientific institution objectively displaying objects. Skeletons of First Nations' great-grandparents were no more privileged than those of whales and dinosaurs.

Notes

1. All letters cited are from the American Museum of Natural History archives, with three different years, as noted in the text for each quotation.

2. Contemporary with museum-sponsored fieldwork to collect specimens, a number of merchants in western North America purchased indigenous craftwork and artifacts to sell to museums, private collectors, and the public. They created a new market for items that had not had prior commercial value (Koffman 2012:175).

References Cited

Bruchac, Margaret M.

2014   My Sisters Will Not Speak: Boas, Hunt, and the Ethnographic Silencing of First Nations Women. *Curator: The Museum Journal* 57(2):151–171.

Carlson, C.

2005   Letters from the Field: Reflections on the Nineteenth-Century Archaeology of Harlan I. Smith in the Southern Interior of British Columbia, Canada. In *Indigenous Archaeologies: Decolonising Theory and Practice*, edited by C. Smith and H. M. Wobst, pp. 134–169. Routledge, London.

Dyck, I.

2016   *The Life and Work of W. B. Nickerson (1865–1926)*. Mercury Series Anthropological Papers No. 177. Canadian Museum of History and University of Ottawa Press, Ottawa.

Freed, S. A.

2012   *Anthropology Unmasked: Museums, Science, and the Politics in New York City.* Vol. 1. Orange Frazer Press, Wilmington, OH.

Koffman, D. S.

2012   Jews, American Indian Curios, and the Westward Expansion of Capitalism. In *Chosen Capital: The Jewish Encounter with American Capitalism*, edited by R. Kobrin, pp. 168–188. Rutgers University Press, New Brunswick, NJ.

Leechman, D.

1942   Harlan I. Smith. *Canadian Field-Naturalist* 56:114. http://canadianarchaeology.com/caa/about/awards/smith-wintemberg-award/harlan-i-smith; accessed November 18, 2017.

Little, M. A.

2010   Franz Boas's Place in American Physical Anthropology and Its Institutions. In *Histories of American Physical Anthropology in the Twentieth Century*, edited by M. A. Little and K.A.R. Kennedy, pp. 55–86. Lexington Books, Lanham, MD.

Miller, C. R.

1984   Genre as Social Action. *Quarterly Journal of Speech* 70:151–167.

Smith, H. I.

1899   Archaeology of Lytton, British Columbia. In *The Jesup North Pacific Expedition*, edited by F. Boas, pp. 129–161. Memoir of the American Museum of Natural History. Vol. 1, Part 3. American Museum of Natural History, New York.

1900   Archaeology of the Thompson River Region, British Columbia. In *The Jesup North Pacific Expedition*, edited by F. Boas, pp. 401–442. Memoir of the American Museum of Natural History, Vol. 1, Part 6. American Museum of Natural History, New York.

1913   *The Archaeological Collection from the Southern Interior of British Columbia.* Publication 1290. Canada Department of Mines, Geological Survey of Canada, Ottawa.

Smith, Mrs. H. I.

1898   Mrs. Harlan I. Smith Makes a Study of the Indians. *New York Daily Tribune*, July 10, 1898. American Museum of Natural History, Anthropology Archives accession no. 1898–47.

Stocking, G. W., Jr. (editor)

1974   *The Shaping of American Anthropology, 1883–1911: A Franz Boas Reader.* Basic Books, New York.

Thom, B.

2000   Precarious Rapport: Harlan I. Smith and the Jesup North Pacific Expedition *Native American Studies* 14:3–10.

2001   Harlan I. Smith's Jesup Fieldwork on the Northwest Coast. In *Gateways: Exploring the Legacy of the Jesup North Pacific Expedition*, edited by I. Krupnik and W. W. Fitzhugh, pp. 139–180. Arctic Studies Center, National Museum of Natural History, Smithsonian Institution, Washington, DC.

Wissler, C.

1913   Societies and Dance Associations of the Blackfoot Indians. *Anthropological Papers of the American Museum of Natural History* 11(4):359–460. American Museum of Natural History, New York.

Contributors

KATHRYN WEEDMAN ARTHUR is associate professor of anthropology in the Department of Society, Culture, and Language, University of South Florida, St. Petersburg. Over the last two decades she has conducted extensive ethno-archaeological research in southern Ethiopia on lithic technology. Her publications and expertise span from gender and technology to community approaches in the study of sacred sites.

CATHERINE C. CARLSON holds a Ph.D. in archaeology from the University of Massachusetts, Amherst. She has conducted field research in British Columbia for several decades and is now senior archaeology manager of a First Nations consulting company, Inlailawatash, owned by Tlseil-Waututh Nation in North Vancouver.

AUDREY HORNING is distinguished professor of anthropology at the College of William and Mary and professor of archaeology as well as Fellow, Senator George J. Mitchell Institute of Global Peace, Security, and Justice at Queen's University Belfast, Northern Ireland. Her work spans the Atlantic, with archaeological investigations in the Chesapeake region and in colonial settings in Northern Ireland, the latter incorporating community engagements as a means of conflict transformation.

ALICE B. KEHOE is professor emeritus of anthropology at Marquette University, Milwaukee, and research associate in anthropology at the University of Wisconsin, Milwaukee. She is the author of eighteen books and monographs, including *The Land of Prehistory: A Critical History of American Archaeology*. She started field research among the Blackfeet people in the late 1950s and has continued to be active in the archaeology and ethnohistory of the Great Plains.

STEPHEN A. MROZOWSKI is professor of anthropology and director of the Fiske Center for Archaeological Research at the University of Massachusetts, Boston. He has examined a broad spectrum of problems in historical archaeology in eastern North America and the Caribbean, ranging from boarding houses in industrial settings to plantation slavery, and more recently practicing community archaeology among Nipmuc descendants in Massachusetts.

GEORGE NICHOLAS is professor and chair of the Department of Archaeology at Simon Fraser University, Barnaby, British Columbia. He has published widely on indigenous and community archaeology for thirty years and developed and directed SFU's Indigenous Archaeology Program on the Kamloops Indian Reserve. As director of the Intellectual Property Issues in Cultural Heritage (IPinCH) Project (2008–2016), he engaged in developing and nurturing community archaeology and heritage projects in international settings.

BILLY Ó FOGHLÚ is a Ph.D. candidate at the Australian National University. His research focuses on the northern Australia, working closely with Traditional Owners, the knowledge-keepers who understand the function of "mound sites" that heretofore have perplexed archaeologists.

INNOCENT PIKIRAYI is professor and chair of the Department of Anthropology and Archaeology, University of Pretoria, South Africa. He began his archaeological career in Zimbabwe, where he became engaged in the archaeology of the Mutapa state, in northern Zimbabwe. He is well known for his definitive research into Great Zimbabwe and for his groundbreaking community archaeology work in southern Africa.

PETER R. SCHMIDT is professor emeritus of anthropology and African Studies at the University of Florida and extraordinary professor of anthropology and archaeology at the University of Pretoria, South Africa. He began his studies of deep-time African history in 1966 when he was a student at Makerere University, Uganda. He is the author or editor of fifteen books, most recently focusing on community archaeology and heritage studies in Africa as well as ensuring that indigenous publications of oral traditions are accessible to wide international audiences.

JONATHAN WALZ is associate professor and academic director of the School for International Training in Zanzibar and research associate of the Field Museum, Chicago. He has engaged in long-term archaeological and ethnographic research in eastern Tanzania, publishing on his comprehensive surveys and findings that shed new light on the interior dimensions of Swahili civilization.

CAMINA WEASEL MOCCASIN received her bachelor's degree in archaeology and geography from the University of Lethbridge. She is a member of the Blackfoot Nation and uses traditional and archaeological knowledge to help people gain a deeper understanding of her ancestors and their way of life. Most recently she has worked as the manager of the Writing-on-Stone/Áísínai'pi Rock Art Monitoring Program as well as the head of education at Head-Smashed-In Buffalo Jump, UNESCO World Heritage Site, Alberta, Canada.

JAGATH WEERASINGHE is professor of archaeology and immediate past director of the Post Graduate Institute of Archaeology, University of Kilaniya, Colombo, Sri Lanka. One of Sri Lanka's most prominent artists, he brings a diverse background to archaeology that includes art restoration and management of archaeology research at Sigiriya, a World Heritage Site.

Index

Page numbers in *italics* indicate illustrations.

Hall, Robert L., North American archaeology, 172n5

Hassanamesit, Massachusetts, 68, 79; Hassanamesit Woods, 66, 86; management committee, 6; project, 65, 71, 74, 84–85

Hassanamisco, 67, 71, 73, 75, 79, 84; Hassanamisco Nipmuc, 77, 87; Hassanamisco Nipmuc Reservation, 71, 84

Haya (Bahaya), Tanzania, 12–13, 17; apprenticeship to Haya history-keepers, 179, 183–84; Bantu-speakers, 177; changing heritage and curation of royal paraphernalia, 193; deep time memorials, 177; heritage, 187; historical writings about, 196; history-making, 178; kingdoms, 191; norms of gender exclusion, 184

Healers (*Mganga*): Tanzania, 14, 113–19, 122–23, 126–28; Sigiriya, Sri Lanka, 229–35, 237–43

Healing (*Mganga*), 113–19, 122–23, 126–28

Heritage (IPinCH project), 156, 162, 169; benefits of, 156; control of, 156; indigenous conceptions of, 157, 162; intangible, 161, 162, 171; management of sites, 157–58, 160, 162, 168–70; tangible, 161, 165, 167, 168; values, 168, 167, 169, 171; Western perspectives or values, 157, 159, 171

Heritage Cooperative, Sigiriya, 243

Hinda (Bahinda) royal clan, Buhaya, 182, 184

Hinterland, East Africa, 114, 124–26

HIV/AIDS: coming to Haya, Tanzania, 185; impact on elderly male knowledge keepers, 197

Hokotehi Moriori Trust, 163–65

Holley, Cheryll Toney, 65–66

Hul'qumi'num First Nation, British Columbia, 157

Human remains (ancestral), 156, 166, 168

Humility (epistemic), 14–15

Hydronyms, 149

IBE (Inference to Best Explanation), 267n4

ICOMOS (International Committee on Monuments and Sites), 224, 226

Indigenous: archaeology, 160, 169, 171n1, 172; knowledge systems, 25, 27, 29–30, 33–35, 41, 99–101, 107, 114, 116, 128, 177, 179, 182–85, 191, 197–98, 157–58, 164, 228, 230–34, 239, 242–44; testing local research hypothesis, 181

Intellectual Property, 161, 170; appropriation of, 171; issues. *See also* IPinCH

Inuit, 169

IPinCH (Intellectual Property Issues in Cultural Heritage), 18, 161, 169, 170, 179n9

Ireland, 15, 202–23

Iron Forge at Kaiija shrine, excavation and dating, 182

James, William, 68, 70

Janja, Rashidi Ali (Zigua healer), 114, 119, 120–23

Jefferson, Thomas, 265–66

Jesup North Pacific Expedition, 272–73, 276–78

João de Barros (Portuguese chronicler), about Zimbabwe, 131

Kahigi II, King of Kihanja Kingdom (Tanzania): political manipulations, 191; involvement in Ngogo River massacre, 196

Kaiija shrine, Katuruka, Tanzania: association with ancient oral traditions, iron forge, 182–84; association with Cwezi and Njeru, 187, 191; association with King Rugomora Mahe, iron tower, 181, 184–85, 194; local preservation by Katuruka citizens, 192; royal rites at, 189; sacred site, place of the forge, 180, 182, 184–85, 187–88; women's testimonies about, 191

Kamaleki, Faustin (Haya male knowledge keeper), 188; testimony about Njeru and her snake, 190–91

Kamloops, B.C., 272–73, 276

Kanyangereko, chiefdom of Maruku (Bukara) Kingdom (Tanzania), 191; King Kahigi's authority over and Njeru's influence, 196

Karagwe Kingdom (Tanzania), 178

Karanga, local and regional histories of, 132, 134–37, 139, 141–42, 148

Karanga people, southern Shona speakers, 132

Kassapa, King of Sigiriya (Sri Lanka), 224

Katuruka village, Tanzania: heritage committee, 192–94, 197; location of Kaiija shrine, 184; map, *180*; research initiatives and female collaborators (Njeru), 185, 187–93, 197

CPSIA information can be obtained
at www.ICGtesting.com
Printed in the USA
BVHW030930260219
541154BV00005B/5/P